Between You and I

SERIES IN CONTINENTAL THOUGHT

Editorial Board

Ted Toadvine, Chairman, University of Oregon
Elizabeth A. Behnke, Study Project in Phenomenology of the Body
David Carr, Emory University
James Dodd, New School University
Lester Embree, Florida Atlantic University
José Huertas-Jourda, Wilfrid Laurier University†
Joseph J. Kockelmans, Pennsylvania State University
William R. McKenna, Miami University
Algis Mickunas, Ohio University
J. N. Mohanty, Temple University
Dermot Moran, University College Dublin
Thomas Nenon, University of Memphis
Rosemary Rizo-Patron de Lerner, Pontificia Universidad Católica del Perú, Lima
Thomas M. Seebohm, Johannes Gutenberg Universität, Mainz
Gail Soffer, Rome, Italy
Elizabeth Ströker, Universität Köln†
Nicolas de Warren, Wellesley College
Richard M. Zaner, Vanderbilt University

International Advisory Board

Suzanne Bachelard, Université de Paris†
Rudolf Boehm, Rijksuniversiteit Gent
Albert Borgmann, University of Montana
Amedeo Giorgi, Saybrook Institute
Richard Grathoff, Universität Bielefeld
Samuel Ijsseling, Husserl-Archief te Leuven
Alphonso Lingis, Pennsylvania State University
Werner Marx, Albert-Ludwigs Universität, Freiburg†
David Rasmussen, Boston College
John Sallis, Boston College
John Scanlon, Duquesne University
Hugh J. Silverman, State University of New York, Stony Brook
Carlo Sini, Università di Milano
Jacques Taminiaux, Louvain-la-Neuve
D. Lawrence Wieder†
Dallas Willard, University of Southern California

Between You and I

Dialogical Phenomenology

BEATA STAWARSKA

OHIO UNIVERSITY PRESS   ATHENS

Ohio University Press, Athens, Ohio 45701
www.ohioswallow.com
© 2009 by Ohio University Press
All rights reserved

To obtain permission to quote, reprint, or otherwise reproduce or distribute material from Ohio University Press publications, please contact our rights and permissions department at (740) 593-1154 or (740) 593-4536 (fax).

Printed in the United States of America
Ohio University Press books are printed on acid-free paper ∞ ™

16 15 14 13 12 11 10 09   5 4 3 2 1

Library of Congress Cataloging-in-Publication Data

Stawarska, Beata.
   Between you and I : dialogical phenomenology / Beata Stawarska.
   p. cm. — (Series in continental thought ; no. 36)
   Includes bibliographical references and index.
   ISBN 978-0-8214-1886-4 (hc : alk. paper)
   1. Phenomenology. 2. Dialogue. I. Title.
   B829.5.S6625 2009
   142'.7—dc22
                                      2009028436

To my grandmothers

In memoriam

CONTENTS

Preface ix
Acknowledgments xiii

Part 1: Classical Phenomenology 1

1 The Transcendental Tradition 3
    The Logical Investigations of the I 6
    From the I to the Ego 17
    The Grammar of the Transcendental Ego (1) 22
    Strawson on the Primacy of Personhood 25
    Wittgenstein on the Lure of Words 26
    The Grammar of the Transcendental Ego (2) 28
    Zahavi on Transcendental Subjectivity as Intersubjectivity 32
    Contemporary Arguments for the Transcendental Ego:
        Marbach, Soffer 39
    Schutz, Theunissen on Social Phenomenology 46
    Husserl's Later Thought 49

Part 2: The Multidiscipline of Dialogical Phenomenology 51

2 Sociolinguistics 53
    Personal Pronouns—Reconsidering the Traditional View (1) 53
    Egocentrism and Polycentrism 57
    Person Deixis and Polycentrism 60
    Anscombe 64
    Wittgenstein 67
    Personal Pronouns—Reconsidering the Traditional View (2) 68
    I and We—A Relational Community 72
    Benveniste and I-you Connectedness 75
    Objectification in the Third Person 78
    Castañeda's Phenomeno-logic of the "I" 81

3 Developmental Perspectives	89
Piaget's Legacy	92
Recent Research on the Sociality of Children	99
Proto-conversations in Infancy	103
The Dialogic Model of Jaffe and Feldstein	105
From Proto-conversation to Conversation	111
Perspectives from Blindness and Autism	114
Polycentrism and Personal-Pronoun Acquisition: Loveland and Others	118
An Egocentric Model of Personal-Pronoun Acquisition: Charney and Others	120
Philosophical Implications and Directions for Future Research	131
4 Philosophy of Dialogue	135
Rosenstock-Huessy's Grammatical Method of Social Research	136
Rosenzweig's Speech-thinking	146
Buber's I and You	149
The Primordial Duality: Buber, Humboldt, Plato	153
5 Buber and His Critics	161
Rosenstock-Huessy: Names and Pronouns	161
Levinas: Reciprocity and Responsibility	162
Epilogue	174
Dialogical Phenomenology	176
The Dialogic Dimension of Meaning and Experience	178
The Practice of Phenomenology	180
Implications for Politics and Feminism	181
Notes	189
References	193
Index	201

PREFACE

My objective in this book is to reexamine the attachment to an egocentric tradition in classical phenomenology and to propose an alternative polycentric view, supported by renewed phenomenological reflection as well as relevant contributions from cognate empirical disciplines and the dialogic tradition in philosophy. I contend that phenomenological approaches, however diverse they might be, have neglected to explore in sufficient depth the communicative structure of experience, in particular the phenomenological importance of the addressee, the inseparability of *I* and *You*, and the nature of the alternation between them. I propose to rectify this neglect by disclosing the primacy of *I–you connectedness* in meaning and experience. I–you connectedness is best thematized within living speech, which is invariably oriented toward an interlocutor, and animated by mutual address. Yet I–you connectedness extends beyond living speech to other modalities of meaning, notably thinking and writing. It also extends beyond discursive experience, and captures the deep dialogic dimension of meaning in prelinguistic and extralinguistic life. The objective of this book is to prepare the ground for thematizing this dialogic dimension in the rich and multidisciplinary manner that is afforded by the multidiscipline of dialogical phenomenology introduced here.

The book is divided into two parts, which strategically contrast classical and dialogical approaches to the social world. This contrast is used partly as a rhetorical device to make the urgency of a deliberately dialogic approach apparent. Needless to say, this project is itself influenced and enabled by classical phenomenology it critically examines; dialogical phenomenology extends some of the directions in which canonical phenomenological authors were heading regarding the inescapable embodiment of experience, embedded in the shared natural and social world. At the same time, I argue that classical phenomenology may be subject to an individualist bias that privileges first-person subjectivity over against communal relationality and leads to the neglect of I–you connectedness. This neglect is most clearly apparent within the transcendental phenomenology of subjectivity, discussed in part 1, chapter 1. A similar oversight of I–you interdependency could be noted within post-Husserlian phenomenology, but is not discussed here at length.

Chapter 1 is devoted therefore to the critical task of challenging the exclusively first-person stance occupied by transcendental subjectivity, and the correlated notion of the social world as an additive plurality of transcendental subjects. I employ notably an original grammatical analysis of pronominal discourse to demonstrate the tension between the usages of the pronoun "I" in ordinary language and in *transcendentalese*. Whereas the former use indicates a social role of the speaker, the latter turns the pronoun into a label for an epistemically construed subject of thought. The former stands in relation to an addressee, the latter loosens these relational ties. The former is caught in a web of I–you reversals, the latter fixed in an irreversible I-stance. As a consequence, the former captures the socially relevant dynamics of spoken discourse, whereas the latter glosses these over.

Part 2 proposes to examine this social dynamics in detail. It provides a relatively wide cross-disciplinary focus on the central question of interpersonal connectedness. In chapter 2, I draw on relevant contributions from sociolinguistics in order to deepen the analysis of pronominal discourse, particularly the pragmatics of personal pronouns, with an eye to articulating the basic thesis of primary I–you connectedness in terms of reversibility, asymmetry, and complementarity. I discuss the interrelated notions of person and spatial deixis, that is, the speech context dependency of "I"–"you" pronouns and "here"–"there" demonstratives, to make a strong case for a polycentric perspectival configuration of experience situated within the shared world. This discussion enables me to put pressure on the egocentric stance of classical phenomenology, and the interrelated transcendental notions of an egological subject and the absolute *here* point of spatial orientation. I propose the alternative dialogical notion of a situated viewpoint for spatial orientation and self-reference in discourse, which reverses into a *you* and a *there* within the social and spatial context construed in first-to-second person terms.

In chapter 3, I turn to relevant contributions from developmental psychology, notably the research on protoconversational or dialogic relations between infants and their caregivers. This empirical research helps to develop an account of the temporal aspects of first-to-second person interaction, such as the turn-taking pattern of dialogue. I hypothesize that these temporally and rhythmically patterned interactions provide the scaffolding for acquiring pronominal markers of personhood. Young children are typically well primed for the acquisition of first- and second-person reference in language since they have been immersed in its prelinguistic pragmatics and dialogical rhythms from the earliest face-to-face interactions with their caregiver. This empirical material provides support for the view that we are steeped in I–you relations long before "I" and "you" markers are fully mastered in complex and varied conversational contexts.

In chapters 4 and 5 I turn to contributions from the dialogic tradition in philosophy. In chapter 4, I provide additional theoretical grounding to the notion of I–you connectedness in terms of primordial duality. The notion of primordial duality is an intrinsically relational category, irreducible to the usual metaphysical categories such as the singularity of the one and an impartial multiplicity of the many. Instead, it captures the first-to-second person relatedness binding the dialogic partners in a nonfusional as well as nonexternal-additive manner, emphasizing that the partners in relation are both connected and distinct, and that they are bound in a way irreducible to the adding together of external enclosed objects. The notion of primary duality finds support both in the grammatical/philosophical category of the dual number, captured by the I–you word-pair, and the mythical accounts of original twin-hood of the human form. This philosophical/grammatical category is therefore especially useful to discussions of social relatedness, and the interdependency and reciprocal engagement binding the partners in relation. It captures the unique dialogic relationality of the two who are not one, and provides a robust alternative theoretical framework to the received configurations of the one and the many.

Chapter 5 has an apologetic tone. It examines the overwhelmingly critical reception of the dialogic tradition within contemporary Continental philosophy, and makes a case for revising this dominant trend. I argue that the validity of the dominant criticism against the ethics of fellowship, issued from the perspectives of ethical responsibility to the face of the other, misconstrues and needs to be reexamined in light of the primary texts belonging to the notoriously underrepresented yet immensely valuable dialogic tradition in philosophy. Finally, I raise some methodological considerations relative to practicing the multidiscipline of dialogical phenomenology and draw some implications of my argument for feminist and political concerns in the epilogue.

ACKNOWLEDGMENTS

I am grateful to colleagues and friends at the Department of Philosophy, the University of Oregon, for supporting my work in general, and this book in particular. I feel privileged to have found a scholarly home where thinking across disciplines is cherished, and contesting the canon graciously received. I would like to thank Scott Pratt for cheerful encouragement of my initial decision to embark on a scholarly journey across some previously unexplored territories; to Mark Johnson for the many friendly conversations and helpful responses to early drafts of the manuscript; to John Lysaker for inspiration. I am especially indebted to Bonnie Mann for sharing her brilliance and humor with me, expanding my phenomenological horizons, and for unfailing friendship. I am very grateful to Ted Toadvine for the interest in this book project, and for shepherding it through the Continental Series at the Ohio University Press. Thanks to Elena Cuffari for help with editing and formatting the text.

Over the years, I have been inspired and motivated by friends and colleagues both in the United States and in Europe. I would like to express special thanks to Shaun Gallagher for his generosity and guidance in my scholarly work, for infecting me with enthusiasm for phenomenology and the cognitive sciences, and for gracefully providing an exemplar of how to conduct rigorous research across reflective and applied disciplines. Thank you for the many conversations, especially the one on the London subway. I am profoundly indebted to Eva Simms for her scholarly advice and comments on portions of the early draft. Thank you for inspiring me and others with groundbreaking research in phenomenological psychology, where poetry and science speak in a unison that is rarely heard in contemporary academia. Thank you also to Sara Heinamaa for letting me bear witness to an astounding intellect, focus, and mount-lifting motivation; I have always felt empowered by our conversations. I would also like to thank Matthew Ratcliffe for his enthusiasm and constructive critique of my work, which helped to balance things a bit. Malcolm Wilson provided helpful comments regarding the use of dual number in Plato.

Over the years, I have also benefited from my exposure to the work of and friendly advice and suggestions from Gail Weiss, Helen Fielding, and Linda Fisher, as well as David Morris. I would like to express my lasting gratitude to Rudolf Bernet for introducing me to phenomenological research and exemplifying extraordinary scholarly rigor. The two anonymous reviewers at Ohio University Press helped to fine-tune the presentation of transcendental phenomenology throughout this monograph.

The debt to my mom, Renata Stawarska, is an infinite one. Thank you for your love and care, and for ever so gently steering me onto the rocky paths of an academic career through your own admirable example. Thank you to my brother, Piotr Stawarski, for love and affection, and explosive humor that shines a light in darkness. I would like to acknowledge my gratitude to Alan Mayhew for encouragement and support during my graduate school years. None of this would have happened without such generosity.

I would like to thank Stuart Murray for being a good friend and inspiring intellectual over the years. Thank you also to Olivier Wehner, Iwona Bogaczyk, Bruce Tabb and Ron Unger, Chris Ogle, as well as Carolyn Culbertson and Miles Hentrup, for your friendship. Thank you to Matt Dold for a life in dialogue.

My thanks go to Springer for permission to reprint portions of "*Feeling Good Vibrations in Dialogical Relations,*" which appeared in *Continental Philosophy Review* 41, no. 2 (2008), as well as portions of "Persons, Pronouns, and Perspectives. Linguistic and Developmental Contributions to Dialogical Phenomenology," which appeared in *Folk Psychology Reassessed* in 2007. Also thanks to Francis and Taylor for permission to reprint portions of "*You and I, Here and Now*. Spatial and Social Situatedness in Deixis," which appeared in *International Journal of Philosophical Studies* 16, no. 3 (2008), and to CHIASMI for permission to reprint portions of "Dialogue at the Limit of Phenomenology" from 2009.

PART 1

Classical Phenomenology

CHAPTER 1

● ●

THE TRANSCENDENTAL TRADITION

In his introduction to the notoriously difficult *Star of Redemption*, titled "The New Thinking," Franz Rosenzweig (2000 [1925]) identifies three main epochs within the course of Western philosophy: cosmological antiquity, theological Middle Ages, and anthropological modernity. Each epoch can be best characterized by the kind of theoretical reduction it enacted: to the cosmos, to God, and, most recently and lastingly, to "the darling idea of the modern era, 'the' I" (115). Modernity institutes "the I" as its central notion, the foundation of independent philosophical inquiry liberated both from the received dogmas of the Church and the traditional cosmological accounts inherited from the Ancients that were being challenged in the face of dramatic advances in mathematical physics (Newton, Galileo, Keplar). As all philosophical children know, it was Descartes' who initiated such a search for absolute certainty in his *Meditations on First Philosophy*, applying systemic doubt to both untrained quotidian and scientifically informed convictions, in view of attaining a piece of truth immune to doubt. The irreducible remainder of Descartes' method is "the darling idea of the modern era, the 'I.'"

What is less often observed is that the reduction to "the I" of modernity does not simply privilege a naturally existing entity (the subject, the self) over others (the cosmos, God), and it does not simply shift the emphasis from the larger-than-human to the all-too-human realm. On such a modest interpretation of modernity, its philosophical figuring of humanity would simply mirror the already-established reality in a neutral manner. Yet it may be more appropriate to interpret the reduction to "the I" in terms of a constructive and profoundly constrictive reshaping of humanity by means of the primarily epistemic lens of philosophical inquiry and the individualist bias imported into it. In this sense the reduction to "the I" does not simply represent but rather produces a novel conception of the person as a repository of inner private events accessible by means of first-person insight, with the kind of intuitive luminosity of rational understanding that no doubt can seemingly obscure. Importantly, the conception of personhood modeled on the ideal of apodictic knowledge gained via intuitive insight leads to an exclusion of second person relatedness, and a forgetting of the inseparability of *I* and *you*.[1]

For the modern turn inward is facilitated not only by a focus on the first-person perspective as the purported point of entry into the rational mind and by a focus on the personal stance of the "I," over against the personal stance cast in other personal pronouns (notably "you" and "we"). It is also the case that a peculiar distortion of the "I's" ordinary linguistic function underpins this turn and produces far-reaching consequences for how we think about who and what we are. Having picked up "the I" or its currently widespread (in both philosophy and psychology, as well as popular parlance) Latin equivalent "the ego," modernity departed from the ordinary use of "the I/ego" as an indicator of the speaker role in discourse (that is, the one who is speaking at a given time) to an unprecedented use of "the I/ego" as a name designating a discourse-independent referent (such as the mind or the thinker), and cast it grammatically as a substantive noun, typically prefaced with a definite article. Modernity therefore divorced the pronoun "I" from its native context of speech and covered over its ordinary discursive role of marking the speaker, who stands in relation to a present or at least a potential addressee. It construed the pronoun "I" as a label for the tacit domain of inner and private thought that can be accessed exclusively in solitude, by means of focused introspective insight with "the mind's eye." Modernity thus divorced the first- from the second-person experience. It produced a construct of a solitary and silent subject, it being optional whether or not this subject may "express" itself to others in public discourse. Interestingly then, the distortion of the ordinary grammatical category of personal pronouns has helped to forge the idea of an extralinguistic, intrapsychic entity, the supposed referent of "the I" or "the ego." It has thus initiated what will be termed in this monograph an *egocentric tradition*, along with its commitment to the conception of humanity as a collective of lone individuals.

The egocentric tradition has deeply informed what Aaron Gurwitsch (1979) calls the "phenomenology of consciousness," which includes Husserl together with Descartes, Locke, and Kant. These authors developed the so-called traditional theory of social relations within phenomenology. The pronouncements of these four philosophers about the social world are, Gurwitsch maintains, derivative of the overriding interest in securing the foundations of philosophic knowledge. The "traditional" account is driven by an underlying epistemological agenda that shapes the resulting theory of sociality in determinate ways. Specifically, it centers the field of inquiry in the exclusively first-person consciousness construed as the site of indubitable knowledge. The "traditional theory" of sociality in modernity and phenomenology is therefore not based on a descriptive account of experience but results rather from a prior effort to establish absolute epistemic certitude and to carve out an ontological niche, where the former aim can be realized or at least preserved as an ideal possibility.

One of the defining components of the traditional approach is that all conscious mental processes have an irreducible relation or "appertinence" to the ego; the ego is a necessary "index" born of mental states and enabling their identification as my own (Gurwitsch 1979, 1–2). Consciousness equals I-consciousness (where "I" is construed as a singular subject). Gurwitsch finds that such an egocentric construal of the mind places the phenomenology of consciousness in sharp contrast to the data of lived human experience, notably the nontheoretical daily conviction that we are in immediate perceptual presence of other persons whose mental life is apparent in and through their manifest behavior (3). Gurwitsch is skeptical, therefore, about the ability of the phenomenology of consciousness ever to produce an adequate rendering of "human encounters in the social world." Within the egocentric construal of the mind, the passage from the ego to other human beings becomes barred, or in Gurwitsch's own words, "'mental processes appertinent to We' [*Wir-Erlebnisse*] become unintelligible" (28) following their initial confinement to the lone "I."

How did phenomenology become confined to this egocentric perspective? Is phenomenology necessarily subject to such a confinement? I believe that the disregard of ordinary language helped to perpetuate this egocentric perspective within classical phenomenology, yet also that a renewed attention to ordinary pronominal discourse may help to liberate phenomenology from this confinement. My positive goal in this critical analysis is to unveil the phenomenological importance of the addressee, the inseparability of *I* and *you*, and the nature of alternation between them. These themes help to highlight the intrinsically dialogic character of experience and the multiple ways in which the first-person stance is entangled with the second-person address. I believe that mainstream phenomenological approaches, however diverse they might be, have neglect to explore this primary connectedness of *I* and *you* in sufficient depth. It is beyond the scope of this project to address each and every canonical figure within the phenomenological tradition and pursue this charge of neglect within their work. I therefore deliberately confine the analysis to a reading of Husserl's relevant works and postpone the debate about the extent of their influence on post-Husserlian phenomenology. Nor do I attempt to deny that the phenomenological tradition offers invaluable resources for thematizing the multiple aspects of interpersonal relatedness. The direct interest of the current work lies however in developing a dialogic perspective on experience; and I believe that this objective is best realized via deliberate engagement with other, nonphenomenological philosophical traditions, such as the dialogic tradition, as well as empirical disciplines, notably sociolinguistics. It is my hope that such a multidisciplinary approach will help to reinvigorate phenomenological reflection on social life, and ultimately reaffirm the usefulness of experientially rooted reflection to contemporary debates about the interdependence of the self and the other. With these considerations in mind, I turn to examine Husserl's classical approach in some detail in the remainder of this chapter.

THE LOGICAL INVESTIGATIONS OF THE I

In the *Logical Investigations* (1970 [1900] Investigation I, ch. 3, §26), Husserl categorized the pronoun "I" (together with other subject-bound terms such as *here, now, yesterday, tomorrow, later,* and so forth) as an *essentially subjective and occasional expression*, to be distinguished from *objective expressions*. What distinguishes the two types of expression is the relative stability of their meaning. An objective expression, for example the word *lion*, pins down (or can pin down) its meaning "merely by its manifest, auditory pattern, and can be understood without necessarily directing one's attention to the person uttering it, or to the circumstances of the utterance" (314). Unlike its subjective counterpart, an objective expression is characterized therefore in terms of both speaker/hearer and speech-context independence, even though, importantly, it is within the context of spoken discourse (noted in the emphasis on the "auditory pattern" of utterance) that the distinction between subjective and objective expressions first takes shape.

Needless to say, as Husserl notes, the objectivity of an expression like *lion* does not in principle preclude the possibility of an objective expression pinning down more than just one meaning, given (or for example) homonyms such as "mean" (adj.) standing for both "average" and "unkind." The resulting ambiguity does not, however, remove the possibility of locating ideal and objective meanings of the word, independent of the speech context, even though the expression may have more than one referent. The differing meanings are self-identical unities unaffected by their common attachment to a single expression. Henceforth, the speaker can limit her expression to a single meaning at the exclusion of others, and so remove the equivocation from her meaning-making acts.

Things stand differently with essentially occasional expressions. Here the meanings are necessarily contextualized by the occasion on which they are produced, and they are inextricably bound to the speaker and to the speech situation. Hence the meaning of the word "I" can be gleaned only at the moment of the "the living utterance" made by a given speaker, and it would fluctuate as soon as another speaker uttered a statement in the first-person singular. The meaning of an occasional expression like the pronoun "I" is inescapably unstable or equivocal since it is inextricably related to the speech situation, which Husserl regarded as the "normal circumstance" of using occasional expressions. Occasional expressions need therefore to be thematized primarily as speech acts, for their meaning is realized fully when they are being spoken. As Husserl puts it, "The word 'I' has not itself directly the power to arouse the specific I-presentation; *this becomes fixed in the actual piece of talk*. It does not work like the word 'lion' which can arouse the idea of a lion in and by itself" (1970 [1900], §26, 316, emphasis added)—presumably, that is, in thinking the word without utterance. Husserl's analysis therefore predicates the realization of the meaning of the word "I," unlike that of the objective expression, on its enactment or performance in speech. Unsurprisingly then, and in often emphasized contrast to Derrida, Husserl postulates a priority of speaking over writing in the context of the usage of the "I." What is less often noted, however, is that the Husserl of the *Logical Investigations* postulates also a priority of speaking over thinking, and is therefore less guilty of a linguistically purged, transcendental notion of consciousness with which Derrida uniformly credits his philosophical works. It may be that Husserl suggests a speech-nourished notion of personhood that would be consistent with interpersonal interrelatedness in an *I-you* mode, even as he does not fully follow through on this project and definitely abandons it in his later, expressly phenomenological, works.

Let me develop Husserl's distinction between speaking and writing in the context of occasional expression in some more detail. Consider that the word "I" becomes divorced from its meaning when transformed to the medium of the written text. "If we read the word [I] without knowing who wrote it, it is perhaps not meaningless, but is at least estranged from its normal sense" (Husserl 1970 [1900], 315). The word "I," and expressions containing a phrase in the first person ("I wish," "I believe," and so forth), differ from objective expressions—such as mathematical expressions of the type 2 x 2 = 4—the semantic content of which is not affected [or realized] by the circumstances of their actual use. The latter expression does not suppose a reference to a subject who would for example make the judgment that 2 x 2 = 4. The statement "I judge that 2 x 2 = 4" intimates something about the speaker's mental state, whereas the statement "2 x 2 = 4" is empty of such intimation. The truth value of the two statements is therefore nonidentical, for the latter statement could be true whereas the former is false (1970 [1900], §25, 313). Importantly then, I-expressions do not translate into objective expressions with fixed meanings. It is correct to say that the word "I" serves to designate the speaker in discourse. However, that does not mean that one could substitute the objective phrase "whatever speaker is designating himself" for the word "I" without producing a profound change in meaning (§26, 315).[2]

I noted that the Husserl of the *Logical Investigations* regards spoken discourse as the typical context of employing the pronoun "I," and so opens the door for a speech-supported and socially mediated conception of personhood. This door seems to get slammed shut when Husserl proceeds to thematize the "I" as a label referencing a speech-neutral self. Seemingly motivated by the lack of a fixed objective meaning in the word "I," and by the semantic fluctuations dependent on who assumes the speaker role at a given moment, Husserl advances the problematic thesis that the word "I" may embody a multiplicity of personal meanings that would be different from one individual to another. It would stand for "the immediate idea of one's own personality" (1970 [1900], 316), that supposedly unique and inalienable core of one's existence available directly to the subject's own intuitive insight. Crucially then, the meaning of the pronoun "I" would be fully realized in the instances of *silent soliloquy* and would not be dependent on *communication with others* for its achievement. Consider that this possibility of noncommunicative meaning fulfillment rests upon Husserl's classic "essential distinction" between expression (*Ausdruck*) and indication (*Anzeichen*).

Following Husserl, signs can be categorized as expressive or indicative. The paradigmatic example of an expressive sign is found in "living discourse," wherein the meaning (*Bedeutung*) of the verbal sign is fully available to the speaking subject. Husserl's usage of the term *expression* is restrictive in comparison to ordinary speech and so does "violence to usage" (1970 [1900] §5,

275), for it excludes facial expressions and bodily gestures from its domain of application. The latter are devoid of meaning; even though they may be interpreted by another as indicating the speaker's thoughts and emotions, their enactment is involuntary and does not follow an express intent to convey one's inner states, whether to oneself or to the other (ibid.) In his monograph devoted mainly to the *Logical Investigations*, Derrida (1973) therefore charges Husserl's account of meaning in expression with being deliberately voluntaristic, driven, controlled, and circumscribed by the subject's will-to-say (*vouloir-dire*). On this account, the speaker's intention is manifest in a transparent and exhaustive manner in her linguistic expression.

In contrast to expressions, indicative signs stand for referents not directly present to the speaker's and/or hearer's awareness. Husserl provides examples of signs "deliberately and artificially brought about" (1970 [1900], §2, 270), such as a knot in a handkerchief, which may serve as a memo to do X, but whose meaning is not contained in the sign but rather is in need of interpretation (in this case, by the subject who tied the knot in the first place). The "'live' functioning" of an indicative sign depends therefore on the connection established by "some thinking being" whose belief in the reality of some objects or states of affairs motivates a belief in the reality of certain other objects or states of affairs (ibid.). For the thinker, "certain things *may* or *must* exist, *since* other things have been given" (ibid.). Husserl insists however that this motivated connection between, for example, a knot in a handkerchief and one's intent to do X is not of a logical but an empirical kind—it is an indicative allusion (*Hinweis*) to what is nonseen and not a deductive demonstration (*Beweis*), which has the evidence of proof. It therefore does not exhibit the objective necessity that binds a premise to a conclusion (§3, 272), but belongs rather to the order of merely probable "modest surmises" (273), wherein the connection between the sign and the signified is external and in danger of being dissipated. Hence, there is the perpetual risk of loss of meaning in the case of indications.

Crucially, the distinction between expression and indication does not map onto two materially distinct regions of signs. As Derrida phrases it, it is not a *substantial* but rather a *functional* distinction, with expression and indication denoting functions or signifying relations rather than terms (1973, 20). The same sign can therefore carry an expressive as well as an indicative function. The case in point is speech. From the viewpoint of the speaker, the utterances are infused with meaning and belong to the order of expression. It would be erroneous to suppose that the speaker needs *to indicate* the meaning of the utterance to herself, as if she needs to interpret the expressive intent from the sequence of the signs uttered. The speaker's expressed intentions are available "at that very moment" (Husserl 1970 [1900], 279/80), but they do need to be interpreted by the hearer, for whom the spoken signs function not as expressions but rather as indications. In communicative speech, the utterance *intimates* to the hearer the inner sense-giving experience of the speaker (§7, 277). Communicative speech appears therefore to blur the previously established "essential distinction" between expression and indication, since "[m]eaning—in communicative speech—is always bound up (*verflochten*) with. . . an indicative relation" (269). As Derrida argues, this entanglement (*Verflechtung*) ultimately undermines the possibility of maintaining the kind of rigid separation between transparent and fully accessible meaning on the one hand, and the opaque physical indicators on the other. For Derrida, all signs are material traces inherently threatened by the loss of meaning, such that no full possession or authorial ownership of intention is possible. Signs circulate in the public space shared by the self and the other, and no single subject could claim monopoly on the interpretation of the meaning of the sign. Husserl's attachment to the purity and ideality of meaning in expression, rigidly demarcated from the materiality of signs and the communicative context in which they circulate, testifies, in Derrida's view, to Husserl's profound indebtedness to the Western metaphysical tradition: its desire for full presence at the exclusion of alterity, its denigration of temporality and fixation with static beings, its epistemological bias at the exclusion of ethical concerns, its ideal of a pure grammar distinct from the multiplicity of natural languages, and its celebration of life that construes absence and loss of meaning as derivative and secondary. Importantly for our purposes, Derrida accuses Husserl of *phonocentrism*, that is, of privileging the voice (*la voix*) over writing, and so of excluding the opaque body of the sign from the domain of meaning.

To be sure, the voice that gets privileged by Husserl is of a peculiar kind, as Derrida notes. It is the voice that "keeps silence" and is confined to the province of silent soliloquy. The voice Husserl privileges is therefore ultimately a philosophical abstraction; it is the substance of mute thought, which serves as an idealized medium wherein pure meanings can be intuitively grasped in their full luminosity by the thinking, and no longer speaking (that is, communicating with others), *I*. "The voice is consciousness" (Derrida 1973, 80); it belongs to the phenomenological interiority stripped of worldly being (76).

This *phone* construed in terms of diaphanous *phenomena* is therefore a mere insinuation of the voice. Derrida insists that it *seems* that the words I utter do not leave me, that speaking and hearing is an auto-affection of a unique kind with no external detour (like the reflective surfaces of the mirror when I look at myself), for it *seems* that I hear and understand (the double meaning of *entendre*) myself at the very instant that I speak, and so it *seems* that the voice does not circulate in the physical space of mundane objects, and that there are no obstacles to its emission. It *seems* that the voice is not coextensive with the world, but belongs rather to the element of ideality (Derrida 1973, 76–79). It *seems* that the voice constitutes together with breath a spiritual medium out of which the metaphysical tradition was keen to derive its conception of the spirit and psyche as the invisible animating principle directing the physical body.³ (Consider that "*psyche*" derives from *psykhein:* to blow, cool.) This spirituality and the attachment to a metaphysically filtered conception of the voice and breath would be preserved in the phenomenological conception of consciousness: "no consciousness is possible without the voice" (79).

To reverse this "traditional phonologism of metaphysics" (1973, 80), Derrida proposes to retrieve the materiality of the sign as a trace, an opaque remainder that resists effacing itself for the sake of the ideality of meaning. The materiality of the sign can be best thematized in the context of the written text. Derrida disputes therefore Husserl's claim that speech provides the "normal circumstance" of language use, even in the case of occasional expressions like the pronoun "I." Recall that for Husserl the meaning of the word is originally established in speaking and divorced from its usual meaning in the written text. Derrida objects that this line of thought supposes the need to have an intuitive grasp of "the object I in order to understand the word I" (96). And it goes without saying that Husserl does regard the word "I" as a label for one's inner presentation of self when he says that "[i]n solitary speech the meaning of 'I' is essentially realized in the immediate idea of one's own personality" (Husserl 1970 [1900], §26, 316). Derrida challenges the need of such intuitive self-presentation by pointing to the continued significance of the word "I" in the absence of the author—the author may be unknown or even dead, as in the case of fictional prose or historical reports. It follows that "the signifying function of the *I* does not depend on the life of the speaking subject.... The anonymity of the written *I*, the impropriety of *I am writing*, is, contrary to what Husserl says, the 'normal situation.'" (Derrida 1973, 97). Writing is therefore, Derrida argues, not added on to speaking from the outside. To speak (*dicere*) is already to dictate a text.

Why did Husserl not draw similar conclusions regarding the relation between speech and text? According to Derrida, the reason lies in Husserl's attachment to the "intuitionistic imperative" (1973, 97), which grounds meanings in the inward silent cogitation, removed from material and perishable texts. Husserl would be guilty of oversight due to his misconception of speech in terms of the spiritual voice that resists being confined to the body of the sign. Had he abandoned this metaphysically filtered conception of speech, Husserl would have been led to embrace Derrida's principle of continuity between speaking and writing, predicated on their shared medium of material signs. Or would he? I believe, contra Derrida, that Husserl may have continued to uphold the separation between speaking and writing, even if he had admitted that both are mediated by historically sedimented material traces and if he had abandoned the intuitionistic conception of meaning to which he largely adhered. He may have continued to argue that a change in meaning occurs when an occasional expression, like the pronoun "I" passes from speech to text, not just for reason of his metaphysical commitments, but rather because of his attunement to the distinctiveness of spoken discourse when compared to writing. He may have objected that, in speech, the meaning of the word "I" is intrinsically context dependent, and that this word would fail to perform its ordinary function of picking a unique speaker out of the multitude of candidates without this contextualization. This performative character and context-dependence of the pronoun "I" provides the basis for making the distinction between spoken and written discourse. In the latter case, the meaning of the word "I" ceases to be contextualized by a given situation and its participants; it no longer connects to a flesh-and-blood individual who vociferates to another. There is therefore no need to rely on an intuitionistic imperative to preserve the distinction between context-dependent and context-independent meanings. Scholars of speech such as Benveniste and Lyons preserved this distinction without invoking a mentalistic subject (see chapter 2).

I conclude therefore, contra Derrida, that Husserl was correct to privilege speech in his account of occasional expressions, and that this privileging is not exclusively a tributary of a preexistent phonocentric tradition and its misconception of the voice but results instead from Husserl's attentiveness to the shift of meaning between spoken and written discourse as far as occasional expressions are concerned. Insofar as Derrida subsumes speaking under writing, he fails to recognize these shifts. In his focus on the text, Derrida glosses over the importance of context for the fashioning and sharing of meaning.

His dismissal of the muted voice of metaphysics seems to lead him to regard just any statement about the specificity of speech as suspect and derivative of this metaphysical tradition. In response to Derrida's charge of *phonocentrism,* we can therefore wonder whether the founder of Deconstruction may not be charged with *phonophobia* in his attack on the founder of phenomenology. After all, it only *seems* that voice lends itself to the confinement to solitary consciousness, and on a different interpretation, voice would not lead us to the compounded metaphysical illusions enumerated by Derrida. It may be that Derrida took the master's voice too seriously and was unable to envisage an alternative perspective that would preserve the specificity of spoken discourse *and* be unburdened by metaphysical baggage. Such an alternative perspective on speech, one which preserves its inherently communicative character, can be found within the dialogic tradition (discussed in chapter 4).

Note also, contra Derrida's uniform criticism of Husserl's conception of meaning, that some ambiguity surrounds the possibility of isolating solitary discourse out of the shared practice of speaking, and so of maintaining an impermeable border between expression and indication even in Husserl's own early text. Recall that in communicative speech, expressions are always entangled with indication. Needless to say, this de facto entanglement did not prevent Husserl from maintaining the distinction between expression and indication as a de jure necessity (Derrida 1973, 20). Husserl firmly believed in the possibility of expression being used in "isolated mental life," with no indicative import (1970 [1900] §1, 269). Furthermore, according to Husserl's provisional definition, "each instance or part of speech. . . shall count as an expression whether or not such speech is actually uttered, or addressed with communicative intent to any persons or not" (275). We witness here a peculiar transformation of speech into a mute mental soliloquy, a clear case of "violence to usage" where public discourse gets distorted into private rumination. This distortion is all the more dangerous in that it effaces itself: Husserl does not regard the case of expression enacted in this "uncommunicated, interior mental life" as deviating in any manner from expression deployed in communication. Implied therein is a principle of the constancy of meaning: "This change in function [from communication to mental soliloquy] plainly has nothing to do with whatever makes an expression an expression. Expressions continue to have meanings as they had before, and the same meanings as in dialogue" (§8, 278). Mutatis mutandis, dialogue consists then in sharing the speaker's "acts of mind" with his auditor, who needs to interpret the speaker's intention. Dialogue appears therefore as a mentalizing process both at the sender and the receiver end, the former channeling mental states through words, the latter intimating the states being expressed.

Needless to say, this conception of expression is ridden with problems. Consider however that some of Husserl's pronouncements partially undermine the very possibility of performing a silent soliloquy in speech, and thus of realizing meaning in solitary mental life. Husserl reminds us that "[e]xpressions were originally framed to fulfill a communicative function" (1970 [1900], §7, 276). In communicative acts "[s]peaking and hearing... are mutually correlated" (ibid.), and so the speaker and hearer roles deployed by self and other are codependent. This acknowledged mutual correlation of speech and its reception by the other, which is integral to "expressions as they function in communication," should have consistently led Husserl to frame the discussion of meaning in social terms. As Gurwitsch puts it, "[f]or a complete account of the essentially occasional expressions, the facts and problems of intersubjectivity must be... taken into consideration" (1977 [1950], 122/23). It is also notable that Gurwitsch drew on linguistic accounts of occasional expressions, especially the work of Wilhelm von Humboldt (discussed in chapter 2), to throw light on the inherently communicative nature of speech in general and personal pronouns in particular. My analyses in this monograph follow Gurwitsch's lead, and they expose the benefits of engaging the linguistic contributions of Humboldt and others for the purpose of developing a nonegocentric phenomenological account of personhood in far more detail than has previously been the case.

Consider that the correlation between speaking and hearing acknowledged by Husserl in the *Logical Investigations* should ultimately throw the possibility of isolating instances of "speech" without an interlocutor into question, thereby undermining the very project of studying "expressions in solitary life." Had Husserl remained loyal to his insight about the inescapably communicative function of speech, he may have been less eager to construct the imaginary scenario of speech that makes no sound, and less eager to locate this artifice of muted discourse on a continuum with communication and speech properly so-called. Husserl may have been less likely to construe "interior mental life," this ghost settlement erected on the ruins of communication, as an instance of speech and a site of meaning. After all, meaning is inescapably filtered through the socially sanctioned and historically sedimented layers of signification. Even if I think or speak to myself in solitude, I continue to partake in the community of speakers whose gift of meaning I carry with me to even in the most deserted regions of the world.

Consider Husserl's example of solitary speech and the ambiguity surrounding it. "One of course *speaks, in a certain sense,* even in soliloquy, and it is certainly possible to think of oneself as speaking, and even as speaking to oneself, as e. g. when someone says to himself: 'You have gone wrong, you can't go on like that'" (1970 [1900], 279/280). In what sense does one speak to oneself here? How are we to understand the mode of address carried by the pronoun "you" introduced into the solitary domain where only the "I" should reign? Husserl hastens to add that "in the genuine sense of communication, there is *no speech* in such cases, nor does one tell oneself anything" (§8, 280, emphasis added). After all, it would be quite purposeless to need to instruct oneself or intimate to oneself the presence of one's own mental states (ibid.). And yet, the silent remorse and exhortation to amendment sounds very much like a voice of a parental authority that has become interiorized and continues to play in the head in the guise of a superego. In Derrida's words (1973, 73), "[t]he problem is whether solitary speech interrupts or only *interiorizes* the dialogue situation." It may be that solitary speech resonates with other voices, making consciousness or conscience (in accordance with the common etymology of the two terms) a polyphonic field where thinking follows in the footsteps of dialogic exchanges with others.[4] In that case, there would be more than just one voice resonating in my head without a necessary charge of madness.

Despite the ambiguity surrounding Husserl's project to isolate solitary mute meanings out of the fabric of communication, it remains unquestionable that the overriding argument of the *Logical Investigations* supposes the hypothetical possibility of such isolation, and that the logical order of "essential distinctions" finds its intelligibility in the extraction of the solitary mental out of sociolinguistic life. Derrida argues that this style of argument is not limited to the 1900 text but exhibits "the germinal structure of the whole of Husserl's thought" (3). Following Derrida, Lawlor (2002, 168) emphasizes that this structure is broader than Husserl's own work; it concerns "the phenomenological project in its essence" and "the historical destiny of phenomenology" (Derrida 1973, 22 and 27). It is beyond the scope of this project to address the exact extent of Husserl's influence on the existential phenomenology and ontology of Heidegger, Beauvoir, Merleau-Ponty, Sartre, and Levinas. I acknowledge that the dialogical phenomenological approach advocated here is extending some of the directions in which these authors were heading, and is indebted to their work in more ways than I can acknowledge or even recognize. The objective of this current project, however, is to advance a multidisciplinary perspective on meaning and experience so as to bring their inherently dialogic dimension into relief. Contra Derrida, I shall not prophesize about the sealed fate of phenomenology, but employ phenomenological resources in order to return to living speech itself, attempting to bracket individualistic and mentalistic preconceptions in the process.

Needless to say, phenomenological description must acknowledge that the experience of speaking, like any other experience, is inescapably situated and bound to a personal perspective. I cannot overleap the first-person position and adopt the perspective of the other. To thematize dialogue experientially is still to draw on one's own experience of dialogue. However, to recognize this inescapable situatedness of living experience need not lead to covering over the intrinsic entanglement of the first-person with the second-person perspective within the very phenomenon of speaking. My experience is situated *and* intrinsically interrelated with the situated perspective of the other to whom my speaking is addressed. The speaking *I* is therefore inseparable from the *you* being spoken to, as well as from the alternating process of speaking and listening as it unfolds between the interlocutors. This I–you relation affords both mutual engagement *and* ineliminable asymmetry between personal and spatial viewpoints. Dialogical phenomenology does not claim that one is able to appropriate the content of the other's experience; however, one's own experience is argued to be essentially enmeshed with (one's own experience of) the other. That means phenomenological reflection practiced from a dialogical standpoint consistently recognizes this inherent first-to-second person connectedness. It does not abolish the first person, but neither does it absolve the first person from the primary interpersonal relationality to past, present, and potential interlocutors, enacted across the modalities of speaking, writing, and thinking.

Furthermore, dialogical phenomenology advocates a deliberately multidisciplinary focus on experience due to the inherent incompleteness of each methodological approach, including the experientially rooted descriptive method of phenomenology. Exclusive focus on first-person experience runs the risk of overshadowing the enabling foundations of individual experience and the larger-than-me social, historical, natural, and cultural contexts that individual experience is immersed in and sustained by, but which it cannot fully recuperate by means of first-person reflection. The recourse to cognate disciplines, which regard meaning within the socially modulated context of language pragmatics, as well as psychological development and language acquisition, is therefore indispensable to do justice to the richness and complexity of the phenomena under investigation. To open up phenomenology beyond the scope of first-person analysis emphatically is not to abandon or discredit its descriptive method. Dispensing with phenomenology would amount to, in my view, dispensing with a concrete, existentially relevant, and experientially enriched philosophical reflection. Yet to enact the phenomenological return to the things themselves means also, in my view, to be mindful of the inherent limitations of individual perspective, and to dialogically engage other disciplinary outlooks on the phenomena of shared interest. Dialogue can be best studied, it seems, in dialogue with others.

FROM THE I TO THE EGO

Following Derrida, the notion of silent speech that underpins the argument from the *Logical Investigations* anticipates the conception of transcendental consciousness as the private domain of mute meaning, crowned with the ego as its subject. Recall in this regard that for Husserl, the meaning of the pronoun "I" is "essentially realized" in solitary speech as "the immediate idea of one's own personality" (1970 [1900], 316). The meaning of the pronoun "I" would be delivered therefore by an intuitive idea belonging to the order of "isolated mental life." Recall also that the meaning accessed in mental soliloquy would be unique to the individual who accesses it from within. The word "I" is, in Husserl's view, "a universally operative indication of this fact" (316). However, as Derrida already noted, "[o]ne can't help being astonished at this *individual concept* and this '*Bedeutung*' which differs with each individual" (1973, 95). After all, the general word "I" would be used throughout to cover an in-principle inexhaustible multiplicity of nonidentical meanings! We can marvel how the practice of shared understanding could be possible in a universe where a single word mobilizes a novel meaning for each speaker. Unsurprisingly, contemporary linguists, Jakobson (1990, 388) notably, challenge "this alleged multiplicity of contextual meanings" attributed by Husserl to the pronoun "I." Even though, in agreement with Husserl, the meaning of the pronoun "I" is context-dependent, Jakobson and other prominent linguists such as Lyons and Benveniste attribute *a general* meaning to this expression: the pronoun "I" indicates the speaker of the utterance to which it belongs (see chapter 2 for further discussion). The linguistic conception of the "I" appears therefore at odds with the transcendental conception of the subject. This tension will need to be examined in more detail.

Even though the absolute majority of Husserl's writings testify to a consistent commitment to the pure ego, in the *Logical Investigations* the author voices doubts about its existence. In the first edition of the second volume, Husserl writes: "I must frankly confess [. . .] that I am quite unable to find this ego, this primitive, necessary centre of relations" (1970 [1900], *Investigation V,* §8: "The pure ego and being in consciousness," 549).[5] The existence of an *empirical* ego, understood in terms of the really existent interweaving of psychic events in the unified stream of consciousness, is unquestioned by Husserl (535). However, this empirical ego gets eliminated once we move away from the psychophysical and henceforth transcendent world to the more primary conception of inner consciousness purified of all content. Importantly, this latter conception of consciousness is modeled by Husserl directly on the self-evidence of the Cartesian conception of *Cogito, ergo sum*, the epistemological precedence of which, that is, its imperviousness to doubt, turns it into a primary datum of study. This Cartesian conception does not prima facie give any credit to a nonempirical conception of the ego—Husserl notes that such philosophical ideas "have always remained questionable" (543). It follows that Cartesian statements made in the first-person singular (for example, "I perceive X") "elude complete conceptualization and expression[;] they are evident only in their living intention, which cannot be adequately imparted in words" (544). The very ineffability of the Cartesian ego makes it initially suspect in Husserl's view. The only valid conception of the ego would belong then to the empirical domain, and be firmly anchored in natural language. And yet, in the notes to the second edition, Husserl qualifies his earlier statements and affirms the necessary existence of the nonempirical ego as the phenomenologically purified equivalent of the empirical one. If the Cartesian statement "I am" is adequately self-evident—the fact that cannot be contested in Husserl's view—then a pure ego must be assumed as its subject. "It is precisely the ego apprehended in *carrying out* a self-evident *cogito,* and the pure carrying out *eo ipso* grasps it in phenomenological purity, and necessarily grasps it as the subject of a pure experience of the type *cogito*" (544, n1). Importantly, it is the Cartesian impulse to isolate a region of apodictic knowledge that motivates Husserl's postulate of a nonempirical ego, and overrides his earlier concerns about this notion. In agreement with Gurwitsch (1979), the pure ego postulate results therefore from a preexisting epistemological agenda and from the unquestioned attachment to the Cartesian conception of truth as absolute certitude obtained by means of intuitive insight within the privacy of subjective life. This preexisting attachment explains Husserl's willingness to posit an entity that he would otherwise be "unable to find."

Husserl's attachment to Cartesian heritage is most clearly expressed in his *Cartesian Meditations*. This text, based on two lectures delivered at the Sorbonne in 1929, reenacts Descartes' quest for certainty pursued in the first two *Meditationes de prima philosophia*. Husserl declares in fact that one could almost call transcendental phenomenology a neo-Cartesianism—not because it retains the *contents* of Descartes' philosophy, but because it is faithful to its *motifs* (1991, 1) and *impulses* (6). It is pertinent in this regard to recall briefly Descartes' classic statement from *Discourse on Method* (1637), which neatly sums up the findings of the *Meditations:*

> I then considered attentively what I was; and I saw that while I could feign that I had no body, that there was no world, and that no place existed for me to be in, I could not feign that I was not; on the contrary, from the mere fact that I thought of doubting about other truths it evidently and certainly followed that I existed. On the other hand, if I had merely ceased to be conscious, even if everything else that I had ever imagined had been true, I had no reason to believe that I should still have existed. From this I recognized that I was a substance whose whole essence or nature is to be conscious and whose being requires no place and depends on no material thing. Thus this self, that is to say the soul, by which I am what I am, is entirely distinct from the body, and is even more easily known; and even if the body were not there at all, the soul would be just what it is.

This passage helps to throw light on the contents and motifs/impulses of Descartes' project. The latter involve the method of radical doubt—the suspension of existential belief in knowledge that fails to yield apodictic insight. The Husserl of the *Cartesian Meditations* embraces this method, and reenacts the modern philosopher's "necessary regress to the ego" (1991, 6) in view of securing unshakable foundation for judgment. It is Husserl's conviction that if performed correctly, Descartes' turn to the *ego cogito* leads directly to transcendental subjectivity (18). Yet, even though Descartes may have had a glimpse into the transcendental field, he failed to preserve its nonmundane purity when he identified the thinking subject with the soul or the intellect (*mens*).⁶ By regarding the ego as the "tag-end of the world," Descartes objectifies subjectivity and is therefore guilty of transcendental realism (24). A rigorous neo-Cartesian method must refrain from smuggling any mundane contents into the ego. This strategy will help produce a transcendental science that is "absolutely subjective" (30), that is, a "pure egology" (ibid.). The pure egological science is intended to be presuppositionless and free from any preexisting metaphysical conceptions. Whether or not the very notion of the pure ego may be an import from a preexisting metaphysical tradition and its intuitionistic conception of truth fails, however, to be examined by Husserl in his *Meditations,* and it obscures the luminosity of transcendental reason as a blind spot.⁷

In line with the Cartesian heritage of his phenomenological project, the Husserl of *Ideas I* retains the broad definition of the *cogito* as the synthetic unity of conscious acts of the affective, perceptual, volitional, imaginary, as well as intellectual sort. "As is well known, cogito was understood so broadly by Descartes that it comprised every 'I perceive, I remember, I fantasy, I judge, I feel, I desire, I will,' and thus all egoical mental processes that are at all similar to them" (1982, §34). However, in agreement with the perspective of transcendental constitution, Husserl theorizes the *cogito* "in the pregnant sense" as the "actional cogito" (1982, §35), wherein particular *cogitationes* are viewed as acts properly so called, that is, as dynamic performances on the part of the ego. Within that perspective, the ego is construed as the seat of an intentionally performing consciousness that constitutes objectivity in manifold ways; it is the source-point of conscious productivity as it spreads out in the manner of visual rays (*Strahlen*) toward the intentional terminus. "The I" provides therefore the subjective pole of conscious activity. In contrast to the notion of the *person* or personal "I" which is subject to change over one's life span as the individual may evolve her political convictions, habits, and preferences, the pure ego-pole is an immutable core within the constant temporal flow of immanent experience. It exhibits therefore a form of transcendence within immanence, insofar as it cannot be identified with the individual cogito-acts, even though it is their necessary substrate (1982, §80). The pure *I* "preserves a numerical identity in contrast with the *cogitationes* which come and go" (Bernet et al., 1993, 208).

Contra his early statements from the *Logical Investigations,* the Husserl of *Ideas I* contends that each act of consciousness can instruct us of the existence of the transcendental *I:* "the isolated experience of a single, simple cogito" offers the best opportunity for realizing the necessity of the existence of the transcendental ego (Bernet et al. 1993, 211). He is quite adamant about the ego's not being eliminable by the phenomenological reduction: "no excluding can [. . .] cancel out the 'pure' subject of the act" (1982, §80). Consistently illustrating his argument with metaphors taken from the sphere of vision, Husserl adds that every act "necessarily includes in its essence this: that it is precisely a ray 'emanating from the ego'" (ibid.). He speaks not only of "rays," but also of the radiating "regard" directed from the pure ego to the object (1982, §84). He insists on the irreducibility of the pure ego by likening it to an eye that cannot see itself and yet has to be presupposed as the source of the look. It may therefore be the case that Husserl's pure-ego postulate is fostered by privileging vision and its organ ("the eye" or the "I") in his discussion of transcendental consciousness, as Richard Rorty (1980) claims. This visual bias is in accordance with the Western tradition of *ocularcentrism,* as discussed by Martin Jay (1993).

Husserl's possible visual bias notwithstanding, another motivation for positing the transcendental ego springs from his concern with accounting for the unity of consciousness and with the possibility of identifying mental processes as belonging to one subject. It was Husserl's conviction that the ego disclosed by the reduction is not individuated or that it is situated prior to differentiations into an *I* and a *you* (1970 [1938], 82). (This apparent nonindividuation raises the questions how to justify the usage of the word "I" in the context of constitution and why not speak of some supraindividual agency akin to Hegel's notion of the Spirit.) The lack of individuation explains why it was a pressing matter for Husserl to find stable criteria guaranteeing the unity of conscious life. As Marbach notes (Bernet et al. 1993, 206), once the perspectives of other consciousnesses were included in the transcendental domain in order to guarantee that the objectivities constituted within phenomenology were not solipsistic but had intersubjective validity, it became increasingly important to identify consciousness not only in terms of its immanent temporal unity, but also in terms of self-containment, so as to delimit successfully one stream of consciousness from another. A criterion that made it possible to secure the self-containment of consciousness was provided by the Kantian principle of the synthetic unity of apperception. As Husserl writes, "In every actional cogito the ego lives out its life in a special sense. But all mental processes in the background likewise belong to it; and it belongs to them. All of them, as belonging to the *one* stream of consciousness which is mine, *must* admit of being converted into actional cogitationes as immanental constituents. In Kant's words, "The 'I *think' must be capable of accompanying all my presentations*" (1982, §57). This necessary conversion of mental processes into I-acts justifies, in Husserl's view, the postulate of the *I* as an irreducible subject of the actional cogito. One can wonder, however, whether this conversion is phenomenologically justified.

Most famously, Sartre (1972, 32) challenged Husserl's move from a de jure ("I think" *must* be able to accompany all my presentations) to a de facto claim ("I think" *does* in fact accompany all my presentations). In other words, Sartre found no phenomenological support for turning the Kantian requirement that it be *possible* to identify any act of consciousness as mine into the claim that the *I* is an *existent* subject of any *cogito*. Contra Husserl, Sartre argues that the synthetic unity of apperception makes no existential claims concerning the *I*. Kant is interpreted to be saying that "I can always regard my thought or perception as mine: nothing more" (ibid.). Ultimately, in Sartre's view, phenomenological evidence suggests that the ego is not a *transcendental* subject of consciousness but rather a *transcendent* mundane entity.[8] His critique extends therefore to contemporary arguments in favor of a phenomenological place for a pure ego, discussed below.

THE GRAMMAR OF THE TRANSCENDENTAL EGO (I)

Let me throw some additional light on the conception of the ego by investigating it via a linguistic lens. Specifically, I wish to retrace the meaning of the word "I"/"ego" as it passes from ordinary language to *transcendentalese*. The term "ego" has become so entrenched in post–Cartesian philosophy, that it often goes unnoticed that a significant grammatical shift occurred when this term was imported into *lingua philosophica*. The word "ego" functions in its native Latin as the first-person pronoun singular, and it therefore serves to indicate who occupies the speaker role at a given moment. In philosophical jargon, and in *transcendentalese,* the same word became prefaced with a definite article, and handled as if it were a noun. In cases where a vernacular rather than the Latin first-person pronoun is used in transcendental philosophy (*das transzendentale Ich* [Husserl], *le Je transcendantale* [Sartre]), we witness an analogous process of nominalization of the first-person pronoun. This shift significantly alters the grammatical, as well as the philosophical, function of the word "I." Consider that first- and second-personal pronouns differ pragmatically from nouns, even though it may seem prima facie that *pro-nouns* are mere substitutes for nouns (see discussion in chapter 2). "I" and "you" enact the speaker and addressee roles in discourse, that is, they do not simply name extradiscursive entities but introduce discursive participants for the first time. Once the shift from the ordinary language to *transcendentalese* occurs, this original pronominal function of indicating the speaker (and the addressee) becomes overshadowed. Specifically, the word "I" gets construed as a label for a stable referent, typically, although not necessarily, an ineffable mentalistic subject. To use Husserl's categories, an essentially *subjective and occasional* expression gets misconstrued as an *objective* one. As a result, the "I"/"ego" ceases to be regarded within its native communicative ground and appears rather as a label for a discourse-neutral referent. I propose to discuss these grammatical shifts and their philosophical implications in more detail in what follows.

Consider first the ambiguous status of the word "I"/"ego" as it enters the transcendental domain.

> All of mankind, and the whole distinction and ordering of the personal pronouns, has become a phenomenon within my epoche; and so has the privilege of the I-the-man among other men [sic]. The "I" that I attain in the epoche, which would be the same as the "ego" within *a critical reinterpretation and correction of the Cartesian conception, is actually called "I" only by equivocation*—though it is an essential equivocation since, when I name it in reflection, I can say nothing other than: it is I who practice the epoche, I who interrogate, as phenomenon, the world. . . with all its human beings; it is I who stand above all natural existence, . . . who am the ego-pole of this transcendental life, . . . it is I who. . . encompass all that. (1970 [1938], 184)

What Husserl outlines here in reference to the pronoun "I" is the delicate issue of, in Fink's words, "transcendental predication." On the one hand, natural language is bracketed and regarded as a phenomenon by the phenomenological onlooker, whose own method is conceived as linguistically neutral. It is a purified form of introspection, intense inner gazing into the constitutive agency of consciousness as it grounds mundane objectivities, the natural languages included. On the other hand, the phenomenologist typically conveys her insights to others in a shared linguistic medium, even though it is unclear whether any transcendental necessity enforces outward expression of the phenomenological findings and is thus possible to wonder, as Fink did, whether "this experiential life [could not] remain then *forever* without language?" (1995, 98). In fact, Fink argued, in two consecutive and contradictory statements, that "there is *no reason* and *no compulsion* for predicative outward expression lying in phenomenologically theorizing experience as such. And yet predicative outward expression is in a definite sense *transcendentally necessary*" (98–99). This blatant contradiction may be partly softened by Fink's invoking an inherent "tendency toward the universal" as the motive for linguistic expression of transcendental meanings (99), as well as "the communicative tendency of all philosophizing" (100). However, for a transcendental phenomenologist it remains undeniable that the *lingua transcendentalis* is not to be confused with the *lingua naturalis*. To be sure, the existing vocabulary stock is not affected by the elevation onto the transcendental level, and no new language is to be devised for accurate articulation of phenomenologically purified experience. However, transcendental statements are not to be read in the same breath as natural ones. For the meaning of transcendental insights can only be grasped in linguistic format by equivocation: while the former capture the preexisting activity of nonmundane subjectivity, the latter are carved out of mundane existence. Hence the "immanent conflict and contradiction in every transcendental predication" (98) and "the constant rebellion against the constraint imposed upon [the transcendental sense] by the formulation in natural words and sentences" (89).

The foregoing discussion suggests that the phenomenological onlooker uncovers a pure transcendental ego, which "would be the same as the 'ego' within a critical reinterpretation and correction of the Cartesian conception." The phenomenologist then baptizes this finding as "I" (or *Ich, Je. . .*) for the sake of shared understanding within a given linguistic community, it being understood that the natural word names its transcendental counterpart "by equivocation" only. Paradoxically, however, the "habituality of language" is retained throughout the epoche (86), and continues to shape somehow the transcendental level of inquiry. This latter point puts pressure on the neat separation between pure transcendental insights and their outward expressions. Instead, we appear caught in a whirlwind of words and meanings, or a natural/transcendental circle. Even though the express objective of the reduction is to locate a preexisting constituting domain of consciousness, which founds the existing domain of mundane existence (including natural languages), it may be that such a separation between the transcendental ground and the natural grounded world proves impossible to accomplish—even as a regulative ideal. If so, the supposed primacy of pure meanings over predication cannot be upheld—they are coprimary. Approached via the question of transcendental predication, the transcendental project as such may therefore be subject to "immanent conflict and contradiction," insofar as it attempts to drive a wedge between meaning and expression.

STRAWSON ON THE PRIMACY OF PERSONHOOD

This point is in general agreement with P. F. Strawson (1991), whose discussion of the pronoun "I" is especially relevant to our purposes. Strawson targeted Descartes' conception of pure consciousness, but his critique extends to Husserl's critically revised conception as well. Strawson challenges the possibility of positing an individuated consciousness accessed in the first-person mode independently of pronominal categories. Strawson argues that the first-person pronoun tacitly employed by Descartes for personal reference is what enables him to theorize a single mind at all. In other words, Descartes continues to rely on pronominal categories as he uncovers the indubitable domain of conscious thought with the classic statement "I think, I am," even though pronouns in particular and language in general must be allocated to the mundane domain whose existence is subjected to doubt. Descartes' project is therefore inherently absurd: the philosopher withdraws the first-person pronoun from ordinary language game and recasts it within the domain of pure thought, where it is forced to perform a task of designating an individual enduring consciousness in the first-person mode—a task that it can de facto play only within language, not outside of it. In Strawson's own words, "We are tricking ourselves by simultaneously withdrawing the [first-person] pronoun from the ordinary game and yet preserving the illusion that we're still using it to play the ordinary game" (1991, 61). The whole conception of a pure ego accessed in isolation from the sociolinguistic community by means of introspective insight and translated *après coup* into a natural language first-person pronoun is therefore founded on a contradiction. This conception needs to be replaced, Strawson (1958) contends, with the thesis of the primitiveness of the *person*, which designates neither the conscious mind nor the body, but a notion more primary than either of these two terms.

Strawson's remarks strongly suggest that the existing natural vocabulary actively shapes the findings obtained on the transcendental plane. Following that line of thought, the pure egological subject of consciousness would appear less as a preexpressive intuitive datum and more as a supposed referent of the nominalized pronoun "I," an element of philosophical jargon inherited from modernity. The nominalized pronoun "I" would therefore produce the phenomenological illusion of a transcendental ego.

This phenomenological illusion would not arise had the word "I" retained its original pronominal function. In that case, as discussed in more detail in chapter 2, it would have been granted that the "I" is a "shifter" (Jespersen 1922, Jakobson 1990), that is, that its referent is not assigned in a relatively stable fashion but shifts according to the evolving conversational context, depending on who adopts the speaker role at a given time. This ordinary conception of the pronoun "I" is at odds with the transcendental notion, which seems firmly attached to an individual subject. However, this latter notion may ultimately distort the ordinary pragmatics of language and consequently the ordinary understanding of who and what we are.

WITTGENSTEIN ON THE LURE OF WORDS

Wittgenstein (1960) clearly identifies this distortion in his *Blue Book*. Once the first-person pronoun is turned into a substantive noun like "the chair" or "the tree," we are being "misled by the similarity of their linguistic form into a false conception of their grammar" (16). In other words, we are duped by the illusion that there is a thing behind every word, especially if that word has a substantive form. "A substantive makes us look for a thing that corresponds to it" (1) in a naive belief in a one-to-one correspondence between a word and its referent. This naive belief, Wittgenstein argues, fuels traditional philosophic questions, such as, what is time? However, it is because "the mystifying use of language" has initially posited time as an objective entity that the "deity of time" (6) can be set on a pedestal for the generations of philosophers to venerate and ponder. Wittgenstein's comment parallels closely the French linguist Emile Benveniste's criticism of the Western philosophical idiom that posits "being" as a substantive noun (1971, 62) and thus "set being up... as an objectifiable notion which philosophical thought could handle, analyze, and define just as any other concept." Both Wittgenstein and Benveniste warn against "the fascination which forms of expression exert upon us" (Wittgenstein 1960, 27). In fact, Wittgenstein believed that philosophy should serve primarily as a therapeutic device helping to dissipate this unacknowledged, unexamined, and thus all the more pervasive lure of words over philosophers' minds by means of a renewed inquiry into language.

Clearly, not all substantive nouns name a physical thing, as the time example shows. Following Wittgenstein, "when we perceive that a substantive is not used as what in general we should call the name of an object, [. . .] we can't help saying to ourselves that it is the name of an ethereal object" (1960, 47). The mental entity designated by the pronoun "I" would be such an ethereal entity. Specifically, Wittgenstein argues, it would be posited as a result of the fact that no description of the physical human body could be substituted for the first pronoun under its subjective use. Consider that Wittgenstein distinguishes between the "use as object" and the "use as subject" of the pronoun "I." To the objective usage of the "I" pronoun would belong phrases of the type: "my arm is broken" or "I am 6 feet tall." In these cases, "I" can refer to a bodily part or the entire body by means of pointing, and locate the referent of the "I" pronoun there. However, "The mouth which says 'I' or the hand which is raised to indicate that it is I who wish to speak, or I who have toothache, does not thereby point to anything" (68). In those latter cases the "I" is used as a subject. Clearly, this subjective use does not undermine the bodily character of the activity I am involved in. However, it is impossible to assign a determined corporeal location to the subject that raises her hand, complains of a toothache, or otherwise communicates with others. This de jure impossibility to "substitute for [subjective] 'I' a description of a body" (74) may lead the philosopher to posit a nonphysical referent of the first-person pronoun. However, Wittgenstein retorts, "to say that the ego is mental is like saying that the number 3 is mental or an immaterial nature, when we recognize that the numeral '3' isn't used as a sign for a physical object" (73). Any claim postulating a nonempirical ego is therefore a product of the compulsion to generate entities, however evanescent, to match and mirror the philosophic idiom.

Even though his critique of the performative potential of language in general and the philosophic jargon in particular is a powerful one, Wittgenstein gives us few positive clues as to what an undistorted grammar of the "I" pronoun would be, or what philosophical consequences for personal identity would follow from it. His objective in the *Blue Book* is chiefly a critical one: to dethrone the "I" from the elevated position it has occupied in philosophy since modernity. We need additional insights, to be gleaned from sociolinguistics, in order to develop such a positive grammar of the first-person pronoun and to spell out its philosophical implications. Furthermore, we may wonder whether Wittgenstein himself was not partially duped by the very illusion he helped to disclose. His distinction between the use as object and the use of subject of the "I" pronoun suggests that this pronoun can, in its objective use, be treated on a par with substantives. In his words, "If, in saying 'I,' I point to my own body, I model the use of the word 'I' on that of the demonstrative 'this person' or 'he'" (68). This modeling suggests that, in its objective use, the pronoun "I" is grammatically equivalent to a substantive noun or a third-person pronoun designating a mundane entity with a definite set of physical properties (size, height, weight), and that problems arise only if we regard the "I" pronoun as a noun designating a nonempirical entity. Both designations are, however, grammatically suspect insofar as they turn the pronoun "I" into a substantive noun. As previously noted, "A substantive makes us look for a thing that corresponds to it" (1), and apparently so does the "I" pronoun construed as an object. Yet it is far from obvious that the "I" pronoun can be construed as a substantive at all. While attacking philosophy for locating an ephemeral referent of the "I" pronoun in its "use as subject" in the pure mind, Wittgenstein is unaware that his own location of the pronoun "I" in its "use as object" in the objective body may be motivated by the same grammatical illusion; that behind the little word "I" there must be a thing. In conclusion, the difficulty resides not only in the nature of the referent of the "I" but in the very assumption that it possesses such an independently identifiable referent. Finally, it may be that Wittgenstein was unjustified in viewing the pronoun "I," in its use as object, as equivalent to a third-person pronoun. As studies in sociolinguistics show, even though the traditional nomenclature aligns the pronouns in a paradigm of conjugation with three terms ("I," "you," "he," "she," "it") and creates the impression of symmetry between the three persons, this symmetry may be merely formal and contradicted by the ordinary distinction between personal pronouns ("I" and "you"), which designate the participants within a conversational exchange, and the so-called impersonal (third-person) pronoun, which designates a nonparticipatory third party that neither speaks nor is spoken to. It follows that we would be yet again "misled by the similarity of their linguistic form into a false conception of their grammar" (1960, 16), were we to regard the first-person pronoun "I" as equivalent to the third. Wittgenstein may not have been impervious to this latter grammatical illusion when he singled out the objective pronoun "I."

THE GRAMMAR OF THE TRANSCENDENTAL EGO (2)

Turning back to Husserl's phenomenology, the reader finds the pronoun "I" being consistently used as a *substantive* (what I will refer to as the substantive

"I," in distinction from the usual pronominal use of "I"), that is, as a label for transcendental subjectivity. One also finds the attribute of "personal indeclinability" (1970 [1938], 185) attached to the "I." As a result, the substantive "I" gets subsumed under the grammatical category termed in Latin *Indeclinabilia*, which includes nouns such as *fas* (divine law); *nefas* (sin, impious act); and *pondo* (pound). Declared indeclinable, the substantive "I" becomes absolved from the grammatical categories of *number, case,* and *gender.* I examine what it means to bracket these categories in the transcendental domain and what philosophical implications for the understanding of personhood follow from this grammatical revision.

Absolution from *gender* does not affect the qualities a pronoun ordinarily bears: the first-, unlike the third-, person pronoun is gender neutral in all languages under discussion. However, the bracketing of *number* does produce far-reaching implications. The ordinary pronoun "I" does have the corresponding plural form, but not the transcendental *I*. For example, Husserl states that any reference to a possible *We* and *Us* is excluded by the *epoche* (1988, §44, 98). On the transcendental plane, I am construed as *one*, absolutely unique. As Husserl puts it, "*In an absolute sense, this ego is the only ego.* It is not meaningfully multipliable; more precisely expressed, it excludes this as senseless" (Fink 1995, quoted in Mensch 1988, 59).

Excluding the possibility of being put in the plural, the substantive "I" is construed as *a nonnumerical singular.* It gets therefore subsumed, as Schutz notes (1966, 77), under the grammatical category of nouns used in the singular only, termed in Latin *Singularia tantum*. Most proper names, as well as mass or uncountable nouns, such as "gold," "faith," "justice," "leather," "wisdom," "garment," "the people," do not figure in the plural and are *singularia tantum* in ordinary languages. The nonnumerical singularity attributed to the "I" generates consequences of interests to grammarians and philosophers alike. It places the "I" within a posture of radical solitude. Once on the transcendental plane, Husserl notes, I become locked in "a unique sort of philosophical solitude which is the fundamental methodical requirement for a truly radical philosophy" (1970 [1938], 184). Or to cite Fink's dramatic formulation, the phenomenological reduction places me "in the monstrous solitude of transcendental existence [*Existenz*] as ego" (1995, 99).

We can wonder whether such monstrous solitude would be assigned to a speaking *I*, caught up in an inextricable bond to a sociolinguistic community and oriented toward a present or a potential addressee. Needless to say, the speaking *I* is inescapably situated within its individuated viewpoint, and phenomenological solitude can be regarded as an expression of this nonoptional situatedness. As previously noted, however, the situated character of experience, notably speech, does not preclude but in fact presupposes an intrinsic connectedness with the other in the *I–you* mode. An exclusive focus on the phenomenological loneliness of the subject may detract from this phenomenological reality of interpersonal connectedness. To reformulate this point in Schutz's terms, there is a difficulty in founding transcendental intersubjectivity on subjective solitude. For Schutz, the difficulty lies specifically in spelling out how the nonnumerical substantive "I" could ever make itself declinable in the plural (1966, 76). Merleau-Ponty who, *nota bene*, adheres to Husserl's notion of the indeclinable "I" in the chapter "Other Selves and the Human World" from the *Phenomenology of Perception,* identifies this difficulty in the following way: "How can the word 'I' be put into the plural, how can a general idea of the *I* be formed, how can I speak of an *I* other than my own, how can I know that there are other *I*'s, how can consciousness which, by its nature, and as self-knowledge, is in the mode of the *I*, be grasped in the mode of Thou, and through this, in the world of the 'One'?" (1994, 348)

The difficulties raised by Schutz and Merleau-Ponty regarding the possibility of multiplying beings construed grammatically and philosophically as nonnumerical singulars does not, however, address the even more urgent question of interpersonal relatedness and communal life. Even if a singular *I* could be multiplied, that theoretical possibility does not capture the phenomenological reality of social life. It is doubtful whether a sheer multiplicity of lone *I*s can yield a communal network of interrelation and interdependency. It leads rather to the notion of sociality as an aggregate or a collectivity of insular individuals. However, the plurality of the *we* is not established by multiplying the referents of the pronoun "I" but rather through an engagement in an *I-you* relation; in other words, the social plurality is not of an *additive* but *relational* kind (see chapter 2 for details). A professed commitment to the multiplicity of *I*s does not therefore serve to establish conditions for a nonempty usage of a communal *we*. The relational fabric of a life shared with others is still missing when we posit a series of solitary selves. The chief difficulty does not therefore reside in how there could be numerically more than just one *I,* but rather in the fact that the relations of the I-you type have not been sufficiently explored.

Indeed as Merleau-Ponty (1964) argues, the professed solitude of the ego is not exclusive of the existence of other egos—its intelligibility may reside in the possible existence of other egos. "To say that the ego 'prior to' the other person is alone is already to situate it in relation to a phantom of the other person, or at least to conceive of an environment in which others could be" (Merleau-Ponty 1964, 174). Solitude supposes the possibility of others in its very experiential character of deprivation from others who are felt as absent.[9] The construal of the substantive "I" as *singularia tantum* may therefore be coextensive with a multiplicity of *I*s. Still, as long as the ego is regarded as an index of inalienable subjectivity, a multiplicity thereof leads to no more than the paradoxical case of multiple solipsism, as Merleau-Ponty also observes (1994, 359). It does not suffice to multiply instances of the singular *I* as long the latter is cast in an uncommunicative first-person mode and precludes the possibility of addressing and being addressed by others in the second person.

To clarify this point, consider briefly the case of the so-called I-you reversibility, discussed in more detail in chapter 2. In ordinary sociolinguistic setting, "I" and "you" are reversible insofar as every "I" uttered by the speaker reverses into a "you" when addressed by another; and analogously the other person addressed as "you" self-refers by means of the "I." These I-you reversals, ongoing within the conversational context, are not extrinsic to either of the pronouns; children master "I" fully only once they have grasped its connectedness to "you." The noneradicable I-you reversibility and the speaker's intrinsic relatedness to an addressee in pronominal discourse are, however, neglected within the transcendental phenomenological grammar of the pronoun "I." Once the "I" has been construed as an *indeclinable nominal*, the I-you reversibility has been covered over.

Consider, finally, the implications of bracketing the grammatical category of *case* in the example of the "indeclinable I." The indeclinable "I" would be immune to placement in the genitive, dative, accusative, and remaining cases. For example, the transcendental *I* would not decline into a *me*, since such declination presupposes an interpersonal framework of interrelated personal perspectives. If the only operational grammatical case is the nominative, then the only personal perspective deployed in the transcendental field is my own. The transcendental *I* becomes therefore construed as a *nonobjectifiable subject*, both grammatically and philosophically. Grammatically, the nominative "I" can function as a subject and not as an object of a verb. It can occupy a preverbal but not a postverbal position. Philosophically, the *I* is defined in terms of world-constituting activity, and not in terms of activity directed upon it by others. To be constituted by others, to be on the recipient side of action, the subject would have to reverse into an object; yet such a reversal is precluded by the confinement of the first-person pronoun to the nominative role.

In conclusion, the ascription of "personal indeclinability" to the pronoun "I" produces a *substantive, singular,* and *subjective* notion of personhood. This notion underscores the separation between the *I* and other persons, and fuels the vision of sociality in terms of an external aggregate of separated *I*s. Phrased in the usual phenomenological terms, it promotes the conception of intersubjectivity as a collective of subjects. Yet an ordinary linguistic conception of the pronoun "I," pursued in this monograph, suggests rather that the *I* is inextricably interrelated with the *you,* and that communal life is sustained by a host of I-you relations. Even though it does not dismiss or dissolve the first-person perspective in language and experience, it underscores its original and irreducible entanglement with second-person relatedness. Thanks to this recognition of the primary I-you connectedness, insights from ordinary linguistic usage can account for the emergence and the relational dynamics of social life.

ZAHAVI ON TRANSCENDENTAL SUBJECTIVITY AS INTERSUBJECTIVITY

My critical engagement with Husserl's work has focused up to now on the neglect of I-you relatedness and the concurrent limitations of the phenomenological vision of the social world. I propose to engage an alternative interpretation advanced by one of the most contemporary defenders of the Husserlian view that helps to further articulate the nature of the criticism developed here. Dan Zahavi (2001) consistently developed the view that Husserl's phenomenology is not bound to a solipsistic subjectivity but offers a compelling transcendental theory of intersubjectivity. Even though Husserl situates the analysis within the solitary subjective viewpoint of the ego, and so may appear to privilege the lone subject over intersubjective relatedness, it is rather the case that Husserl develops a theory of primary intersubjectivity with the full methodological rigor called for by the phenomenological style inquiry. Phenomenology does not regard intersubjectivity on a metalevel above and beyond the experience of individual *I*s, but rather as exhibited in individual life of consciousness. Intersubjectivity cannot be pursued as a transcendental problem from an external third-person perspective, but only through an interrogation of first-person experience (2001, 18). The confinement to solitary subjectivity is therefore not an expression of implicit solipsism; it manifests rather Husserl's ongoing commitment to the primacy of intersubjectivity as manifested within subjectivity. Zahavi concludes therefore, in open disagreement with the linguistic pragmatic approaches to intersubjectivity formulated by Apel and Habermas, that a properly philosophical understanding of intersubjectivity requires not a break with but rather a turn to and a radicalization of the phenomenological (that is, transcendental) philosophy of the subject (2001, 209). This is in fact one of the distinct advantages of the transcendental phenomenological over the linguistic pragmatic approaches to intersubjectivity: the former avoids conceiving subjectivity and intersubjectivity as irreconcilable alternatives standing in mutual opposition or contradiction (205).

Zahavi focuses his discussion of transcendental intersubjectivity on its constituting rather than constituted aspects, primarily because he locates Husserl's true contribution to the phenomenology of intersubjectivity therein (2001, 21). Intersubjectivity is therefore thematized phenomenologically within the perspective of world constitution, notably the intersubjective validation of the objective world. From a phenomenological point of view, the transcendence and objectivity of the world do not arise for a solipsistic subject but suppose, and are mediated by, an experience of a mundane givenness to another subject. It is only because I experience that others experience the same objects I do that I experience these objects as objective. Objectivity of the world is predicated upon intersubjective validation (34). Zahavi is careful to delimit two types of relations to others within the context of intersubjective validation: a contingent a posteriori actual experience of others, and an a priori intersubjective openness of subjectivity itself. Since the latter type of relation is primordial for Husserl, transcendental intersubjectivity is not made dependent on encounters with contingent others but precedes the experience of flesh and blood others and belongs necessarily to the a priori structure of subjectivity (52–57). The solitary constituting subject itself discloses therefore, in its predicative experiences, a cofunctioning intersubjectivity (61), thus averting once and for all the threat of transcendental solipsism.

Contra Schutz, the transcendental *I* is therefore emphatically not a *singulare tantum*. "If there is one transcendental I, there is necessarily the possibility of *more than one*, for it is only in inter-subjectivity that this I is a constitutively functioning I, i. e. a transcendental I" (Zahavi 2001, 65, emphasis added). Transcendental solitude does not preclude but presupposes (transcendental) plurality; subjectivity *is* intersubjectivity (exhibited within subjectivity). In agreement with Husserl's conception of the other as another *I* or *alter ego* (19), the plurality is composed of transcendental subjects (24) or monadic *I*s (63). It is a transcendental community of *I*s disclosed through the solitary ego (20). The solitary *I* is said to be equipped with we-consciousness (99), even though it is needs to be emphasized, in accordance with the transcendental method, that every *we* is centered in the *I* who has we-consciousness (64).

I previously argued that a notion of plurality based upon the more-than-one *I* does not provide a phenomenologically rich and accurate conception of social life. What is needed is not a collective of *I*s, but I-you connectedness. Zahavi's defense of Husserl's transcendental intersubjectivity remains therefore neglectful of this basic interpersonal duality of first- to second-person relation, and remains committed to an isolated first-person stance that fails to yield a relational plurality of interdependency and mutual coexistence. Zahavi emphasizes the necessary relatedness (2001, 84) and connectedness within a community (75), but it remains doubtful whether an account centered on the first-person stance alone provides the resources needed to thematize this communal connectedness in phenomenologically concrete terms. Phrased in pronominal terms, it is questionable whether the collective of *I*s produces a *we*. Ordinary language analysis drawn on in chapter 2 makes manifest that, contrary to received notions, the first-person plural does not arise via multiplication of the referents of the pronoun "I," but rather is predicated on I-you relatedness. The transcendental account cannot *both* employ pronominal categories *and* disregard their ordinary meaning in use. The transcendental account of we-consciousness should therefore make transcendental room for the *I and for the (relatedness to the) you*. Yet, there is no room for a transcendental *you*, and henceforth the passage from I-subject to we-community is blocked.

Zahavi's reading of Husserl supposes a radical disjunction between, on the one hand, the *I* regarded as "subject per se," and, on the other hand, the field of I-you relations, which are assigned to "the personal subject" (2001, 83).

> It is. . . . extremely important to note that Husserl differentiates between various levels of I-structure. Thus there is a distinction between the subject as such (or the I as a unity in the stream, i.e., as a pole of affection and action) and the personal subject. When Husserl writes that it is true a priori that. . . there is no I without Thou . . . and that each I is what it is only as "socius" of sociality, as a

member of a community... this concerns precisely the I as a person, and not the I as a pole of affection and action. (193)

Needless to say, as Zahavi admits, a full and concrete story of the *I* needs to include this interpersonal connectedness (83). Henceforth, the *I* cannot be characterized without the *you* in a phenomenologically primordial manner. The transcendental subject would therefore be personal and embedded within a host of interpersonal relations. However, ultimately only the first-person subject, an absolute and originally unique *I*, is deemed transcendental, whereas the (inter)personal subject is regarded as secondary and derivative. Zahavi therefore rebuffs the objection raised by Zeltner (1959) and Theunissen (1986) that Husserl neglects to describe a genuine concrete sociality found in the I-you relation by stating that Husserl was interested above all in a transcendental elucidation of transcendence and objectivity, and not in a detailed presentation of personal experience (18). However, it is unclear why sociality regarded primarily as a means to an end within the perspective of world constitution should exhaust or overdetermine the phenomenological conception of social life. The distinction between I-subjects and I-thou persons may be motivated by the interest of the phenomenological perspective of constitution, but it could be cast within the transcendental theory of intersubjectivity rather than motivate a split between transcendental and personal regions. The ego-alter ego schema carries over to the discussion of interpersonal relations in their concreteness, and thus comes to provide the basic paradigm for thinking about sociality in all regions within Husserl's phenomenology; whereas the I-you duality is more appropriate for capturing the phenomenological reality of relatedness to the other addressed frontally and not thematized from a disengaged lateral standpoint as another "I," a cosubject presupposed within the transcendental project of world constitution.

The transcendental conception of sociality as I-collective ultimately neglects the ordinary meaning in use of pronominal discourse, whereas it may itself be shaped by a traditional, epistemically filtered, take on pronominal discourse and its conception of the "I." Let me unpack this principal point of contention in what follows. Zahavi revisits and substantiates Husserl's notion of the indeclinable (nonnumerical singular) "I" by emphasizing its indexicality (82). He is careful to emphasize that the uniqueness of the "I" is not to be thematized in substantial but rather indexical terms—only I experience myself as "I" (even though others may experience themselves as "I," too). However, this emphasis on the subjectivity of the "I" neglects the social role played by the "I" in discourse, which ordinarily designates a speaker, regardless of whether it is uttered or heard, and does not therefore stand in a privileged relation to the self but does stand in a privileged relation to the realm of speech. The emphasis on indexicality regards the "I" within the context of silent soliloquy wherein the "I" is thinking to itself, while the speaking "I" plays *both* a subjective/indexical *and* a socialized/discursive role.

The latter point gets occluded, since the indexicality of the "I" is ultimately deemed linguistically neutral.

> This emphasis on indexical uniqueness. . . . is by no means to be understood as a merely contingent linguistic fact. The relatedness of sense back to an I-consciousness is not dependent upon the factual availability of linguistic terms such as "I," "ich," "je," "jeg," etc., rather, it is a matter of a fundamental transcendental relationship that is ultimately linked with the problem of individuation and self-awareness. (82)

An alternative reading offered here suggests that the transcendental perspective of I-consciousness is predicated on a tacit employment of the pronoun "I" and so is shaped by linguistic facts. As Strawson notes, there is a contradiction inherent in a philosophical project that both draws on *and* claims immunity to pronominal discourse. I-consciousness may seem like a transcendental given uncovered by neutral phenomenal seeing. However, upon investigation, I-consciousness is tributary of an epistemically driven tradition of inquiry, which construes I-consciousness as the domain of apodictic knowledge. I analyze a contemporary example of this epistemically determined I-consciousness in some detail in chapter 2, in light of Castañeda's philosophy. In this section, my aim is to show its influence on I-consciousness within Zahavi's defense of Husserl.

Zahavi discusses the reference of the word "I" in some detail, because it reveals—albeit is not a precondition of—some peculiar features of self-awareness (1999, 3). The pronoun is peculiar because, when correctly used, its reference never misfires. Following the Cartesian intuition, the person who says "I" not only guarantees the existence but also the experiential presence of its reference every time the "I" is uttered. First-person reference or subject-use of "I" is therefore contrasted with third-person descriptions and names, which attribute objective characteristics to self. I would still be referring to myself when I believe that I am Billie Holiday, but the description "one of the greatest female jazz vocalists" surely applies to someone else (see chapter 2 for further examples and discussion).

It is therefore customary to oppose the subject-use of "I," predicated on nonobjectifying self-awareness, to an objectified knowledge of oneself, for example, gained by watching one's reflection in the mirror (Zahavi 1999, 6). The latter denotes an external encounter with oneself, and is subject to misrecognition and error. For example, I may see my reflection in a store window, identify it as a disgruntled DMV customer, only to recognize that this customer is indeed *me*. An internal reflexive reference is, on the contrary, invariably accompanied by self-awareness and enjoys the so-called immunity to error through misidentification.

The subjective/internal view is modeled on the peculiar reference of the pronoun "I," its unfailing referentiality independent of any identificatory knowledge. However, as discussed in chapter 2, the emphasis on immunity to error (through misidentification) is fueled by a quest for apodictic knowledge and effectively overshadows the properties of the word "I" that would muddy transparent self-awareness. In the ordinary pragmatic context, the pronoun "I" carries both subjective and objective references, that is, statements capturing mental states ("I am happy," "I feel sick"), but also physical states ("I dress in black," "I am myopic"). The latter are subject to error through misidentification and do not yield Cartesian knowledge about the existence and existential presence of the self. To privilege subjective I-reference is therefore to glean over the complexity of I-referentiality and to single out only those aspects that fit the preexisting project of securing apodictic knowledge. The resulting epistemic construal of self-awareness is therefore reductive of the existential complexity and opacity of the self, as expressed in the ordinary pragmatic usage of the word "I." It should not be unequivocally naturalized as preexisting transcendental I-consciousness, but inscribed within the intellectual history of epistemic quest and its ideals of knowledge as transparency and apodicticity.

Consider also that the opposition between first- and third-person perspectives covers over another aspect of I-referentiality and interpersonal relatedness. Following Zahavi:

> whereas Others refer to me using identifying and discriminatory means such as proper names, demonstratives, or definite descriptions, these third-person references are not merely unnecessary but ultimately insufficient if I am to think of myself as myself, that is, in the proper first-person way. (1999, 10)

The opposition between first- and third-person referentiality mapped onto the self and the other respectively does not account for second-person reference, and the ways in which the "I" is interrelated and alternates with "you" in ordinary context of pronominal use. This neglect of an I-you connectedness fuels the notion of internal reflexive subjectivity, and gives a discursively unwarranted impression that other viewpoints are necessarily objectifying and potentially falsifying. To be sure, others can do exactly that. However, the opposition between internal first person and external third person is shaped by an epistemic hierarchy of superior and inferior knowledge—whereas pronominal discourse in ordinary use serves not only to establish claims with truth value (including claims made about the self and the other), but also to enact dialogical relations between interlocutors. The latter dialogical function is of a performative rather than representational kind, in that it enacts speaker and addressee roles in discourse (as discussed in chapter 2). It therefore gets occluded from an account that regards I-referentiality exclusively from the standpoint of the ideal of apodictic knowledge.

In conclusion, any discussion of I-referentiality needs to account for the rich and complex pragmatic context of "I" use, which includes the subjective and objective referentiality, as well as the connectedness and alternation between "I" and "you." The notion of I-consciousness shaped by an epistemically motivated focus on first-without-second-person reference does not appear linguistically neutral, but rather shaped by a historically specific take on language, which strategically illuminates certain aspects of pronominal discourse and obscures others. The task left to the philosopher seems then to consist in a turn to ordinary linguistic use of pronominal discourse, in view of retrieving the aspects that have been traditionally neglected. I believe that it is urgent and useful to pursue this project in order to develop a properly philosophical understanding of sociality.

To advocate a return to pronominal discourse does not limit the inquiry of sociality to the linguistic level. Zahavi raises a charge of such limitation against the linguistic pragmatic approaches of Apel and Habermas, and emphasizes that transcendental phenomenology of intersubjectivity is not limited to linguisticality (2001, 203). For Husserl, the subject is already prelinguistically intersubjective (ibid.). However, the prelinguistic notion of intersubjectivity in terms of I-consciousness and I-multiplicity is, as argued above, shaped by a determinate, epistemically driven take on language; rather than radicalize *this* notion of subjectivity and/as intersubjectivity, it is more advisable to reexamine language within a social context of use. At the same time, importantly, a deliberate turn to pronominal discourse in social context does not limit the inquiry to linguisticality alone. Zahavi is right to critique purely linguistic accounts on phenomenological grounds, arguing *both* that an openness to others and to the world needs to be shown at the pre- and extra-linguistic level *and* that sociality must be irreducible to factual and contingent relations (205). Dialogical phenomenology advocated here meets these two conditions. Firstly, it develops a rich narrative of prelinguistic ontogeny (chapter 3), and makes a strong case for a development of *I* and *you* discourse out of the earliest protoconversational interactions between the infant and the caregiver. Drawing on the dialogic tradition in philosophy, especially Buber, it makes a case for I-you connectedness within in utero existence (chapter 4). Dialogical phenomenology draws on empirical and dialogical traditions to complement phenomenological accounts of prelinguistic experience, which is notoriously difficult to capture by means of methodologically trained first-person description. It shows how linguistic competence emerges out of prelinguistic life and connects with extralinguistic aspects of communicative experience.

Secondly, dialogical phenomenology is not limited to enumerating purely contingent and factual aspects of experience. I-you connectedness is regarded as necessary to meaning making. However, it may be that dialogical phenomenology does not draw the boundary between factual and necessary claims as sharply as transcendental phenomenology does. For example, in utero existence and the care received in early infancy are factual *as well as* necessary conditions of selfhood and sociality. It is impossible to disentangle these strands within a phenomenologically concrete narrative, since these factual conditions are essential to the very emergence of selfhood and sociality. From a dialogical perspective, it would be an abstraction to regard a subject outside of these factual contexts of support, sustenance, and care received from others. Every project enacted in philosophical solitude has been so sustained. Dialogical phenomenology does therefore share the commitment to identifying eidetic structures of experience, but reads them off factual, embodied life enabled and sustained by the natural and social world.

CONTEMPORARY ARGUMENTS FOR THE TRANSCENDENTAL EGO: MARBACH, SOFFER

I'd like to examine contemporary views suggesting that there is good evidence for a phenomenological place for an ego. According to Marbach (2000), this evidence is to be found in the workings of memory as well as imagination. Marbach opens the discussion of how memory and imagination may provide a phenomenological, that is, experientially validated rather than rationally posited, basis for the transcendental ego by harking back to Husserl's notes from a 1907 manuscript wherein the philosopher raises the question of "the evidence of the I as an identical, which therefore can surely not consist in a bundle" (2000, 80). In this passage, Husserl clearly contrasts his understanding of an enduring *I* with Hume's conception of the mind as "successive perceptions only," with no centralized core self (1967 [1739], 253). Husserl then proceeds to ask about the phenomenological evidence for this *I*, describing it "as an apperception, but one that was precisely in contrast to what is empathized, in contrast to other I's (*andere Ich*)." What is at stake in Husserl's preoccupation with the ego question is accounting for how the conscious experience of other persons, which must be *somehow* manifest within the transcendental domain if phenomenology is to stay true to its project of founding transcendental intersubjectivity, does not merge with the philosopher's own introspectively gained experience and is accessed otherwise than through her own phenomenologically purified conscious acts. In Husserl's own words, "Were that the case, were that which is essential to the other's own self accessible in a direct manner, then it would merely be a moment of my own essence, and finally, he and I would be one and the same" (Husserl 1988, quoted in Bernet et al. 1993, 156).

Turning to the question of memory and fantasy as possibly privileged sites of the transcendental ego's existence, consider that Husserl's investigations led him to regard these acts under the complex category of re-presentation (*Vergagenwartigung*, also translated as *presentiation*), rather than as simple cases of a consciousness of an image, or mental depiction of an elapsed, or imagined, event. Up to 1904–5, in his *Phantasy, Image Consciousness, Memory (1898–1925)* lectures, Husserl did construe memory and imagination as acts of consciousness of an image, and he modeled their conception on his analyses of the perception of aesthetic images or pictures. Pictures, such as portraits, represent an absent entity (*Bildsujet*) by means of a material content such as canvas and paint (*Bildding*), which becomes transformed by the pictorial consciousness into a representational object (*Bildobjekt*) rendering the absent referent (for instance, Queen Victoria) quasipresent. The consciousness of a physical picture combines a perceptual apprehension of the pictorial thing in this material presence (which provides it with intuitive rather than purely conceptual character) with a nonperceptual act that "fantasizes" a nonpresent entity into the physical content and turns it into a picture properly so called. It was Husserl's initial conviction, closely paralleled in Sartre's treatise *L'imaginaire,* that acts of pure fantasy and memory, which do not require the material support of paint and canvas, consist in similar pictorial representation, with the external picture becoming replaced by an internal image perceived with the mind's eye. As a result, a unifying theory of picture consciousness that groups aesthetic objects and mental images can be put forward.

Despite its unifying potential, the pictorial model applied to pure fantasy and memory encounters a serious difficulty. The difficulty in question is how the mental image grasped in a perceptual manner by the recollecting or fantasizing consciousness succeeds in preserving the nonpresent character of recollected and fantasized events, rather rendering them present in the manner of an illusory perception or hallucination. If it is true that images are contents of consciousness, then it is unclear how the elapsed or imaginary events represented by them do not merge with the experience lived in the here and now. This apparently insurmountable difficulty ultimately leads Husserl to revise his theory of memory and imagination. Their representational character is located not in the sphere of mental imagery alone but rather in the double intentionality of representational consciousness. Categorized as re-presentation or presentiation (*Vergagenwartigung*), memory and imagination, as well as empathy, are found to display a complex structure that coinvolves the present act of consciousness that recollects an elapsed event or imagines a merely possible one *and* the act of consciousness retrieved from the past or imagined. Limiting the discussion to memory for the time being, it can be said that remembering an elapsed event consists not only in bringing the contents experienced in the past back in the present but also in the *reproduction* of the past experience. In recollection, a present act of consciousness reproduces or intentionally implicates an act of perceptual consciousness realized in the past. This act of reproduction succeeds in preserving the distance between the present and the past in that the present act of consciousness involves the past perceptual act without coinciding with it. This impossibility of reducing the past "life" of consciousness to the present "life," due to the internal division of temporal consciousness, makes the recollection of the past as absent or "passed" in the present possible.

Something similar is at work in imaginary consciousness, whose object appears equally distant and evanescent. Following Husserl, fantasy, in a way analogous to memory, involves a perceptual consciousness and effectuates a *reproduction* of perception. Yet the imaginary reproduction, unlike the perceptual one, takes the form of a *neutralization* of perception or of a neutralization of the belief in the existence of the object of perception. Perceptual consciousness and its positional thesis (the belief in the existence of the object) are implicated by the imaginary consciousness by means of the suspension of the existential thesis. The imaginary subject apprehends something absent not by means of an image but through the mediation of another (perceptual) act of consciousness. Note that the perceptual act in question need not stand for an actual perceptual experience: perception is taken here in the sense of a merely *possible* experience that need not be accomplished prior to the imaginary act. Neutralization at work in imagination, rather than modifying a preexisting perceptual act, *stages* perception as an act that could in principle be realized, even though it need not be.

The re-presentational character of consciousness operative in imagination and memory lends credence to the transcendental ego hypothesis in Marbach's view. The author relies on an example of recollection of his visit to Café Florian in Venice to make the point. The recollection occurs necessarily in the first-person perspective. The café with its tables and chairs, musicians playing the piano under the awning, the bustle of waiters coming in and out, the crowd of other patrons, as well as the life of the city in the distance, are experienced as spatially oriented from my point of view, even though this point of view does not coincide with the current one of the person engaged in recollection but consists rather of a quasi-bodily orientation from which I see and hear in an *as if* fashion the events unfolding in and around the café. As I recollect, I may be seated in a comfortable armchair in my study, but the dominant vantage point remains that of the elapsed consciousness of the visitor to Café Florian seated at the table and enjoying a glass of wine. Following Husserl, Marbach refers to the so-called phenomenon of overlapping (*Verdeckung*) or interference of experiences to make his crucial point. As long as I am absorbed in the process of conjuring up the elapsed events, my quasi-experience of the past, together with its quasi-bodily viewpoint and quasi-perceiving, overlaps or interferes with my simultaneous actual bodily viewpoint and perceptual awareness. The more attentively I immerse myself in the elapsed experience, the less vivid is the perceptual givenness of my present surroundings and of my place therein. Such interference of the past experience, necessarily relative to my position there and then, testifies, in Marbach's view, to the occurrence of "mental I-displacement" in memory (and analogously, in imagination). Were we to discredit the idea of mental

I-displacement, Marbach contends, we would be led to the image/picture consciousness theory of memory (and the imagination), in which it is the mental image of the Café Florian that facilitates the activity of remembering an elapsed event. However, such a pictorial theory of imagination gives rise to the difficulties examined above. Furthermore, Marbach argues on phenomenological grounds that he has no awareness of an image or depiction of the café but rather of the café itself, *as it were*. Hence, from a phenomenological point of view, there is no basis for postulating a second object, a replica of the existing venue visited in the past, to explain the mechanics of recollection. The author concludes that "recourse to a mental image of the Café, supposedly present in the mind, cannot be accepted as an account of the phenomenon of re-presenting the event to be preferred to the descriptive account in terms of I-displacement" (Marbach 2000, 86).

Instructed by the overview of the difficulties raised by the image/picture consciousness theories of memory and imagination, we may be willing to accept the hypothesis of mental I-displacement in its stead. The latter hypothesis accounts both for the first-person character of recollection as well as for the quasipresent character of recollected events. We should, however, waver at the conclusion drawn by the author that the hypothesis of mental I-displacement lends credence to the postulate of the transcendental ego. The transcendental ego apparently accounts for how it is that I experience myself as identical over time despite the fact that I may continuously evolve, as being numerically *one* even though I may not feel that qualitatively the same as the person I used to be in the past. In Marbach's words, "It is this experientially, subjectively unified consciousness that is alive in performing acts of re-presenting something that gets marked with the little word 'I'" (2000).

In response to Marbach, such a postulate of a pure *I* is not indispensable to the temporal unity of consciousness. As Sartre argues, referring to Husserl's own analyses for the purpose, temporal synthesis need not require the intervention of an underlying ego-subject. Sartre observes that "it is characteristic that Husserl, who studied this subjective unification of consciousnesses in *Vorlesungen zur Phänomenologie des inneren Zeitbewusstseins*, never had recourse to a synthetic power of the I. It is consciousness which unifies itself, concretely, by a play of 'transversal' intentionalities which are concrete and real retentions of past consciousnesses" (1972, 39). Sartre adopts this idea of auto-temporalizing consciousness in his argument against the transcendental ego, and refers to as the "flux of consciousness constituting itself as the unity of itself" (1972, 60). This phrase is an almost verbatim paraphrase of

Husserl's own statement from the lectures on the consciousness of internal time: "the flow of consciousness constitutes its own unity" (1991, §39).

Rather than representing a phenomenological datum, the ego hypothesis may have been motivated by the need to demarcate the phenomenologist's consciousness (including elapsed and fantasized events) from the consciousness of another person, on the supposition that they co-appear in the transcendental domain yielded by the phenomenological reduction. In fact, it was Husserl's conviction that the previously discussed structure of re-presentation discernible in acts of recollection and imagination is to be located also in the acts of empathic understanding and so may open new avenues for the study of other minds.[10] In the latter case, a re-presentational structure is also found operative, even though, as Marbach clarifies, "I experience the re-presented consciousness with an understanding of its being originally experienced by another creature that is (or has been or would be) simultaneously bodily present with me" (2000, 89). It is imagination rather than memory that serves as a privileged candidate in the context of interpersonal re-presentations. When I recollect elapsed events, such as a previous visit to a Venetian café, I reproduce a past consciousness that I have lived in the first person, as a living perceiving bodily organism, and that belongs therefore to the history of my life. When I *imagine*, however, the fictional events do not belong to my personal history. That is why, for Husserl, imaginary consciousness may serve as a matrix for relations to another conscious self: just as I can experience another perceptual consciousness in an "as if" fashion when I fantasize, so can I "quasi" participate in the life of another person by intentionally implicating or "imagining" her conscious life. In both cases we may witness a dehiscence between the experience of fantasizing and the experience fantasized about, and a possible case of alterity that cannot be reduced to the same. Imagination turns out to be a possible field of study for interpersonal relations, and acts of empathy may be grouped under the heading of re-presentation.[11] Even though the other's conscious experience is foreign or distinct from the field of my consciousness, the structural character of the conscious act involved in empathic relations would be analogous to the one at work in imagination. Both involve a conscious act intentionally implicating another conscious act.

However, once empathic interpersonal acts are included under the category of re-presentation in the transcendental field of inquiry together with intrapersonal acts of imagination and memory, the pressing question for Husserl—and Marbach—becomes just whose acts are thematized after the phenomenological reduction? and how may the conscious acts of others be demarcated from one's own?[12] In Marbach's view, the I-involvement in intrapersonal re-presentation can be justifiably contrasted with my representing conscious experience of other minds in empathy (2000, 88), and the issue of self/other demarcation in the transcendental sphere thus settled. The author proposes the example of re-presenting the perception that someone else has of a window that I do not see to make the point. Following Husserl's line of thought, I am cognizant of the other's experience by means of imaginary re-presentation. This re-presentation is arrived at by means of my imaginative positing of experiences of my own—it is the same experience that I would have were I to adopt the other's point of view. Unlike in the case of imaginary re-presentation pure and simple, I posit an actual experiencing that is not mine when I empathically relate to someone else. Finally, and here the contrast between intra- and interpersonal re-presentations becomes apparent; even though I am copresent in the understanding of the other mind, the "superposition of identity" between my *I* as reproducing the other's experience and the "alien I" (*fremdes Ich*) undergoing the experience in an original mode does not obtain. Henceforth, empathic relations to another *I* may be contrasted with the mental I-displacement operative in the context of intrapersonal re-presentational acts. However, the question remains whether the agency of transcendental ego, which is charged with delimiting the field occupied by "my I" from the "foreign I," is not motivated by the specific needs raised by Husserl's transcendental theory of intersubjectivity. This theory gleans intersubjective structures from the subjectivity itself, and models empathy on internal relations of recollection and fantasy. The difficulty inherent in transcendental theory of intersubjectivity as subjectivity, however, is how intrasubjective and intersubjective relations differ. If the other is posited in analogy with my own experience, what transcendental conditions guarantee that the "foreign I" is not a figment of my imagination or a replica of my past experience? As Pol Vandevelde (1996) notes, the theory of empathy based on an enlargement of the field of subjective experience attributes too much of a positive role to imagination.

In a more positive response to Husserl, Gail Soffer (1999) proposes a partial defense of his theory by calling for "a general transformation of intersubjective empathy, a widening of the contextual horizon of evidence upon which empathetic appresentations are formed, a more complex use of memory, openness to correction, and humility about accuracy" in her genetic account of sociality (165). Sofer's qualifications, however insightful they may be, do not, however, challenge the basic set of problems associated with the re-presentational model. Within this model, interpersonal relations are theorized in third-person terms, by means of a mentalizing strategy of imaginatively projecting conscious experiences of another person, with no clear sense of whether and how the individuals in question *relate* to one another. (Recall in this regard the aforementioned example of empathy as re-presenting someone else's perception of a window that I do not see.) If empathy is to capture interpersonal relations properly so called, it needs to focus on interpersonal interaction in the I-you form, rather than on the analogizing strategy of the I–other I, or ego–alter ego, schema, which posits that the other person is analogous to albeit distinct from myself. Focusing on the dialogical mode of direct address and response at work in interpersonal relations properly so called removes the need to posit a transcendental ego as a guarantor of self-containment, and thus for a transcendental ego *tout court*.

SCHUTZ, THEUNISSEN ON SOCIAL PHENOMENOLOGY

Another question to be raised in this context is whether the domain of transcendental consciousness allows for thematization of sociality at all. This question was previously raised by Alfred Schutz (1957). Focusing his discussion primarily on *The Cartesian Meditations,* Schutz contended that it is doubtful that "Husserl's attempt to develop a transcendental theory of experiencing Others (empathy) as the foundation for a transcendental theory of the objective world was successful, and what is more. . . *that such an attempt can succeed at all within the transcendental sphere*" (55, emphasis added). Schutz challenged therefore the possibility of developing a transcendental theory of subjectivity and applying phenomenological constitutional analysis to the social sciences.

Consider Schutz's objections to Husserl in more detail, this time in light of the classic fifth "Cartesian Meditation" and its famous analysis of the constitution of the alter ego. Schutz recalls that the project of phenomenological reduction carried out by Husserl in *Cartesian Meditations* (1988) leads to an abstraction from "all that is other than myself" (*Fremden*), including not only other living beings but also cultural artefacts that indirectly indicate other minds, as well as the intersubjectively shared world. This abstraction allows Husserl to separate meanings that belong properly to the ego from those that related to the subjectivity of others. The resulting immanent domain is denoted as the sphere of *ownness* or the primordial sphere—my private world in the most radical sense. Following Husserl's analysis, within the sphere of ownness certain natural bodies (*Korpern*) appear that are distinguished from my own living body (*Leib*), to which I ascribe sensations and the ability to hold sway. Specifically, another human being emerges first of all as a natural body. By means of an "apperceptive transfer" from my own living body, I bestow upon it the sense of a living body distinct from, even though analogous to, my own. The bestowal of sense upon the other involves an analogy (*analogisierende Auffasssung*), even though Husserl stresses, contra his contemporary Theodore Lipps, that it is not an *inference* by analogy (*Analogieschluss*). Contrary to an inferential process, the analogy does not consist in an actively executed projection of my experience onto the foreign body but rather a passive process of association within which the actually present body of the other refers back to the merely appresented domain of her field of sensations and holding sway.

This apperceptive transfer of sense is enabled by the so-called phenomenon of *pairing* or coupling (*Paarung*). Whether or not I am expressly aware of it, the copresence of the other's body and my own establishes a unity of *similarity* within the couple. The two paired bodies are said to overlap intentionally, engaged as they are in reciprocal stimulating and coinciding. It is my own primordial living body that provides the ground for constituting the other as a body similar to my own (*Leibkorper*). However, even though the other is an intentional modification of my self, she is not a mere reduplication of my own body. Whereas my own body provides the index of "here," the body of the other has the index of "there"; although for her, the body indicates an absolute here. The association between my bodily here and the other's there facilitates the grasp of the other as a spatially removed other self or ego, rather than extension of myself.

This constitutive analysis of the alter ego raises a host of difficulties in Schutz's view. For one, as already indicated by Scheler, the condition of similarity between the body proper and the other's body is a problematic one. This condition contradicts the phenomenological datum of perceptual asymmetry between the other's body, which is visually available in its totality, and the body proper, which can only be partially seen. A more fundamental objection concerns the very possibility of enacting a constitutive analysis of the other from within the transcendental domain: What sense at all does it make to derive the other out of the primordial sphere of ownness, which appears in the *Cartesian Meditations* as radically asocial (Schutz 1957, 95)?

Does that not amount to deriving sociality from out of a solipsistically construed consciousness? As previously discussed, Zahavi (2001) makes a strong case against a solipsistic construal of solitary consciousness. However, there is extant textual support for a solipsist construal of the egocentric sphere in Husserl's *corpus*. For example, in a text stemming from 1934 (and so postdating *Cartesian Meditations*), Husserl refers to the abstractive elimination of all empathies in the reduction, stipulating that the sphere of ownness can be read in an unambiguously solipsistic sense (see Bernet et al. 1993, 159). Schutz's concern with reconciling sociality with solipsism does therefore carry some weight. Most importantly, however, even if the ego is not a *solus* but a *socius ipse*, the difficulties surrounding an external additive conception of sociality remain. As Schutz argues, it does not suffice to establish a collection of isolated individuals to found a human community—it is also necessary to explain *how this community stands, potentially at least, in communication* (1957, 75). The transcendental method encloses its practitioner in an uncommunicative turn to consciousness, which is by definition performed by annulling interactions with others. Schutz reminds us that the practice of the epoche is necessarily solitary, even if others were to perform the epoche together with me (74). The epoche plunges its actor in isolation from consociates, and its constitutive analysis applies exclusively to the world as experienced from the single phenomenologist's point of view. A shared practice of the epoche can therefore yield a cosmos of monads without windows, where each monad reflects but does not coinvolve others in a participatory, mutually relational manner. The project of founding the social sciences on transcendental phenomenology of intersubjectivity is therefore, in Schutz's view, misguided from the start.

In his influential study *The Other* (1986), Theunissen also challenges the ability of transcendental phenomenology to found social ontology. He argues notably that the express preoccupation with establishing an objectively known world by means of transcendental constitution subsumes the entire analysis of social relations under a predetermined agenda. The other is regarded primarily as a coconstitutor of the world coestablishing the validity of objectivities, rather than a social partner. Theunissen argues further that no attempts to revise the transcendental framework by incorporating insights from the disciplines that pay heed to the reality of social phenomena—notably the philosophy of dialogue—can ever succeed. It does not suffice to add the dialogical *Thou* form to the egocentric framework of Husserl's philosophy. Henceforth, Theunissen was skeptical of the phenomenological sociology of

Alfred Schutz (1967), particularly his analysis of the *Thou*-orientation. The result of dialogical contributions being integrated into phenomenology without revising its ego-centered base is only an *illusion of dialogue*.[13]

I agree with Theunissen that mere addition of dialogic contributions to an uncritically maintained model of epistemic subjectivity is insufficient to make a strong case for I-you connectedness. However, contra the view that Theunissen may have embraced, I do not call for a replacement of phenomenology by the philosophy of dialogue.[14] I believe that phenomenology can be preserved as a descriptive method firmly rooted in situated experience, but that experience is communicative, and first person entangled with the second, from the start. I call therefore for a renewed examination of the dialogical dimension of experience, especially but not exclusively in terms of living speech.

HUSSERL'S LATER THOUGHT

In concluding this opening critical chapter, let me examine a possible objection that the foregoing analysis fails to address the developments of Husserl's thinking in his later texts. This was in fact one of the critical remarks made by Fink to Schutz during the discussion following the latter's talk on "The Problem of Transcendental Intersubjectivity in Husserl." Fink refers to the manuscripts written after the *Cartesian Mediations,* in which Husserl

> arrives at the curious notion of the primal ego [*Ur-Ich*], of primal subjectivity which is prior to the distinction between the primordial subjectivity and the transcendental subjectivity of other monads. He seems to try to some extent, to withdraw the plurality from the domain of the transcendental. . . . According to Husserl's ideas in these very late manuscripts, there is a primal life which is neither one nor many, neither factual nor essential; rather, it is the ultimate ground of all these distinctions: a transcendental primal life which turns itself into a plurality. (Schutz 1957, 86)

And in *The Sixth Cartesian Meditation*, Fink clarifies that the primal ego (*Ur-Ich*) is "an ego that is prior to the distinction, ego–alter ego, being an ego that allows the plural to break forth from itself" (quoted in Mensch 1988, 396).

Does the *primal ego* notion remove the concerns raised earlier about transcendental theory of intersubjectivity? James Mensch (1988) responds in the affirmative. Although acknowledging that phenomenology can be subsumed under the heading of transcendental idealism insofar as it makes the knowable world dependent on consciousness, and that it may be subject to the solipsistic limitation in the reduction of the world to the transcendental ego, Mensch argues that phenomenology itself provides a solution to these constraints. The solution is located in the "radically pre-egocentric" level located by Husserl at the original level of constitution, prior to the distinction between self and others (*Zur Phanomenologie der Intersubjectivitat, dritter Teil,* Mensch 1988, 19). According to the author, this preindividual level, wherein we exist in an original identity, is required for the subsequent recognition of the difference between persons. The original identity at the level of constitution is the ground making possible the plurality of selves in the constituted world. Henceforth, Mensch concludes that "transcendental idealism has within it the solution to the problem of intersubjectivity it raises. [. . .] The reduction, which raises the problem of transcendental solipsism, overcomes this problem when pursued to the end" (1988). By positing a preindividual ground, termed the *primal ego,* transcendental phenomenology ceases to advocate a *solus ipse* that generates a private world, and so evades the threat of solipsism. The objections raised to Husserl by Schutz thus lose their force.

Or do they? As previously discussed, there is room for a plurality of egos in Husserl's project even up to *Cartesian Meditations*. In that case, it is not clear that a preindividual ground is needed to account for a plurality of individuals. Furthermore, Husserl may have already been working with such a preindividual ground in his earlier conception of the world constitution, wherein he posited a nonindividuated agency as the motor of the constitution. In that case, the apparent novelty of Husserl's later texts in comparison with his better-known works is less obvious. Furthermore, positing the pre-egological ground ultimately multiplies rather than reduces the difficulties: it is unclear how and whether the shift from the original prepersonal identity to interpersonal difference can be accomplished. Rather than solving the problem of plurality, the later developments threaten to effectively dissolve it. That may be the reason why Fink, in a somewhat cryptic concluding statement of his discussion with Schutz, notes that "the substantive difficulties" uncovered by the latter in his discussion of the texts up to the *Cartesian Meditations* "would be. . . only increased" by the developments in Husserl's later philosophy. The difficulties discussed earlier remain untouched. Transcendental phenomenology of intersubjectivity developed in the later texts is equally if not more vulnerable to the objections raised to the earlier works.

PART 2

The Multidiscipline of Dialogical Phenomenology

CHAPTER 2

SOCIOLINGUISTICS

In this chapter I turn to linguistics in view of spelling out the ordinary grammatical conception of personal pronouns with the aim of demonstrating the philosophical thesis of primary *I–you connectedness*. As will become apparent in the course of this discussion, linguistic contributions are not extrinsic to phenomenological accounts of sociality in terms of embodiment and perception but intrinsically interconnected with them. The traditional separation into distinct regions of inquiry may be a trait of the institutionally sanctioned divide between the disciplines of phenomenological philosophy and linguistics that serves to confirm the perceived divide between phenomena and language, rather than a trait of human life examined afresh and with a critical eye to the historically constituted "naturalness" of disciplinary borders. I hope that this critical stance helps to expose the permeability of the perceived borders between their regions of study (lived experience and speech/language). I also hope that by adopting an approach of deliberate suspension of commitment to disciplinary divides, the phenomenon of sociality will reemerge in its embodied/perceptual/linguistic complexity.

PERSONAL PRONOUNS—
RECONSIDERING THE TRADITIONAL VIEW (1)

Let me begin this analysis with a discussion of the traditional view regarding the grammatical function of personal pronouns. The dictionary definition states that the pronoun is a word serving to replace a previously mentioned noun or name. For example, the name Victoria may be replaced by the personal pronoun "she," as long as no ambiguity arises within the narrative as to who this pronoun refers. Pronouns would thus be shorthand expressions designating a previously established referent in order to avoid repetition.

This traditional definition has been playfully rendered in the following extract from *The Little Grammar People* (Mass 1947, 21):

> "My whole life is one of deep thought, because, as you can tell by my name, I have to stand in the place of Miss Noun."
> "Whatever do you mean?" asked Linda, puzzled. "Doesn't Miss Noun stand in her own place?"
> "Oh yes, certainly. Sometimes she does, but not always. You must remember that she leads a very busy life and has to be in an awful number of parts at once, and it's my business to help her whenever I can."
> "That's interesting," said Barry.
> "Let me explain myself more clearly," Sir Pronoun went on. "When Miss Noun is needed in a sentence she makes quite sure she is there to begin with, but hops away again like quick-silver, partly because she has so much to do and partly because she's afraid people may grow tired of her. I then step along and say, 'Ladies and Gentlemen, with your kind permission, I shall represent Miss Noun for a short time, as she was afraid of tiring you and has gone.' Sometimes I am greeted quite amiably, but other times everybody gets very annoyed, says I don't make myself at all clear and throws me out of the sentence. Miss Noun then, realizing the situation, appears again in person, and all is well—although, I must admit—" he added dolefully, then paused.
> "—that all isn't as well as it might be with you," Linda suggested.
> "Exactly," he replied. . . . .
> "But Sir Pronoun, just why is it that you have to think so much?" Barry asked.
> "Because," the long boy explained, "Miss Noun is so terribly changeable, and as I have to take her place I must be changeable too. I'm positively the whole time trying to decide whether I should now be a 'personal,' 'demonstrative,' 'relative,' or 'interrogative' pronoun."

This little amusing dialogue destined for children does not deviate from the widespread adult conception: the pronoun is a grammatical category resembling a mixed bag into which diverse items are stuffed. There are *personal* pronouns, wherein the first and second persons ("I," "you," ("thou"), plural "we," "you," with their cases) stand for the names of the speaker and the person spoken to. Those of the third person ("he," "she," "it," "they," with their cases) avoid the repetition of a name already mentioned or indicated. Closely related to them are *possessive* pronouns: adjectives arising out of the original genitive case of personal pronouns ("my/mine," "your/yours," "our/ours," and so forth). *Interrogative* pronouns ("who?" "what?" "which?") ask the name, and so on, of a person or thing unknown. *Relative* pronouns ("who," "which," "that") subordinate one sentence or clause to another, as "I met a friend *who* told me" for "I met a friend, *and he* told me." Furthermore, several definitive adjectives are classed as *adjective pronouns* or *pronominal adjectives*. These include the *demonstratives* ("this" [pl. "these"], "that" [pl. "those"]); *distributives* ("each," "either," "neither"); indefinite numerals, and so forth ("any," "some," "one," "other" ["another"]).[1] Following the dictionary definition, all pronouns are united by the common feature of deputizing syntactically and semantically for nouns, despite a wide array of functions (to indicate a person or possession, to interrogate, to demonstrate) performed in the process. Sir Pronoun stands in for Miss Noun—that's the basic principle of pronominal functioning. This deputizing feature is enshrined in the etymology of the word: from Latin *pro* ("instead of" or "in return for") and *nomen* (personal name, proper name, proper noun, noun).[2] Upon inspection, however, this grammatical categorization, based on a uniform ascription of a deputizing function to diverse parts of speech, turns out to be problematic.

Lyons (1977, 637) points out two problems associated with the traditional view. Taken literally, the *pro-noun* would have to stand in for a single noun, while pronouns may serve as substitutes for complex-noun phrases or nominals ("the vase that I broke last Christmas at my friends," "Ann and Mary's house"). More significantly, to define pronouns in terms of substitution, whether for nouns or nominals, is to imply that their so-called *anaphoric* function is more basic that their *deictic* function—a point which Lyons hotly disputes. Let me begin by defining the terms. *Anaphora* comes from Greek *anapherein,* which means "to bring back," "recall," or "repeat." An *anaphoric pronoun* stands as a deputy for an expression with which it is semantically and syntactically identical. The *anaphoric function* is typically defined as reference to either an antecedent-noun phrase or possibly to what an antecedent-noun phrase refers. For example, having declared that "my friend Victoria is a swimmer," I can subsequently refer to Victoria by means of the demonstrative phrase "this woman" as well as the pronoun "she."

As Lyons points out, the anaphoric function is typically, but not necessarily, exercised in relation to an expression that has been recently mentioned and precedes the pronoun in the text. The expression may also follow the pronoun with which it is correlated. For example, it is possible to say "When she woke up, my friend smiled" wherein "she" refers in an anticipatory manner to "my friend."

Deixis, the *deictic function,* comes from the Greek "to point" or "to show" (Greek *deiknunai*). Deictic pronouns relate utterances to the spatial and temporal coordinates of the act of discourse. They are equivalent to Husserl's *subjective and occasional expressions* discussed in chapter 1, and are also known as the *indexicals* in philosophical scholarship. Consider Lyons' definition:

> By deixis is meant the location and identification of persons, objects, events, processes and activities being talked about, or referred to, in relation to the spatiotemporal context created and sustained by the act of utterance and the participation in it, typically, of a single speaker and at least one addressee. (1977, 637)

Here are some examples. Demonstrative pronouns and adjectives like the English "this" and "that" are deictic expressions, and so are demonstrative adverbs, such as "here" and "there," and "now" and "then." The first two pairs of expression denote spatial proximity and distance with regard to the speaker's point of view at the time of the utterance, whereas the last pair denotes temporal proximity and distance with regard to the time of the utterance. Whereas "here" denotes the position occupied by the speaker at the time of the utterance, "now" refers to the moment when the utterance is made. These spatial and temporal coordinates are therefore meaningful only if referred to by a speaker who is situated in the spatial and temporal context. Furthermore, the act of utterance is an event involving the speaker's entire living, breathing body. As Ryle (2000 [1949], 179) reminds us, "the moment at which 'now' is breathed is the moment which it indicates," whereas "here" indicates, if it functions in a deictic context, "that particular place from which the speaker propagates the noise 'here' into the surrounding air."

Similarly, the uttered word "I" indicates the particular person from whom the sound "I" issues, whereas "you" refers to the person who receives the sound produced by the speaker. Carried by the elemental air, traveling between the organisms that breathe and receive vibrations from their environment both in their auditory tracks and in the entire bodily column, the deictic expressions connect, as if via umbilical cords, to the speaker's and addressee's communicating bodies as well as to the context of the utterance. Deictic expressions involve speakers and hearers in a *situation,* taking this word in its original sense of being in situ or in a location. Speakers and hearers must be embodied perceivers who are supported by the firm ground of the earth if they are to acquire, employ, and comprehend deictic expressions correctly. Their embodiment and perception, their ability to indicate things in the environment and to grasp the significance of indication by others, provide therefore both the prelinguistic conditions and the paralinguistic features of deixis. This point will occupy us at some length when we turn to the question of "I" and "you" acquisition in chapter 3. It is important to note at this stage, however, that deixis is *not* to be narrowly construed as an exclusively linguistic category, but that it denotes a social and corporeal expertise, which harnesses and mobilizes our abilities to orient in a shared spatial environment using the repertoire of available perceptual skills. That is why deixis in general and person deixis in particular cannot be accounted for in terms of syntax and semantics alone but necessarily also in terms of perception and embodiment.

EGOCENTRISM AND POLYCENTRISM

Lyons (1977) concludes from the speaker involvement in spatial referencing that the deictic situation is *egocentric,* since the speaker relates everything to her perspective and casts herself in the role of ego (638). The speaker's situated vantage point provides, in Lyons' words—which resonate with Husserl's terminology—*the zero-point* of the deictic space (669), that is, an absolute *here* that never acquires a plus value. Lyons approximates in this regard Husserl's conception of the body proper as an absolute *here* that never reverses into a *there*. The perceiver's own body provides a reference point for constituting an environment configured by spatial vectors such as close/distant, low/high, to the left/right, in front/behind, and so forth. The intelligibility of these terms is relative to the irreversible *here* occupied by the solitary perceiver, which is typically regarded as the principal phenomenological determinant of spatial orientation.

Lyons, on the other hand, regards spatial situatedness expressly within the terms of the "canonical situation of utterance" (637), that is, the face-to-face interaction between at least two participants of discourse. He is thus able to bring the social aspect of spatial orientation into relief. In Lyons' words, "canonical situation of utterance"

> involves one-one, or one-many, signaling in the phonic medium along the vocal-auditory channel, with all the participants present in the same actual situation able to see one another and to perceive the associated non-vocal paralinguistic features of the utterances, and each assuming the role of sender and receiver in turn. (ibid.)

The canonical situation of deixis thus throws a new light on spatial situatedness, and endows spatial categories with an inherently communicative value. Within this situation, I am explicitly reminded of situated viewpoints other than my own. Significantly, I need to allow for an encounter with another perceiver/speaker, who addresses me as "You, over there" and to which I may respond with "Here I am." If I fail to grasp this here-there reversal, and fail to understand that the demonstrative "there" reverses into a "here" following the change of speaker roles from the other to myself, I have not grasped the meaning of "here" fully and am unable to use this deictic expression in the canonical situation of utterance. Similarly, had I not grasped the I–you reversal and understood that the personal pronoun "you" addressed to me by the speaker reverses into the pronoun "I" in my response, I have not grasped the meaning of the first-person pronoun fully either. The canonical situation of spatial orientation and deixis discussed by Lyons thus ultimately undermines the validity of an egocentric perspective, and helps to establish a *polycentric* orientation in its place.

My argument for the primacy of polycentrism in spatial orientation to the shared world is in agreement with Elmar Holenstein (1985), who argued that an egocentric construal of the perceiver's body, as in Husserl's emphasis on the first-personal zero-point, ultimately fails to account for the actual mechanism of spatial orientation. Holenstein noted that the perceiver does not rely exclusively on bodily location but also on the multiplicity of salient reference points and on the relations to coperceivers as she locomotes and orients in the spatial milieu. This multireferentiality is evident even when no other perceiver is present in the perceptual field. When standing in the market square surrounded by houses, it is the center, possibly accentuated by a clearly visibly monument, that provides the reference point with regard to which I orient myself, and not the other way round (18). The reference point is likely to be housed in a dominating element of the perceptual field, whether because of its shape or meaning. The body proper assumes this central referencing function only when it happens to occupy such a dominant position, not by default (19). Holenstein advocates therefore a *polycentric* givenness of experiential space over against the *egocentric* subjectivism espoused by Husserl. Such polycentrism is integral both to the navigation in the shared spatial environment *and* to the mastery of deictic terms such as "here"–"there" and "I"–"you."

Consider then that the egocentric conception of space in terms of an irreversible *here* produces the paradoxical scenario of an aspatial and unsituated category enabling the navigation of the shared spatial world. It is puzzling just how a spatially configured environment would be constituted by a viewpoint that is not subject to spatial configurations. This unsituated viewpoint of the absolute *here* may provide an appropriate *locum* for the transcendental irreversible *I* but it does not capture the body-situated-in-the-shared-world. It ultimately distorts the ordinary conception of spatial deixis as it is used in the ordinary practice of referring to manifest locations of people and things alike.

By contrast, in a nontranscendental polycentric perspective on spatial orientation and deixis, the *here/there* and *I/you* reversals are easily granted and, importantly, they are interconnected. The perceptual/navigational space exists on a continuum with the deictic space of interpersonal discourse; speakers are situated in space. The pronoun "I" plays a double role of indicating the speaker *role* and *perspective*, that is, the location from which the speaker addresses another in discourse. Gurwitsch (1977 [1950]) notes, following Humboldt, that "I" and "you" form an invariant system of relations realized between addressor and addressee in every actual case of speech. "I" and "you" designate therefore the places occupied by members within this relational system, and the place needs to be taken here in the literal sense of spatial location occupied by the interlocutors. The "here"/"there" indicators of location bear a profound affinity with the "I"/"you" indicators of speaker/addressee role occupied in discourse. This intuition is confirmed by Humboldt's study of languages in which adverbs of place are closely related to personal pronouns, lending support to their common origin.[3] As shown in chapter 3, there is also empirical evidence that a polycentric orientation in space provides a necessary condition for the mastery of "I" and "you" pronouns in children. In conclusion, the meaning of the personal deictic terms "I"–"you" is not limited to the metalinguistic and intralinguistic role of indicating the speaker/addressee role in discourse, but includes also the extralinguistic role of situating discourse in the shared spatially configured field, as may be expressed by the spatial deixis "here"/"there."

PERSON DEIXIS AND POLYCENTRISM

Returning to the question of deixis and anaphora, consider that personal pronouns are a prime example of why the deictic function of pronouns is more basic that the anaphoric one, and why the traditional definition of "I" and "you" as *pro-nomen* is unfounded. "I" and "you" pronouns do not serve as semantic and syntactic deputies for proper names or definite descriptions. The pronoun "I" does not *mean* the same thing as Beata Stawarska, professor of philosophy at the University of Oregon. If it did, the rest of the English-speaking population would be deprived of the ability to self-refer by means of the first-person pronoun. An analogous case can be made about the pronoun "you." Its reference is not to be identified with the reference of proper names or definite descriptions. It is not fixed in a stable manner, for first- and second-personal pronouns refer to the roles played by the participants in dialogic interaction rather than to events or entities situated outside the dialogic space. These roles are principally those of the "sender" and the "recipient" of a message, or in less technical terms, of the speaker and the addressee. Successful performance of speaker and addressee roles is not in need of a previous (or any) mention of the referent in discourse. "I" and "you" do not therefore typically serve the anaphoric function traditionally applied to pro-nouns but rather the deictic one. Rather than depend on a previously established place in discourse, "I" and "you" pronouns introduce entities into discourse by assigning them dialogic roles; they *produce* the speaker and addressee in and through their utterance rather then reproducing an already-established referent in discourse.

It is this independence from previous mention that makes deixis more basic than anaphora in Lyons' view (1977, 673). In fact, the linguist adds, speaker involvement in discourse is ineradicable and cannot be analyzed in terms of anything else (646). Contrary to the widespread impression that personal pronouns have an ancillary role with regard to nouns, and could therefore in principle be dispensed with, speaker and addressee markers such as "I" and "you" pronouns are intrinsic to speech qua speech. As Humboldt (1999 [1836], 95) argues, person deixis is the most elementary and primitive stratum of language; it would therefore be erroneous to regard (personal) pronouns as a relatively late development, whether in evolutionary or developmental sense. In this latter view, a "narrowly grammatical mode of conceiving the replacement of the noun by the pronoun has. . . supplanted the insight more deeply drawn from language" (ibid.). This deeper insight suggests that the emergence of personal pronouns is enmeshed with the emergence of language itself as long as we thematize language as speech, that is, a medium of communicative engagement between embodied perceivers situated in the environing world. From that point of view, linguistic empirical data regarding speaker–addressee connectedness are not regarded as merely contingent facts pertaining to a select group of natural languages, but rather as an indispensable and necessary aspect of language qua speech. They are therefore raised to an ontological level, even though they are located within the empirical stratum of discursive experience.

Consider that the best way to characterize person deixis in linguistic terms is by means of the *shifter* category. "Shifter" was introduced by Jespersen (1922, 123) and taken up by Jakobson (1990) as a handy term for the words whose meaning differs according to the situation, and can be applied to one thing at one time, and a different thing at another. Examples of shifters could be "enemy" and "home," whose referents shift depending on the speaker and the situation, but most paradigmatically include the personal pronouns. Their referents are not assigned in a fixed fashion but fluctuate according to the evolving conversational context. Who the pronoun "I" refers to depends on who takes up the active speech role at a given point in time. Its reference is therefore fixed in *performative* rather than *truth-conditional* terms. As Lyons puts it, "It is [the speaker's] performance of [this particular deictic] role, and not the truth of any presupposed identifying proposition which determines the correct reference of 'I'" (1977, 645). With reference identified in terms of a performance, the first-person pronoun harkens back to the original meaning of the word *persona,* which indicated "mask" in Latin and was used to translate the Greek word for "dramatic character" or "role" in the theater. However, insofar as personal pronouns function as shifters in the conversational context, they are not bound to a single persona but are interchanged between the interlocutors as the conversation progresses and the addressor/addressee roles reverse.

In somewhat more technical terms adopted by Jakobson (1990) from Peirce's classification of signs, shifters are hybrids that combine the functions of a *symbol* and an *index*. According to Peirce, a symbol like the English word "red" is associated with the represented object by a *conventional rule*, whereas an index, like the act of pointing, is in *existential relation* with the object it represents. Consider the first-person pronoun in this context. On the one hand, the sign "I" represents its object by being associated to it "by a conventional rule," and so different languages or "codes" assign the same meaning to different words, like the Latin *ego,* the English *I,* the German *Ich,* French *Je.* . . . On the other hand, the sign "I" represents its object by "being in existential relation with it"—the word "I" points to or indicates the person making the utterance. As an indexical symbol, a shifter is therefore an element of the "code" (or language), whose meaning cannot be defined independently of the "message" (or speech–act/utterance), and must therefore be thematized in terms of a speech situation. Jakobson notes also that "every shifter. . . possesses its own general meaning" (388), "I" standing for the addressor and "you" for the addressee of the message to which it belongs. Contra the Husserl of *Logical Investigations,* the word "I" does not designate "a different person in each case. . . by means of a new meaning." Instead, each shifter possesses its own general meaning, dependent exclusively on the role taken up by the person in dialogic interaction. This generality of meaning enables personal pronouns to serve their primary function in natural languages: to manage dialogic roles regardless of individual differences.

Note that personal pronouns can function efficiently as shifters on the condition that the information they provide about the referent is minimal. Typically, first- and second-person pronouns provide no clues regarding the person's race and gender, social status, physical characteristics, and so forth. If a person knocking on the door responds to "Who is it?" with a laconic "It is I/me!," the host has no means of identifying the visitor based on the content of their utterance alone and may only hope for nonverbal clues such as the tone of voice to discern the visitor's identity. Such semantic poverty of personal pronouns is striking compared to the relative semantic richness of other lexical units, for example, the nouns and noun phrases that enable us to paint a fairly detailed picture of a given individual's life. It is this semantic poverty, however, which enables the pronouns to serve as indicators of speech roles in an undiscriminating manner. As Bhat (2004, 42) notes, personal pronouns successfully fulfill their function of being the same for all speakers or addressees since they are not burdened with information specific to the individuals who enact those roles. Not everyone can be described as "the 21st century Queen of England" or "the world's first light-weight boxing champion"; in principle, however, in a nonhierarchical society, everyone can take up the speaker role and address another in second-person terms. "I" and "you" pronouns are literally democratic in that they facilitate equal representation of all speakers and listeners within public discourse.

To be sure, such representation of persons on the arena of public discourse does not always take place. For example, women were historically denied access to vocal representation in the church community, as testified by Paul's Letter to the Corinthians (14:34–35), and its stipulation to "Let the women keep silent in the churches." Speech and public representation in spoken discourse is therefore not to be thematized only as a natural ability but also an ethical and political right. It therefore straddles the usual disciplinary distinction between descriptive and prescriptive sciences, for it bears not only on the *is* but also on the *ought* of human life, on human capabilities of vociferation and expression, grounded in their embodied existence *and* on the rights of representation and recognition in the public domain of political life, which may or may not be granted and respected.

Returning to the discussion, consider that the semantic poverty of personal pronouns implies that they are dissociated from their specific referents. They do not designate anything particular about the speaker and the addressee; Benveniste even goes so far as to claim that "I" and "you" pronouns refer exclusively to the "reality of discourse" and that persons are linguistically constituted entities. "'Ego' is he who *says* 'ego'" (1971, 224). Holenstein (1985, 59–67) therefore terms the pronoun "I" a metalinguistic expression— "I" turns back to the speaker of the utterance in which it occurs. Hence the pronoun "I" boasts a "guaranteed reference"—it reliably indicates the speaker in the production of the utterance in which it occurs. Such guaranteed indication and inherent reflexivity of the pronoun "I" have been epistemically construed in the modern and idealist traditions as indubitable proof of the existence of a thinking substance attainable in the first-person singular only. Holenstein counters that the certainty afforded by the pronoun "I" is not that of a *Cogito*—an absolute and ineffable standpoint of pure thought. Instead, in the right (that is, speech) context, the pronoun "I" unambiguously facilitates the performative production of the speaker as the ineradicable subject of speech acts. The correct usage and understanding of the word "I" do not document therefore an introspective insight into the Cartesian theater of thought but rather a socialized speech role or, in Holenstein's terms, "practical mastery of one's own relativity and of the reversibility of standpoints and roles, which one assumes as a member of a community" (68). Rather than a testament to egocentrism, the pronoun "I" evidences therefore the existence of a communicative space with a vibrant polycentric orientation, wherein each individual speaker role is performed relative to other speakers via an ongoing reversal of addressor/addressee roles. The emphasis on an absolute here-point runs the risk of covering over this plurality of perspectives and deprives the pronoun "I" of the communicative potential it ordinarily possesses.

The communicative conception of the pronoun "I" is at odds with the notion that the first-person marker is indicative of what is unmistakably *my own*. This conception is typically substantiated by the fact that the pronoun "I," *in my use of it*, indicates consistently and exclusively nobody else but me. Other pronouns, it is said, such as "you" or "she" may indicate different people at different times.[4] However, if the pronoun "I" was ego-bound, then it would fail to function efficiently as a shifter and the back-and-forth movement of a conversation would be brought to a halt. Yet the word "I" is generally intelligible to the members of a linguistic community, whether it is uttered or heard; it belongs to the realm of shared understanding and resonates in the public space of speech, rather than being a subjective possession. The egocentric conception of the "I" unduly privileges the philosopher's own use of the pronoun and covers over the ordinary linguistic fact that personal pronouns are intelligible for speakers and hearers alike. Put differently, the egocentric conception relies on the philosopher's own use of the pronoun "I" within silent soliloquy rather than spoken interlocution and is therefore forgetful of its inherently communicative role. Needless to say, the pronoun "I" continues to perform its addressor function even in silent soliloquy; but this is regarded as secondary to the epistemically construed first-person stance. The grammatical first person is thus regarded as ontologically first, and the ontological primacy of I–you connectedness gets covered over.

ANSCOMBE

The preceding analysis of personal pronouns as nonappropriable, semantically poor shifters, is in general agreement with G. E. M. Anscombe's essay "The First Person" (1991), even though I believe the author does not fully appreciate the philosophical implications of the grammar of the first-person pronoun. In this essay, Anscombe challenges Descartes for using the "I" pronoun as if it were a name for a disembodied mind. She reminds the reader that Descartes' meditations in the first person need to be distinguished from a third-person inquiry. An inquiry in the third person could be compatible with ignorance that one is its object. For example, "When John Smith spoke of John Horatio Auberon Smith (named in a will perhaps) he was speaking of himself, but he did not know this" is a possible situation (72). However, a reference in the first person, using the "I" pronoun, is such that the object reached by it is necessarily identical with oneself (the "guaranteed reference" of Holenstein). Surely, as Anscombe is quick to point out, to talk in terms of object-reaching is to treat the pronoun "I" as a quasiname and to assume that it functions syntactically as a proper name. This is problematic, she notes, since every English speaker uses that quasiname, and so its ability to single out individuals from a crowd would be limited. We would risk finding ourselves in an equivalent of a Monty Python sketch in which the name *Bruce* refers to just every philosopher at the table. However, she notes further, even if all individuals carried the same name, there still remains a difference between the first-person pronoun and proper names in that "each one uses the name 'I' only to speak of himself" (73). Is that to say that those whom she terms "our logicians," those who regard the pronoun "I" as a proper name, happen to have dim eyes? (73) The philosopher answers in the affirmative.

Contrary to the logicians' traditional belief that models the "I" pronoun on a proper name (in agreement with its etymological meaning of pronomen), that is, "a singular term whose role is to make a reference" (76), Anscombe argues that "I" is not a referring expression at all. Problematic consequences follow from the logicians' unexamined assumption that the pronoun "I" *is* a referring expression. The consequence is a commitment to the Cartesian Ego as the sole referent of the word "I"—or to some post-Cartesian version thereof, such as the transcendental ego. However, this commitment produces the "*intolerable difficulty* of requiring an identification of the same referent in different "'I'–thoughts" (77, emphasis added), that is, of locating a stable subject among the first-person acts that come and go. It was Hume who testified most famously to the impossibility of locating such a persistent mental self, and Sartre followed in his footsteps by declaring the ego transcendent rather than transcendental. In line with these authors, Anscombe submits that "There is no such thing [as the I]" (79) and that the mental is a "grammatical illusion" (81). This illusion has the misfortune of fueling endless, irresoluble debates about the exact status of this mute and invisible subject and how we can thematize it without objectification. To be sure, Anscombe does not doubt the possibility of identifying different "I"–thoughts as belonging to the same human being. However, she sees no need to posit an ego to get the job done. This reidentification may be an acquired ability to give a narrative account of what one has done—an ability learned from others and, in part at least, for the sake of others to whom one tells the story of one's life.[5]

Anscombe's claim that the pronoun "I" does not refer and that the philosophical notion of a subject is a grammatical illusion will be less shocking if we supplement her argument with an important distinction between two modes of reference: denoting and indexing. Traditionally, "denoting" is regarded as the manner in which names or definite descriptions pick out an extralinguistic entity for both the speaker and the hearer. For example, the sentence "Victoria is a swimmer" helps to pick out a particular girl out of the group. However, the sentence "This is Victoria" contains an indexical reference since it is inextricably related to the moment of the utterance—for example, to the event of introducing my friend Victoria to another guest at a dinner party. Consider this denoting/indexing distinction in the context of personal pronoun use. Descartes believed that "the I" serves to pick out an entity, the thinking thing, housed within the material body. As such, he interpreted the pronoun "I" (handled as if it were a noun) as a denoting expression, a point that Anscombe disputes. However, to argue against an extralinguistic referent is not to deny the pronoun "I" indexical value. It is not to declare that the pronoun "I" is a meaningless expression. The "I" is not semantically empty for lack of external referent. It is however contextually bound and its meaning indissociable from the utterance—a point that Anscombe does not make but which makes her argument more persuasive. Recall from earlier discussion that as a shifter, the pronoun "I" must be dissociated from its referent in order to fulfill its dialogic function of designating any speaker efficiently. The dissociation from the referent that Anscombe rightly insists upon in her discussion of the first-person stance is therefore a necessary feature built into the grammar of the pronoun "I"; it needs to be brought into account to make the de jure and not merely de facto character of this nondenoting character of the pronoun manifest. Supported with grammatical insights, Anscombe's argument carries more weight, for the pronoun "I"'s lack of reference ceases to appear as a purely factual, however problem-ridden, occurrence. This strategy demonstrates the usefulness of bringing explicitly linguistic analysis into philosophical argument.

WITTGENSTEIN

A similar case could be made regarding Wittgenstein. Recall his criticism discussed in chapter 1 of the philosophers' search for an ethereal object behind the pronoun "I" construed as a substantive, closely paralleling Anscombe's own critique. Pointing out the ordinary function of the pronoun "I" as a shifter indicating the speaker role in dialogic context provides positive insight into what an undistorted grammar of the "I" pronoun would be—a positive perspective missing in Wittgenstein's critique. This gesture shows that the semantic poverty of the pronoun "I" resists being turned into a content-bearing substantive in ordinary use. Grammatical analysis helps therefore to bolster the philosopher's argument. Finally, on a more critical note, the grammatical analysis challenges Wittgenstein's distinction into the subjective and objective uses of the pronoun "I," the latter modeled on the demonstrative "this person" or "he" (68). As previously discussed, this modeling suggests that, in its objective use, the pronoun "I" is grammatically equivalent to a substantive noun or a third-person pronoun designating a mundane entity with a definite set of physical properties (size, height, weight), and that problems arise only if we regard the "I" pronoun as a noun designating a nonempirical entity. However, this designation appears to attach a referent to the "I" pronoun and burden it with content. It follows that Wittgenstein's posit of the pronoun "I" in its use as object deviates from the ordinary grammatical conception of the pronoun "I" as indicator of the first-person stance, which does not split into subjective and objective aspects but is unitary.

I hope that armed with contributions from linguistics, as well as phenomenological philosophy, I have helped to dispel the myth that pronouns in general and personal pronouns in particular stand in for nouns. It turns out that personal pronouns "I" and "you" resist this grand concept of noun-substitution, just as much as they depart from the denoting type of reference traditionally attributed to nouns. As such, they put pressure on the received view that the chief function of speech is to name or label entities. This view has retained credence up to the present day in some authors, for example, Russell and early Wittgenstein. On that view, the naming relation is a standard model for meaning, and the meaning of a name resides in its bearer. *Any* speech part would thus need to stand in a naming relation, or some variant thereof, to a referent in order to possess meaning. This traditional definition of pronouns as stand-ins for names is thus deeply rooted in the soil of the

Western philosophical conception of how meaning comes to language. However, this conception covers over the real foundation of communal-meaning making in the communicative acts of speakers situated in the world. Importantly, it serves to efface the speaker and hearer, these nonobjectifiable performers, from the domain of meaning and turns the linguistic markers of personhood into labels without having asked who the labelers are. To ask the latter question is to enact a Copernican turn from the object to its foundation. However, the foundation is not located within a solitary cognitive subject but rather in the shared communal-meaning making practice enacted by embodied speakers firmly rooted in the environing world.

PERSONAL PRONOUNS— RECONSIDERING THE TRADITIONAL VIEW (2)

Having stripped off the layers of the traditional conception of *pro-nomen*, we are in a better position to appreciate the primacy of *I–you* connectedness. Consider in this regard yet another myth about personal pronouns that finds expression in another traditional paradigm: the table of conjugation. This table typically includes three terms, "I," "you," and "s/he," and serves to conjugate a verb according to the first, second, and third persons. This paradigm widely used in the nomenclature creates the impression of strict symmetry between three types of person cast in the three types of pronouns. Unsurprisingly, this impression is reinforced in the dialogue between Sir Pronoun and the children from *The Little Grammar People* (Mass 1947, 22–23).

> In Grammar Kingdom, there are three types of person, and to distinguish them we call them 'first,' 'second,' and 'third.'... 'I' is a first person pronoun.... And, being a pronoun, it must stand for a noun. Now, what is that noun?"
> "Why, Barry, of course. That's your own name, isn't it?"
> "Yes, yes," said Barry eagerly. "And that's a proper noun, because it belongs to me only."
> "And the word 'you' would be a second person pronoun, wouldn't it? Because it stands for the one or thing being spoken to," said Linda.
> "Quite right,'" replied Sir Pronoun. "You'll find, as you go on thinking, that there are any amount of occasions on which I am 'personal.'"

"And then, what about third person pronouns?" asked Barry. "They would be 'they,' 'their,' 'him,' 'it,' 'she,' 'he'—oh, lots and lots of them—as those stand for the things or people being spoken about. How easy it is after all, isn't it, Lin?"

Sir Pronoun's instructions are easy enough to follow, but the instructor is guilty of perpetuating an illusion. As Benveniste (1971, 221) notes, the impression of symmetry between the three persons is merely formal. The first- and second-person pronouns need to be distinguished from the third-person one. Benveniste claims in fact that only the former two can justifiably be termed *personal*, whereas the third designates a nonpersonal entity, which could refer to a thing or a corpse. He follows the definitions used by Arab grammarians, for whom the first person designates "the one who speaks," the second "the one who is addressed," while the third is "the one who is absent" (197). The third-person pronoun lacks what the other two pronouns capture, namely positive participant involvement in discourse. That is why the referents of the third-person pronouns may be seen as "nonpersons," since their position in the speech act is defined in exclusively negative terms, in contrast to the referents of "I" and "you" (Lyons 1977, 638). Contrary to "I" and "you," the third-person pronoun referents are not defined in terms of speech roles. Furthermore, in accordance with the Arab classification, while the referent of the third-person pronoun may be absent and yet identifiable, in order to identify the persons indicated by "I" and "you" one needs to be present in flesh and blood in the event of discourse (this is the existential relation identified by Jakobson).

The distinction between "I"–"you" and third-person pronouns can be cashed out in terms of their semantic load and gender marking. The former are semantically poor and carry no information about the discourse participant. Third-person pronouns, on the other hand, do typically carry a small semantic load. The third-person pronouns are typically marked for gender, whereas gender distinction is generally absent in first- and second-person pronouns. Bhat (2004, 109–11) lists some exceptions to this rule; however, he explains them in terms of speech roles rather than the specific individuals performing those roles. When gender distinctions occur in first- and second-person pronouns, he notes that their purpose is not to identify the referent but rather to indicate social distinctions or to comply with social requirements.

Note also that the third-person pronoun could feasibly be, and in some languages is, dispensed with altogether in favor of demonstrative pronouns

(Lyons 1977, 639; Bhat 2004, 13). Furthermore, the demonstrative pronoun is the source of the third-person pronouns (as well as the definite article) in the Germanic and Romance languages (Lyons 1977, 646). It is therefore unsurprising that there are many languages that do not have an equivalent of the English "she," "he," "it." However, "there is perhaps no language. . . in which there are no first-person and second-person pronouns" (639). Or, focusing on the speech roles rather than on their specific linguistic markers, there is no spoken language devoid of *some kind of marking of addressor and addressee.*

To be sure, Lyons' claim of translinguistic universality of *I–you* has recently been challenged by a consideration of Asian languages such as Burmese, Thai, and Japanese, which do not possess special lexemes of the personal pronoun form (Bhat 2004, 30). These languages use a wide array of nouns rather than a limited set of personal pronouns for the purpose of self-reference and address. In Japanese, these are terms of occupation or status title, and are marked for gender, age, perceived social status, and emotional correlation between the speaker and the addressee (Hinds 1986, 241, quoted in Bhat 2004, 31). Unlike the previously discussed shifters, these expressions appear therefore to closely tie speech roles to the specific individuals who perform these roles, in observance of the specific culturally constrained code of appropriate social interaction for differently marked (by class, gender, age, status) individuals. Hinds concludes, however, that despite their nominal origins, and despite the fact that these expressions show nominal characteristics (they occur after demonstratives and are modified by relative clauses), these expressions display some characteristics of their own and thus need to be grouped in a distinct pronominal category. Furthermore, as Bhat (31) and Wales (1996, 56) observe, during the language-acquisition period, the parent speakers of languages with personal pronouns may use expressions "mother" and "father" to refer to themselves and to use the child's name rather than the second-person pronoun in order to ease the potential confusion resulting from the shifting nature of personal pronouns. "Mommy will give Amelia a cookie" is a possible example of direct address that bypasses the "I"–"you" reversibility for the sake of unambiguous reference.

Consider also that self-deprecating expressions (for example, "your humble servant") as well as honorific expressions (for instance, "her" or "his majesty," "sir" or "lady"/"madam") may be used in the place of personal pronouns to follow the rules of social appropriateness, especially if a strong attachment to vertical distinctions between groups construed as "higher" and "lower" on the social ladder, whether due to class privilege, age, gender, or race, exists rather than attachment to a horizontal relation typically cast in "I"–"you" terms. Such expressions have enjoyed a firm footing until quite recently in the English-speaking world. They are still being consistently used, for example, in familiar relations between parents and their children in the southern states of the US, where some children are still required to address their parents as "sir"/"ma'am." Note that this polite form of address may exploit the history of racial oppression in this part of the country, as when white parents who adopted black children insist on the formal "sir"/"ma'am" type of address, thus inadvertently reviving the long-standing history of inequality between the blacks and the whites within the context of children-parents relations.[6] Furthermore, the widespread custom to have the children address the parents using "mom"/"dad" in the US rather than by means of the second-person pronoun may be a reflection of a similar desire to use a mediatory term anchored in the socially construed specificity of nuclear-family relations rather than the nonspecific "you." Interestingly then, utterances of the type "Mommy will give Amelia a cookie" may play a complex role of easing the potential confusion regarding correct personal-pronoun use *and* instituting the habit of using nominal expressions denoting parental power and privilege over the child, a dynamic that the second-person pronoun would by necessity fail to convey.

Self-deprecating and honorific expressions, as well as parental titles, can therefore feasibly be used for the purpose of self-reference and address, even in the absence of personal pronouns. These expressions, when used in the context-dependent utterance, therefore perform the speech roles typically assigned to the "I"–"you" pronouns. Surely, the examples above also import a semantic load representative of the power relations within a given social hierarchy, together with the twin history of oppression and privilege based on gender, race, class, social status, and age. This importing of oppressive relations into speech prevents the participants from being placed on an equal footing. Forms of interpersonal address marked by socially construed advantage/disadvantage are therefore at odds with the objectives of egalitarianism and equal representation. It is also important to emphasize, however, that even the honorific and self-deprecatory expressions continue to perform the function typically assumed by personal pronouns: they identify the participants in the dialogic context. This shared dialogic space may itself produce an equalizing effect—hence the significance of sitting down together with the opponent at the negotiating table in conflict-resolution strategies. Speaking and listening to one another in face-to-face contexts may help to subvert the rigid regiments of oppression, and destabilize the opposition between the "powerful" and the "powerless" individuals or groups.

Recall Wittgenstein's stipulation (chapter 1) not to follow a purely formal approach to language but to examine how the word is being used in ordinary context. This rule is directly applicable for present purposes. Even though the expressions of address discussed above belong formally together with the nominals, they may be used to indicate participant involvement in discourse and thus serve to specify speech roles and not only the specific individuals performing these roles; this indexical/deictic function provides therefore the central cue for interpreting them, rather than their nominal form. It follows that even in the absence of first- and second-personal pronouns, the twin-speaker/addressee category continues to be expressed in discourse. This category is indispensable for any language, as long as the latter is founded on and serves as the vehicle of interpersonal communication and shared understanding of the world. The speaker-addressee relation is built into the structure of any language, regardless of the cultural differences in the specific grammatical and lexical expressions of person involvement. I call this basic relation *the deep grammar,* insofar as it reveals not only the factual but also the indispensable aspects of spoken language, and I contend that it is rooted in the communicative potential of the living, perceiving, and interrelating human bodies. I therefore do not posit transcendental conditions of possibility of communication by advocating the deep notion of I-you connectedness; neither do I regard I-you connectedness as a transcendent surface fact. I contend rather that I-you connectedness ultimately undoes these technical distinctions and functions in the manner of a necessary dimension of language, which can be gleaned from the actually existing languages and which supposes an already established foothold within a living language.

I AND WE—A RELATIONAL COMMUNITY

Up to now, I have employed insights from ordinary pronominal discourse to disclose the interpersonal dimension of meaning that may be occluded from a phenomenological inquiry conducted typically in the first person. Insights from ordinary pronominal discourse help also to situate the interpersonal relatedness in the I-you mode within the context of communal life, or what would be cast in pronominal terms as the "we" of larger social groups. Even though communal life may seem at first sight to exceed the interpersonal dynamics of direct first-to-second-person relations, it turns upon, on inquiry, to extend and presuppose them. As such, I-you connectedness appears to organize social life both within and beyond the range of proximal face-to-face relations. To help make this point, consider another unique feature of first- and second-person markers in discourse, which sets them apart from the third person. The feature in question is captured by the grammatical category of *number* (Bhat 2004, 10).

In the case of the third-person pronoun, the category of number denotes the plurality of referents. Hence "they" is constituted by adding up instances of "she" and/or "he." Plurality in the third-person pronoun is therefore of a straightforwardly *additive* kind. In the case of the first-person plural, the situation is more complex. It is not the case that "we" denotes a plurality of "I"s. As numerous linguists, for example Jespersen (1924, 192), Benveniste (1971), and J. Lyons (1968, 277) have pointed out, the terminology used for describing the nonsingular forms of both first- and second-person pronouns is misleading since these forms do not stand in the same type of relation to singular forms as "girls," "telephones," stand to "girl," "telephone." The word "girls" indicates several girls, but the pronoun "we" does not indicate several "I" referents, that is, speakers. "We" indicates just one speaker, that is, the speaker of the utterance in which it occurs, and one or more nonspeakers. In its minimal form, the "we" pronoun indicates the speaker and the addressee—as in "We are leaving," wherein the referents are the one who makes the utterance and the one at whom the utterances is aimed. This is the so-called *inclusive* case of the first-person pronoun in nonsingular use. It is also possible for the "we" pronoun to be exclusive of the addressee—as in "We are leaving," wherein the referents of the pronoun are the speaker, and one or more nonspeakers, who address another person or group and inform the addressor(s) of their imminent departure. This distinction between the inclusion and the exclusion of the addressee is not a distinction in *plurality*, but rather in the kind of *relation* established between the addressor and the addressee. Furthermore, the relation to the addressee is always involved in the utterance of the "we" pronoun, whether the addressee is included or excluded from its referents. This demonstrates the intrinsically dialogic—rather than additive—character of plurality in the pronoun "we": the pronoun "we" is not founded on an external collective of the referents of the pronoun "I" but rather on the *I-you* type of relation, even though it remains true that the speaker uttering "we" speaks on more than her own behalf (speaking on behalf of the addressee in the inclusive form and on the part of nonspeakers who are not the addressee(s) in the exclusive form). It is only once this intrinsic relation between the speaker and the addressee is undercut that it becomes feasible to think of the "we" pronoun as a sheer multiplicity of the referents of the pronoun "I."

One could object that there are cases in which the pronoun "we" has more than just one speaker as its referent. A case cited by Jespersen (1924, 192) involves a body of men who in response to "Who will join me?" respond with a unison "We all will." Jespersen comments that despite the de facto plurality of speakers voicing the pronoun *we*, its meaning should be read as "I will and all the others will (I presume)." Even though Jespersen's interpretation of the example seems correct, the example itself is somewhat contrived, as one rarely hears an extemporaneous "we" uttered simultaneously by a group of people without prior consultation with the others (how would you know that the others are going to join in?). Furthermore, even though the pronoun "we" is used to express the opinions of many, it typically issues from a single mouth. Unlike the pronoun "I," the pronoun "we" is representative of its referents but not necessarily performed by its referents. That is why in some situations a referent may feel alienated from the inclusive "we" produced by a spokesperson and feel that she herself is not represented in the utterances including this pronoun in a way that would be difficult to realize in the typical instance of the pronoun "I." To revise Rimbaud's classic statement, *we is an other*—at least sometimes. That is why a nonalienating "we" is dependent upon ongoing deliberative engagement within the I-you mode within the referent group; otherwise, the common "we"-front risks being fractured by dissenting voices and the larger representational potential of the first-personal plural may be lost. Needless to say, such deliberative engagements are possible as long as the one who speaks on behalf of others by means of "we" listens to their speech too. The speaker's *I* needs to reverse into the addressee's *you* for the communal *we* to be possible.

Consider how the problematic additive nondialogic conception of plurality in "we" continues to inform the understanding of sociality in the transcendental phenomenological tradition, as if it sufficed to multiply monads to produce a community. In §54a of the *Crisis* entitled "We as human beings, and we as ultimately functioning-accomplishing subjects," Husserl raises the question of the constitution of intersubjectivity. He notes that a more careful than hitherto provided analysis of the ego brings up "the phenomenon of the change of signification of [the form] 'I'—just as I am saying 'I' right now—into 'other I's,' into 'all of us,' *we who are many 'Is,'* and among whom I am but *one* 'I.'" (1970 [1938], 182, emphasis added). This change of signification should provide a transcendental meaning to the community as the more-than-one subject enacting the universal constitution. However, this conception of transcendental intersubjectivity as "we who are many *Is*" rests on the misguided assumption that a community could be founded by adding up multiple referents of the "I" pronoun to form the plural "we." As noted above, the pronoun "we" is not a sum total of speakers who self-refer by means of the pronoun "I"; there has to be an interpersonal relation of direct address for the pronoun "we" to arise, whether this relation is internal (the inclusive "we") or external (the exclusive "we") to the referents of the pronoun. In either case, the pronoun "we" arises within a dialogic context, and such a context is missing within the transcendental conception of intersubjectivity. The latter operates with the widespread yet illusory notion that the referents of the "I" pronoun add up like the referents of "apples" or "oranges" to form larger groups.

In line with the traditional view that the chief purpose of language is naming or labeling, the pronoun "I" is viewed in transcendental phenomenology as a label for the self. On this account, it should suffice to multiply the labels to obtain a set containing many selves. It is important to stress that this traditional view is perpetuated in transcendental phenomenology despite—if not because of—its consideration of language as extrinsic to its own method. This stance of determined disinterest does not result in the phenomenologist's emancipation from language, if such were possible, but rather in the importing of the unexamined preconceptions about how words function into the heart of the inquiry. Should the phenomenologist take a closer look at grammar and personal pronoun pragmatics, she would be in a better place to appreciate that I-you relations are necessary to forge communities founded on mutual coexistence. It is the I-you relation rather than the lone "I" that provides the building block of sociality and the starting point of analysis for any social theory. As Martin Buber would put it, there is no I as such, but I exists necessarily in relation (see chapter 4).

BENVENISTE AND I-YOU CONNECTEDNESS

The above discussed differences between "I"–"you" and third-person pronouns (gender marking, plurality) have incited some linguists to depart from the all-inclusive "pronoun" category and adopt two separate categories, one including the pronouns that participate in the conversational exchange (typically, "I" and "you") and the other for all the remaining pronouns. Bhat adopts this distinction and proposes using two separate terms: *personal pronouns* and *proforms*. The adoption of the term pronouns for "I" and "you," despite the fact that clearly they do not stand in for nouns, has, he says, the backing of an extended grammatical tradition (5). An appealing alternative terminology is provided by Showalter (1986, quoted in Bhat 2004, 5) who distinguishes between *interlocutory* and *substitutive* pronouns. This terminology has the advantage of clearly marking off the "pronouns" belonging to the conversational exchange from the ones that do not. It is therefore tempting to coin a new term, *interlocutives,* to once and for all dispel the twin myth of noun substitution and of strict symmetry between first, second, and third persons that has served to occlude the primacy of I-you connectedness and facilitated the philosophical construct of an isolated *I.*

Consider now why "I" and "you" are necessarily connected. Benveniste provides a number of valuable clues in this regard. To begin, he distinguishes between discourse and language. Discourse is shorthand for actual interpersonal communication, whereas language stands for a system of signs and syntactical rules which could be exemplified by an "impersonal" scientific text wherein neither "I" nor "you" ever need to be mentioned. In discourse, however, the first-person pronoun is necessarily taken up by the speaker as another is addressed in the second-person mode. "I use *I* only when I am speaking to someone who will be a *you* in my address." "I" and "you" are therefore complementary: "neither of the terms can be conceived of independently of the other." (p. 225). As Humboldt put it, "in the I, the Thou is also given automatically" (1999 [1836], 95). This interconnection between "I" and "Thou" demonstrates, according to Humboldt, the presence of a dual number (*Dualis*) in speech, to be distinguished from the singular and the plural numbers. This original duality, based on the insight about personal pronouns "more deeply drawn from language" than the received view of *pro-nomen* could ever yield, reflects the inherently dialogic nature of speech in its ineradicable dependence of the "I"-sayer on a conversational partner.[7] Humboldt confirms therefore our earlier insight (from the discussion of the pronoun "we") that the "I" and "you" couplet is not a sum of singulars and needs to be pluralized in relational and intradiscursive terms, rather than in additive terms appropriate to extradiscursive entities. Note finally that this original I-you duality is preserved even in solitary thought whose unfolding is dependent on an engagement with a virtual *you* (an imagined interlocutor); this apparently asocial activity continues therefore to be informed by social inclination (see chapter 4 for additional discussion of the dual number in relation to Buber).[8]

Turning back to Benveniste, note that the I-you complementarity does not mean that the two terms are equivalent or symmetrical. Benveniste points to the contrast between "I" and "you"—*you* is the non-*I*, that is, the one who I am not and with regard to whom I am transcendent. This difference between "I" and "you," however, "does not suppress the human reality of dialogue" (Benveniste 1971, 201). It is a difference that makes communication *between* persons possible, a difference internal to the dialogic relation. Contrary to the egocentric tradition, the other person is not construed in a strict symmetrical fashion to oneself as another I or alter ego; such a construal undercuts the possibility of grasping the other within the context of direct address.

Together with *complementarity* and *asymmetry*, Benveniste views *reversibility* as a key characteristic of the I-you relation (1971, 199). "I" and "you" are reversible insofar as every "I" uttered by the speaker reverses into a "you" when the speaker is addressed by another, and analogously the other person addressed as "you" self-refers by means of the "I." These I-you reversals, ongoing within the conversational context, are not to be thought of as extrinsic to either of the pronouns, as if one could use and comprehend "I" with no grasp of "you," and vice versa. Furthermore, regarded from a developmental point of view (discussed in more detail in chapter 3), the pronoun is fully acquired by the child only once she understands that whereas proper names such as the name "Amelia" apply regardless of who the speaker is, the choice of personal pronouns is affected by the participant role in discourse, and that different lexemes are being used depending on whether the child is speaking or being spoken to. The child must therefore acquire the "I"–"you" couplet and understand how the reversible relation between these two words is modulated by the interrelated perspectives and roles of speaker and hearer in order to fully master either pronoun. Contra the egocentric tradition, the first person is inextricably connected with the second person in the ordinary grammar of personal-pronoun acquisition and use.

I-you reversibility further exemplifies their complementarity. This I-you complementarity is not, however, confined to the early stages of human development when pronouns are acquired. Benveniste emphasizes that a peculiar "polarity of persons," which always posits "you" as an echo of "I," and vice versa, is a permanent trait and fundamental condition of language

(1971, 225). Language is dialogical through and through, and the pronouns provide a privileged locus for witnessing its dialogic dimension. Hence the linguist's assertion that "The importance of [the] function [of pronouns] will be measured by the nature of the problem they serve to solve, which is none other than that of intersubjective communication" (219). Viewing either of the pronouns in isolation from their inherently communicative role therefore conceals the fact that interpersonal communication is the driving force of language and reduces living discourse to the sterility of impersonal scientific text.

I-you reversibility is artificially suspended in *transcendentalese*. Rather than thematize interpersonal relations in terms of the dialogic I–you, transcendental phenomenology posits an *ego–alter ego* schema, where my consociates are conceived in strict analogy and symmetry with the solitary *I*. This ego–alter ego schema preserves, to be sure, the first-person pronoun within the transcendental inquiry, but this pronoun fails to reverse into the second-person form. Henceforth, neither the ego nor the alter ego is subject to direct address. Construed as acommunicative self-enclosed beings, the ego and alter ego by necessity fail to relate, no matter how multitudinous they may be. Both constructs are lifted out of the communicative context, they are *ex-communicated* in the literal sense of the word. The ego–alter ego model forecloses the possibility of the second-person type of relation, having expunged the second-person mode out of transcendentalese.

OBJECTIFICATION IN THE THIRD PERSON

To revisit the contrast between "I"–"you" and the third-person pronoun, consider that although "I" and "you" posses the "correlation of personality," the third-person pronoun appears impersonal or a nonperson (Benveniste 1971, 228). It falls outside the scope of direct address and so loses the peculiar discourse-dependent meaning. It indicates neither to the one who speaks nor the one spoken *to* but the one spoken *of;* it might be an inert object or a dead body that does not reverse between *I* and *you* but freezes into an irreversible *it*. Static, fixed, the third-person pronoun referent is deprived of speaker/addressee involvement. Even though this pronoun is consistently ascribed to people, it designates them as a nonparticipatory third party, as passive, distant, nonpresent, even though they might be in physical proximity.

Consider some real-life examples of the nonidentity between the interpersonal "I"–"you" pronouns and the nonpersonal third-person pronoun, notably the profound transformation that occurs in a shift from direct address to a third-person relation. John Hull, a religious-education professor suffering from recent onset blindness reports the unsettling change of attitude among some of his acquaintances. Accompanied by his wife at church, he finds that he is no longer directly addressed but rather spoken about, as when one of the vergers asks his wife, in his presence, "Marilyn, is it John's wish to go forward to the communion rail?" (Hull, 2001, 101). Even though Hull appreciates the verger's concern, he is nonetheless upset not to be spoken *to*, and notes that "to speak *about* me, in the third person, to someone else, is another matter." Hull feels relegated to the status of an object through the "Does he take sugar?" approach, forcibly removed from the conversational context, even though he is not deaf but blind! His inability to return the gaze, which is often accompanied by a shift from a *facing* relation to a *lateral* ear-to-mouth relation to others in the blind population (face-to-face relations are predicated upon, as is often glossed over, intact visual sense in both parties), is misinterpreted in our predominantly *ocularcentric* society as a linguistic inability to engage in a dialogic exchange. This misinterpretation deprives the blind person of the rights to engage and be engaged as an equal partner in the social setting.

Consider another example, which for some readers may be closer home. At a cocktail party, you make some pleasant small talk with an acquaintance. Turning to mingle with others, but still within earshot of your previous interlocutor, you find yourself transformed into a *she* spoken of in a hardly complimentary manner. ("She put on weight, did you notice?") You find yourself objectified, petrified, silenced. Your fury is only a testimony to your powerlessness. This moment is reminiscent of the transformation produced by the look of the other in Sartre's famous analysis from *Being and Nothingness*. Here is the story. Engaged in the process of eavesdropping on a conversation through a keyhole, you find yourself suddenly spotted by another person who happens to pass by in the hallway. With her gaze she fixes your crouching pathetic figure in the hallway, reducing you to a humiliating caricature of yourself. For the other, you have become congealed into the manifest facade of an eavesdropper, a role that you now live in the manner of a thing (in Sartre's ontological system, an *in-itself*) rather than as a free project of consciousness (*for-itself*). Even though the objectification by the foreign gaze temporarily freezes up your freedom, you continue to experience it consciously as humiliation and shame in front of the other. In fact, Sartre argues, the affective states of shame, as well as pride, arise exclusively within the interpersonal world.[9]

The Sartrean moment of objectification through the gaze is analogous to the objectification in language through the shift from interpersonal to impersonal pronouns, which effectuates a similar congealment of the subject into a thing or an *it*. They share the observational or third-person stance adopted by another person toward you. Even though Sartre contends that this stance typifies interpersonal relations in general, and accounts for their intrinsically conflictual nature, the insights gained from sociolinguistics suggest rather that they are but one type of dynamics operative within the social world, one that disrupts rather than preserves the interpersonal relation based on reciprocity, equal partnership, and communicative engagement within the I-you mode. I believe that Sartre's analysis of the social world in terms of the objectifying foreign gaze is wrongheaded in that he takes as paradigmatic the third-person type relation, which arises de facto as a disruption of the more fundamental interpersonal relation in the second-person type. However, his analysis is helpful in that it illuminates the nature of this third-person relation and its marked difference from the interaction of the I-you type.

Transcendental phenomenology privileges the third-person type relations by its ego–alter ego model. The alter ego is syntactically equivalent to a third-person pronoun and would be complemented by a verb inflected in the third person (for example, "the alter ego thinks. . . ," which can be replaced by "s/he thinks."). As such, the alter ego belongs to the nonpersonal grouping even though verbally it claims allegiance to the personal pronouns properly so called. This allows both the ego and the alter ego to appear not as partners in communication but primarily as depersonalized nonparticipatory third parties. Each one may think or speak *about* the other, whether casually in gossip or thematically as part of a philosophical project to resolve the problem of the transcendental constitution of intersubjectivity. However, no party needs to speak and relate *to* another in the process.

The insights gained from linguistics substantiate earlier criticism of the transcendental phenomenological conception of sociality. They reinforce the earlier argument that importing the first-person pronoun into transcendental phenomenology leads to an oversight of ordinary grammatical principles regarding ordinary pronominal discourse. Notably, I-you complementarity, reversibility, and asymmetry are left out of account, reinforcing the notion of an isolated *I* or ego, defined in terms of separation, irreversibility, and symmetry with other *I*s/egos. These oversights motivate the construal of personal identity in terms of a first-person subject and of sociality in terms of a detached third-person relation between this subject and analogous others. However, insights from ordinary pronominal discourse demonstrate that I-you connectedness is indissoluble and basic. A first-without-second person subject appears as a product of an epistemically overdetermined intellectual tradition that disrupts this primary relational stance for the sake of securing an intuitive grasp of apodictic knowledge. This tradition has fostered the myth of individualism, according to which persons are "naturally" egoists, self-centered, and concerned primarily with private interests, unless they heroically abandon this primitive egoism in a generous altruistic gesture of investment in community life.

The ongoing egoism-altruism debate in moral theory is but a proof of how entrenched the opposition between the self and the consociates still is in contemporary mindset, and how difficult it is to think of one's own interests as continuous with those of one's community. This egoism/altruism opposition rests on the intellectual thesis of the primacy of the ego. However, as ordinary language analysis helps to reveal, the ego is an abstraction from a more primary interconnectedness of the first and second persons. To found a philosophy of sociality on the ego that is a product of the dissolution of this primary interconnectedness is thus to put the cart before the horse, and to regard the product of a split as the basic reality. In order to avoid such a wrongheaded approach, an inquiry of sociality must begin there where social relations themselves are forged and preserved: in the dialogic space opened up by first- to second-person interaction. Only a philosophy firmly rooted in this dialogic space may help retrieve the basic reality of social life and abolish the myth of inescapable egocentrism.

CASTAÑEDA'S PHENOMENO-LOGIC OF THE "I"

Before pursuing the inquiry into I-you connectedness further, with the help of developmental psychology (chapter 3) and the dialogic tradition (chapters 4 and 5), I propose to contrast the contributions from sociolinguistics and phenomenology discussed in this chapter with the thought of a philosopher—Hector-Neri Castañeda (1999)—who occupied himself extensively with personal pronouns, notably the first-person pronoun, but whose conclusions depart significantly from the evidence for social and spatial situatedness of self mounted in this chapter. I propose to examine his approach in some detail, because it helps to contrast the polycentric view developed here with an egocentric one and to further expose the epistemic bias that produces the egocentric perspective on personal reference. Even though this bias has a well-established history in philosophy, it distorts the conception of personhood in favor of an asocial and nonsituated self. As such it helps to make apparent the need for an alternative inquiry, which is not driven by a quest for transparent knowledge but responds rather to the great complexity of the phenomenon under investigation. The phenomenon of personhood is complex because it is inherently embodied and embedded within the social and the natural world. A phenomenological inquiry into personhood needs to resist the urge to reduce its complexity for transparency, preserving the multilayered patterns that shape, organize, and situate personhood within natural, social, and linguistic contexts. I believe that Castañeda's otherwise insightful and instructive account of the pronoun "I" does not preserve this inherent complexity of personhood.

Castañeda's central thesis developed in *The Phenomeno-Logic of the I: Essays on Self-Consciousness* (1999) is that the analysis of the first-person pronoun provides direct support for an inner private self. His thinking is therefore reminiscent of Husserl's postulate of the transcendental ego, construed as a linguistically neutral agency located by the phenomenological onlooker in the purified field of consciousness, which is equivocally expressed in the natural language by the pronoun "I." The transcendental order of inquiry proceeds therefore, so to say, from top-to-bottom. Castañeda's thinking follows the reverse bottom-to-top direction by deriving an egocentric mentalistic subject from the personal pronoun "I." Both derivations are fueled by a preexisting philosophical agenda of securing apodictic knowledge, as discussed below. Yet they also serve as a useful reminder that language alone cannot perform the task that linguists like Benveniste assign to them: creating personal marking ex nihilo by the sheer fact of uttering and comprehending personal pronouns. Castañeda is right that something more than linguistic competence is needed for developing personal identity, and that the sense of self (whether construed in individualist or social terms) exceeds its linguistic expression. However, he is wrong to posit an isolated transcendental subject to accommodate this need.

In agreement with the linguists discussed in this chapter, as well as with Anscombe, Castañeda views the first-person pronoun as a unique expression that cannot be reduced to or replaced by names, definite descriptions, and third-person pronouns. For example, a philosopher might say, "The one who wrote this sentence about the transcendental ego is not very bright" to express a belief not expressed by "I am not very bright," even though the philosopher wrote the sentence in question (say, on a misplaced scrap of paper later discovered at a friend's house). Contra the linguists, however, Castañeda does not think it suffices to explain first-person reference as the reference to the speaker of the utterance in which it occurs. For the speaker must *thinkingly* refer to herself in order that she be able to use the little word "I" in the first place (1999, 256). Following Kant's Copernican revolution, Castañeda argues that there is no direct word-to-world correlation without invoking the *thinker*, whose internal self-reference provides a necessary condition of possibility of linguistic self-reference via personal pronouns. To argue otherwise would be to assign too much of a productive role to language and assume that the speaker's utterance of the first-person pronoun initiates self-reference ex nihilo. However, the person who says, for example, "I am hungry," is not determining the "I"-referent *après coup*. Were such a search for the author of an utterance necessary, we would be at a loss to explain how "I"-references could ever get off the ground. It follows from Castañeda's argument that we need to presuppose a preexistent reflexive self in order to account for how first-person reference ever gets initiated.

This preexistent self must exhibit a special kind of reflexivity. Consider another example.[10] Oedipus may think or say that the slayer of Laius should be killed, without realizing that he himself is the slayer. So even though Oedipus refers to himself when he speaks or thinks about the slayer of Laius, *he does not know it*. His self-reference lacks self-awareness. Similar examples abound in the literature. Borges may read a story about the man named Borges, without being aware that he himself is the person featured in the story. When he does come to realize it, a new element is added to the story that does not have to do with its semantic content but with his reading of the character in the first- rather than the third-person mode. What exactly does this new element consist in? According to Castañeda, it has to do with a reference to oneself qua self. It is a reference that has to do with the internal reflexivity of self-awareness, and it differs profoundly from any external encounters with oneself.

Castañeda distinguishes between two types of reflexive reference: external "pedestrian" and internal "exciting" ones (1999, 252). Let me begin with the pedestrian. Seeing oneself in the mirror is a good example of external reflexive acts. For example, Ernst Mach who notices "a shabby old pedagogue" approach him as he is boarding a tram in fact sees his own reflection in a mirror, but does not recognize it as such. His demonstrative reference of the mirror image is not made in the first person, even though the *demonstrandum* stands in fact for the demonstrator himself. Such external encounters with oneself need to be neatly separated from the internal reflexive reference. The latter is realized in thought accompanied by self-awareness. Castañeda stresses that internal self-reference is of a *mental* or *thinking* kind—it is a conceptual ability that, for example, small children do not have (4). This conceptual ability is only known from within. It is an index of subjectivity, realized within episodes of self-consciousness. Unlike Descartes, Castañeda does not attribute an ontological substantive status to this transcendental self. He views it along the Kantian lines of the transcendental prefix, the "I think that" of Kant's transcendental principle of the unity of apperception, which is beyond doubt. Unlike Kant, and like Husserl, Castañeda does not consider the transcendental *I* to be a product of transcendental deduction (an a priori condition of experience), but rather a phenomenological datum (215) located by the thinker during the episodes of self-awareness. This transcendental ego is not, in Castañeda's view (unlike Husserl's), an enduring entity out of which particular instances of thought spring forth. There is rather a series of transcendental *I*s, that are subjective particulars existing with certainty during the thinking experience only (247). Castañeda spells out this idea by means of the so-called *I*-guises: different thoughts, which are the same as their corresponding *I* (216).[11]

What is interesting about Castañeda's approach, and what sets him apart from transcendental phenomenology, is his express preoccupation with ordinary language. Castañeda claims to develop a material and experiential semantics for ordinary language (1999, 226). He argues, quite rightly, that to investigate first-person reference one needs to study the living semantics and the pragmatics of first-person language (234). However, his conclusion that what one refers to by means of the first-person pronoun is the internal/mentalistic/private self (257) is not based on unprejudiced analysis of language use but rather on a preexisting philosophical agenda. Had he looked into how the pronoun "I" is employed in ordinary language, Castañeda would have noticed that it captures not only mental states ("I am hungry," "I am feeling sad") but also physical states ("I weigh 130 pounds," "I am 6 feet tall"). As Strawson (1991) pointed out, the pronoun "I" does not discriminate between "internal" and "external" or public references; it carries both. To single out only a specific set of "I"-references that fit one's preexisting assumption of a mentalistic subject is *not* to pay heed to the complexity of ordinary language and to the intrinsic ambiguity of the first-person pronoun, which resists being construed along the traditional subject-object binary. It is rather to follow the epistemic concern of securing the domain of knowledge immune to error through misidentification. After all, the subjective "I"-thoughts are traditionally deemed to yield the kind of apodictic certainty that is not provided by references to oneself in the so-called external reflexivity: seeing one's expression in the mirror, referring to oneself by means of a definite expression like "the slayer of Laius," contain the danger of misidentification. Similarly, the first-person statement of the type "I weigh 100 pounds" could be invalidated by external evidence, such as reading the subject's real weight off the scales, while it is senseless to mount evidence against the person who confesses "I am feeling sad." This distinction between the statements subject to verification and those that are not motivates the isolation of an inner mental self as the locus of unshakable knowledge. After all, in the spirit of Descartes' quest for indubitable truths, Castañeda is "considering entities as they are thought of and referred to by a thinker putting her world together after the skeptical devastation brought about by the Mad Scientist, or the Evil Demon" (224).

The transcendental self stands as an entity that survives this skeptical devastation and "is putting the world together" (Castañeda 1999). However, the self construed in the quest for apodicticity clearly conflicts with the self attained via ordinary language analysis. Although the former is defined by the philosopher in purportedly unambiguous terms (certainty, interiority, privacy, mentality), the latter is notoriously ridden with ambiguity—it is internal *and* external, private *and* public, mental *and* mundane, and so it perpetually frustrates the traditional epistemic quest for absolute certainty and colors the supposedly transparent spiritual substance with sociolinguistic pigment. Rather than acknowledge and embrace this ambiguity, Castañeda prefers to project the unambiguous subject of the epistemic quest for apodicticity onto the phenomenon of ordinary language and to force it into the exclusively first-person stance. By doing that however he loses his footing in the ordinary grammar of the pronoun "I" and reverts to the intuitionist paradigm of transcendental philosophy.

Unsurprisingly, Castañeda contrasts and privileges the first-person reference (to an internal self) over the third-person reference to an external public facade that is available in equal measure to the self and the others. Consider this passage:

> What one thinks, *de dicto,* i.e., the internal content that one thinks, when one thinks in the first-person way, is entirely different from

what others think in the third person way. Yet a necessary and sufficient condition of being a person, or being fully a person, is to be able to think of oneself as *oneself*, in the first-person way. Others must perforce think of one in the third person way. This contrast is enormous and enormously important (232).

What is strikingly missing from this opposition between first- and third-person reference is the second-person type of referentiality. Castañeda construes relations to others exclusively in the third-person mode, in terms of the external reflexivity noted above, whereas relations to oneself would follow the mode of internal reflexivity of the first-person stance. However, a philosopher keenly interested in ordinary language should note also the interconnectedness between the first and the second person. He should be aware of the I-you reversibility, which makes it de jure impossible to thematize the pronoun "I" in isolation from the pronoun "you." As discussed earlier, the speaker masters the pronoun "I" fully if she understands its reversibility into "you" within interpersonal address. The failure to master I-you reversibility results in the concomitant failure to employ the pronoun "I" for the purpose of self-reference. This is a big loss for Castañeda and other philosophers of subjectivity, for it means that the thinker who purportedly references nothing other than her internal/private self by means of the first-person pronoun would be unable to master the pronoun "I" and thus to enact self-reference in language. Contra Castañeda, the pronoun "I" does not simply point inward, toward some ephemeral and evanescent cloud of self-awareness, but it points in two directions at once: toward the narrating self *and* toward the potential or present addressee. The pronoun "I" is necessarily bidirectional; like the Janus head, it coexhibits inseparable facets of *self-awareness* and *addressability*. It does not internalize into an index of subjectivity unless it is forced to fit a preexistent philosophical agenda. The discussions of subjectivity that disregard this inherent two-facetedness of the "I" tacitly assume an individualist bias, even though they may draw on phenomenological evidence of some ineffable inner experience in the process. If such experience is to be had, it cannot be attributed to a socialized self and prefixed with the ordinary pronoun "I." The problem of self-awareness is ill-posed as long as the self is forced into an exile from the region of first-to-second person interdependency. Such an exile from dialogue does not seem to reinforce self-reference but rather to abolish it.

Despite its individualist bias and intuitionist commitment, there are positive lessons to be learned from Castañeda's discussion of the first-person pronoun. Recall the philosopher's argument that the pronoun "I" cannot on its own initiate the task of first-person reference. I believe that this basic point—that linguistic reference is founded on prelinguistic conditions—merits careful attention. Otherwise we risk theorizing the self exclusively in terms of participation in discourse, as Benveniste in fact does. For him, the self is a linguistic entity, whose existence is coextensive with each instance of discourse and thus, of a momentary nature (1966, 226). This view is guilty of the charge of linguistic optimism, which makes language appear as a superpower that creates entities ex nihilo in the creationist style recounted in the Book of Genesis. I believe that Castañeda's project may be read as a warning sign against attributing an ex nihilo creationism to language and abstracting the latter from the nonverbalized modes of expression. However, it is doubtful that we need to invoke a transcendental self in order to account for first-person reference broadly construed. If it is true that first-person reference is inextricably interconnected with second-person reference, then an inner private mental self would not do the job; that is, it would not be a sufficient condition of possibility of mastering the pronoun "I." In fact, it would hinder rather than help in the pronoun-acquisition process by forcing the child to perform a conceptual leap from an asocial self to a socialized speaker.

Furthermore, the transcendental thinking self is not necessary to account for the linguistic mastery of the pronoun "I." Recall that on Castañeda's reading, the internal-self reference (required for the "I" pronoun mastery) is a cognitively sophisticated mental operation. Children would thus be required to cogitate privately à la Descartes in order to establish a foundation for a linguistic first-person reference. However, it is doubtful that we need to postulate a philosopher in the crib to account for how personal pronouns are acquired. To be sure, a sense of self is needed for the child to acquire, produce, and comprehend personal pronouns. But up-to-date empirical research shows that this sense may be present, in however primitive a form, at birth, as well as be of bodily and perceptual rather than intellectual kind. After all, nonphilosophers and their children typically master personal reference just fine. Rather than posit a cogitating self as a precondition of personal reference, we need therefore to trace the gradual emergence of linguistic competence from out of lower-level skills anchored in the communicative potential of the body. This approach dispenses with the need to establish transcendental conditions of possibility in favor of a developmental story of gradual emergence of language use from the host of skills involved in perceptual and spatial orientation to the world via the mastery of polycentric perspective. This approach succeeds where the transcendental approach necessarily fails. It demonstrates that the child is born into a nexus of interpersonal relations that approximate conversational exchanges between competent language users, and so it accounts for the readiness to acquire markers of personhood relative to one's position vis-à-vis the other. It points to the child's embeddedness in the shared social and natural world which puts pressure on philosophical attachments to egocentrism. It proves what proficient language users know through unthematized daily praxis: that personal reference is inescapably interpersonal, enabled and sustained by the living practice of dialogue.

CHAPTER 3

DEVELOPMENTAL PERSPECTIVES

In chapter 2, I discussed I-you connectedness from sociolinguistic and phenomenological perspectives. I focused especially on (inter)personal deixis, that is, the ways in which meaning is contextualized by the spatial and temporal context of utterance, which coinvolves the reversible speaker and addressee roles. Deixis in general and personal pronouns in particular are therefore inescapably rooted in an existential context. In this chapter, I propose to continue examining interpersonal pronouns in context, but to focus the discussion on developmental aspects and interrogate the emergence of linguistic symbols for speaker and addressee from presymbolic patterns of interpersonal interaction. This developmental story will enable me to expand the validity of primary I-you connectedness beyond the domain of verbalized interaction to the earliest stages of human life. At the same time, the developmental story will enable me to meet the challenge raised by Castañeda and other philosophers of subjectivity by showing that self-reference does indeed precede the mastery of the pronoun "I," but, in contrast to the philosophy enclosed in the epistemically construed first-person perspective, that self-reference is a *relational* feature, which coinvolves first- and second-personal perspectives and roles from the start.

Consider how cognitively complex personal pronoun acquisition is. Importantly, the child must understand that even though she uses "I" (and cognate possessive forms "my," "mine," "me") for self-reference, others address her with "you" (as well as "your" and "yours"). The child must, in other words, understand how the "I" and "you" pronouns (and their cognates) interrelate in the conversational context in order to be credited with full acquisition of speech roles. In the words of Benveniste, the child must acquire I-you reversibility in order to master either of the first- and second-person pronouns fully. Merleau-Ponty brings this important point into relief in the following passage ("Child Relations with Others" [2000, p. 150]):

The 'I' arises when the child understands that every 'you' that is addressed to him is for him an 'I'; that is, that there must be a consciousness of the reciprocity of points of view in order that the word 'I' may be used. . . . The pronoun 'I' has its full meaning only when the child uses it not as an individual sign to designate his own person—a sign that would be assigned once for all to himself and to nobody else—but when he understands that each person is an 'I' for himself and a 'you' for others. It is when he understands that even though others call him 'you' he can nonetheless say 'I,' that the pronoun is acquired in all its significance. In order for it to have been a real acquisition, he must have grasped the relations between the different pronouns and the passage from one of their designata to the others. In other cases the sound 'I' is used mechanically. . . but it is not used in its fullest linguistic and grammatical meaning.

As discussed in this chapter, the road to the mastery of personal pronouns in their fullest linguistic and grammatical meaning may be a long and winding one. The fact that the pronoun designating self and other issues from the child's mouth need not alone testify to what I would like to call a *conversational competence* in the domain of personal pronoun use, that is, the ability to use personal pronouns as markers for speaker and addressee roles and points of view. Needless to say, the challenge faced by the child is not limited to the linguistic coding of persons but extends to phonological and syntactical abilities necessary for the mastery of language in general. At the same time, the acquisition of personal pronouns in their "fullest linguistic and grammatical meaning" depends upon a series of cognitive prerequisites, such as the consciousness of the difference and the reciprocal interrelation between one's own and the interlocutor's points of view. As argued below, presymbolic practices of infancy and childhood such as face-to-face interactions (for instance, imitation of facial gestures) and joint attending to the perceptual environment (for instance, looking and pointing at a common object of interest) provide a fertile ground for the mastery of spatial and personal points of view, which are subsequently taken up in the linguistic marking of speaker and hearer perspectives. However, the perspectival configuration of spatial environment alone does not suffice. Consider that if the child is to grasp personal pronouns as shifters that follow the deployment of speaker/hearer roles by the interlocutors at a given conversational turn, she must also grasp the alternating turn-taking pattern in conversation in order to master the "I" and "you" pronouns fully. "I" and "you" reversibility is a temporal phenomenon that unfolds in the conversational flow wherein interlocutors assume the speaker roles in a sequential rather than simultaneous fashion. As argued below, presymbolic practices of infancy typically grouped under the heading of protoconversation, which exhibit the turn-taking character of dialogue even though the medium of communication is limited to nonverbal vocalizations and gaze, serve as a field wherein the infant can practice proto-conversational roles and as a precondition for the subsequent mastery of "I"–"you" pronouns in a conversational context. On this account, the child acquires linguistic markers of conversational roles with relative ease since she is already embedded in an interpersonal conversational context. To sum up, there are personal, spatial, and temporal preconditions of full "I"–"you" mastery in conversation. In this chapter, I examine empirical evidence for the existence of these personal, spatial, and temporal skills in infancy and childhood and their role in personal-pronoun acquisition.

A word of caution is due before turning to the empirical material. Due to its developmental focus, the discipline I will rely on most extensively in this chapter is the psychology of infancy and childhood. However, there are both merits and pitfalls in extending one's philosophical arms to embrace the contributions from psychology, especially as far as the question of sociality is concerned. As James Wertsch (1991, 3) soberly observes, psychology in general and child-development studies in particular are dominated by an individualistic orientation. In the words of Barbara Rogoff (1990), "an emphasis on the individual has characterized decades of research carried out by American investigators studying children's intellectual milestones, IQ, memory strategies, and grammatical skills. It has also been characteristic of the incorporation of Piaget's theory into American research in the modern era" (quoted in Wertsch, 4). That is why I agree with Wertsch that integrating developmental psychology into the study of social relations does not mean simply applying existing theoretical constructs, but also devising new models and articulating the guiding assumptions about what it means to be human, at the risk of having to venture beyond the comfort zone of dominant post-Cartesian interpretations. Only then can we engage the cognate disciplines of philosophy and psychology in a truly interdisciplinary relation of mutual influence rather than unilateral dependency of the theoretical and expressly reflective discipline on the contributions provided by its empirical sister. Philosophy should not simply adopt the relevant research results, especially if the latter are obtained within a questionable theoretical framework that prejudges both the experimental design and the interpretation of the data by the psychologist. It should help to disclose the implicit assumptions the empirical scientist brings to her lab and possibly point to alternative theoretical models with which to set up experimental studies and to use as a heuristic lens through which to view the findings obtained in those studies. It is my aim to provide an example of how to accomplish such interdisciplinary interpenetration in this chapter.

PIAGET'S LEGACY

First, however, it is necessary to set up the stage for the discussion. As previously noted, the major influence on contemporary research on child development is by the giant of French psychology, Jean Piaget. Piaget deserves enormous credit for establishing child psychology as an autonomous scientific discipline, and his studies impress with their careful balance of intellectual rigor and wealth of empirical material. Importantly, his conceptual framework continues to bear significant influence on the empirical research in contemporary child psychology. In the late 1970s, Ragnar Rommetveit (1978, 113) noted that "recent literature [on cognitive development] is replete with replications and modifications of earlier studies [by Piaget and the Genevan School], yet—despite numerous declarations of discontent—nearly devoid of significant reorientations and genuine innovations."

In the recent decades, Piaget's scientific legacy has been subject to a wave of critical tests by some of the leading researchers in the United States. They have used state-of-the-art technology and innovative experimental design to test and shake up some of the foundation stones of the Piagetian edifice and demonstrated that the master may have erred in at least some of his statements on children's early competence. Notably, it has been shown that infants can imitate facial expressions of others, despite Piaget's claims to the contrary (Meltzoff, Meltzoff, and Moore 1977; 1989). It has also been shown that infants have a sense of object permanence, contra the French psychologist's own views (Spelke, 1991). By and large, the recent tendency in experimental psychology has been to return the credit to young children for cognitive abilities that Piaget openly denied them, a concerted scientific trend that recently received a mock response in the satirical magazine the *Onion*, which published a feature detailing an ersatz experimental study to the effect that babies are really dumb.[1]

Piaget's complex legacy in contemporary studies on child development is clearly visible in the field of language acquisition. Even though some researchers have complained that "attempts at transcending tradition-bound premises for inquiries into language and thought are hampered by an undue transfer of respect from Piaget's impressive work on thinking to his far more sporadic comments upon the nature and role of language" (Rommetveit 1978, 113), Piaget's central thesis of the child's initial egocentrism, derived from his studies of language, continues to inform the field of language-acquisition studies, including the mastery of personal pronouns. This centrality persists despite the illogicalities the egocentric thesis gives rise to in the domain of language acquisition, such as the notion of potential full mastery of personal pronouns in childhood, but only insofar as they refer to the child's own self and not to others (see further discussion below). Piaget belongs to the intellectual tradition of modernity discussed previously in reference to Descartes and Husserl insofar as he advocates egocentrism as the original state of the human mind. Piaget found evidence for egocentrism especially in the young child's cognitive abilities—the child is declared unable to experience the world from a different point of view from her own or fails to appreciate a diversity of perspectives (cognitive as well as social and moral). Consider that if true, the egocentric predicament would have disastrous consequences for the child's ability to acquire deictic terms like "I"–"you" pronouns. Recall that "I" and "you" are shifters that indicate speech roles rather than persons, and so their referents shift constantly between the speaker and the addressee in a conversational context. Recall furthermore that "I"–"you" are reversible in that the speaker who auto-refers by means of the first-person pronoun is addressed with the second-person pronoun. The grasp of the shifting and reversible nature of "I"–"you" by the child supposes what she apparently lacks—a polycentric understanding of role and perspective as component of meaning. This tension between, on the one hand, the child's initial egocentric mindscape pervasive till the sixth to seventh birthday, and, on the other hand, the child's indisputable ability to master "I"–"you" pronouns in a typically effortless and error-free fashion around the second and third birthday, leaves two basic options ahead of us. We may, as Piaget does, posit a revolutionary process of decentering, which would help the child break out of an initial egocentrism. The disadvantage of this line of thought is that it makes the appearance of polyperspective on the developmental curve appear as an ex nihilo event that cannot be traced back to any cognitive precursors in the child's life. This line of thought violates what Cromer (1974) called the "cognition hypothesis," which stipulates, among other things, that "we are able to understand and productively to use particular linguistic structures only when our cognitive abilities enable us to do so" (246). Devoid of the cognitive ability to include other perspectives in our experience, we would however be unable "to understand and productively to use particular linguistic structures" such as the reversible and shifting structures of personal pronouns (ibid.). Another option open to us, which has the merit of sparing us such an explanatory cul-de-sac, is to follow the recent revisionary tide in developmental psychology and subject Piaget's statements on the child's cognitive abilities to a critical test. It means, first, reevaluating the merit of Piaget's own statements in favor of initial egocentrism. Second, it involves consulting recent empirical studies on interpersonal relations in infancy and early childhood that provide evidence for the existence of temporally coordinated turn-taking and role-switching exchanges between the infant and caregiver via the voice and the gaze, strongly suggesting that the infant is well primed for the acquisition of dialogic roles in symbolic interactions. Combined, these strategies help make a case for an originally decentered condition and attunement to other perspectives from birth on, which is continuous with the later stages of the acquisition of perspective-dependent deictic terms, such as personal pronouns.

Piaget first identified the child's egocentrism in his studies on language even though he and other researchers made attempts to extend it to other aspects of the child's cognition—perception, moral judgment, and reasoning—in view of potentially teasing out a single egocentrism factor operative in these domains. Piaget regarded egocentrism as an unquestionable original state of intellectual naïveté typifying the human mindscape. He thought it was "a mode of spontaneous apperception, which is common to every individual and as such needs no preliminary explanation" (1959, 275). This is a striking statement for an empirical psychologist to make, especially as, on Piaget's own admission, the evidence mounted to support egocentrism is fragile (286). Ultimately, Piaget seemed to regard egocentrism as an irreducible component of the human intellectual development, which can be cashed out in logical and mathematical categories (285). However, he also construed egocentrism as a concrete perceptual tendency of the child's mind. To exemplify it, he devised concrete experimental situations wherein the children of up to about six or seven years systematically fail to take someone else's spatial perspective into account. The classic example is the Three Mountains demonstration (Piaget and Inhelder, 1956), in which children are shown a three-dimensional model of a landscape with three mountains, a tree, and a house. They are asked, first, to choose a picture that represents what they saw, and then a picture representing what a doll standing at another location would see. Children consistently selected the picture representing their own view, thus lending support to the thesis of their inability to appreciate and adopt another spatial perspective.

However, more recent experimental research by Hobson (1980) challenges Piaget's conclusions and shows that even very young children (between two-and-a-half and seven years) have the potential to coordinate points of view in spatial tasks, such as playing a hide-and-seek game around a matchbox with pipe-cleaner figures. According to Hobson, under appropriate conditions, the young child can comprehend a coherent system of relations of viewpoints independent of himself. In Piaget's Three Mountains task, the child has a more or less side-on view of the three-dimensional display, which differs only in detail from that of the doll he is required to judge. That is why, Hobson notes, the child is liable to confuse his own view with his image of the view of the other, and may fail to disambiguate between the two views. Now, in Hobson's hide-and-seek task, the child has an overview perspective on all pipe-cleaner figures, which is in clear contrast to each pipe-cleaner man, and so the confusion between the details of his own and the other views is less likely than in the Three Mountains task (329). In conclusion, the child's appreciation of multiple perspectives is not an "absolute" cognitive skill but rather it is contextualized by the spatial setup of the specific perceptual situation the child is engaged in and enhanced by the possibility to monitor the other perceiver's perspective from his own vantage point, a possibility that is missing in Piaget's task of mental inference of the other's view.

Let me say more about Piaget's conception of egocentrism. Piaget lamented its misunderstanding by his peers and stressed that the choice of the term does not imply that the child is consciously and reflectively pondering her own self. To be sure, the child is thought to be de facto confined to her own perspective in transactions with people and things. However, the child is unaware that her experiential viewpoint is just one among many. If the stance is narcissistic, as psychoanalysis has it, it is narcissism without a Narcissus, that is, without an identifiable individuated self. For instance, citing an example of Brunschvicg, Piaget notes that a boy of six to seven who counts the number of people in a room will not include himself in the head count. The same child declares that he has a brother but that his brother has no brother (1959, 280). This anecdotal evidence is used to support the thesis that the child is both locked into his own experiential viewpoint (unable to adopt the perspective of his brother) *and* oblivious of his own presence in the experiential field.

One of the implications of egocentrism is, following Piaget, that the child is a victim of excessive realism that fails to disentangle between a subjective take on the world and the objective world itself. The child is initially a subject-object adualist, radically turned toward the world, and has no sense of the separation between inside and outside, thought and thing. The developmental goal for the child will be to disambiguate between psychical and internal and material and external events. As Eva Simms (1999) notes, there is a clear teleological ideal of the child in Piaget's thinking as a radical dualist who situates thinking in the head.[2] The child's grasp of the objective world is predicated, in Piaget's view, on grasping physical categories of the sciences, such as causality as grasped by an impersonal rational mind (1959, 275). There is therefore also implicit scientism in Piaget's view of human development. The child's immediate lived experience is deemed profoundly anthropocentric; the child tends to endow inanimate objects with intentionality and purposefulness, thinking, for instance, that the balloons go up because "they love the air" (1959, 279). In other words, the child attributes her own mental propensities—intention, desire—to inert things, because she lives in a symbiotic fusion with them. In order to break away from egocentrism, the child will then need to accomplish two things: overcome the early subject-object adualism and decenter her absolutist perspective on the world by acknowledging, and reciprocally relating to, perspectives other than her own.

I now turn specifically to Piaget's studies of language as privileged site of uncovering the child's egocentrism. Piaget studied children attending the *Maison des Petits de l'Institut Rousseau* in Geneva in the context of their spontaneous play. He noted down everything said by the children in its context. The children's age ranged from four to seven. The material accumulated during the visits suggested to Piaget a high "coefficient of egocentrism" in children's language. In other words, the majority of children's utterances was apparently not directed at a particular interlocutor and gave the impression of the child talking to herself. Typically, the child was commenting on and reinforcing the progress of the activity she was currently involved in (drawing, playing, and so on), with the words serving as a "stimulus to action" rather than a means of communicating with others. Piaget notably identified patterns of repetition (close to identical reiteration of another person's utterance), monologue (utterance in which the child is the only speaker), and collective monologue (a choir of simultaneous utterances wherein no one seems to be listening to what the others are saying) as key components of the child's noncommunicative speech. Combined, they make up more than half of the child's utterances and give credence to the claim of a pervasive egocentrism in the child's speech. Examples of the child's *socialized* speech serving a communicative function include sharing information with another, criticism, and derision; commands, requests, and threats; and questions and answers.

What characterizes the child's egocentric utterances is primarily that they treat of the child herself (for example, the activity she is currently engaged in), with no apparent attempt to influence or even catch the attention of the persons within hearing range. Importantly, these utterances are made typically in the presence of others (other children and the teacher, and at least Piaget's own). However, insofar as the child does not appear to discriminate between the hearers—anyone can serve as audience—she is said not to attempt to place herself at the point of view of her hearer. The child does not seem to care whether she has been understood—or even heard—by the interlocutor. The dominant perspective in the child's utterances appears therefore to be the child's own.

Consider an example of apparently asocial speech—repetition—in more detail. Jac says to Ez: "Look, Ez, your pants are showing." Pie, who is in another part of the room immediately responds. "Look, my pants are showing, and my shirt, too" (13). Piaget comments that there is not a grain of truth in Pie's repetitive statement, nor is he using the words for the sake of adapting herself to the conversation—but only for the sake of play. However, despite their lack of truth-value, Pie's utterances may also, contra Piaget, be interpreted as conversational. Pie does not repeat what he hears verbatim, but responds *as if* he joined in the conversation. Importantly, he shows proficiency in his use of "I" and "you" pronouns, and as such may be credited with a grasp of the speaker/addressee perspective in the speech context rather than with an aperspectival disposition. Piaget views repetition (or a close-to-repetition, as in the example above) as consistently demonstrating the child's lack of differentiation from her consociates. Imitation (or near-imitation) counts as the case of the child's confusion between *I* and non-*I*, an initial adualism between the activity performed by self and perceived upon the other (1959, 12). Henceforth, even though it may *appear* that the child is engaged in a pervasively social activity when she mimics others, since she clearly mirrors their gestures and movements, upon inspection, it turns out that the child does not differentiate between her productions and those of other people, and so she is caught in a symbiotic fusion that precedes interpersonal relations properly so called. This apparently fusional quality of the child's experience leads Piaget to state that there is "no real social life between children of less than 7 or 8 years" (1959, 41).

Note also that Piaget makes use of the thesis of adualism to discredit the argument that the child must have been socialized if she has picked up the given natural language spoken in her social milieu. After all, is linguistic competence not sufficient proof of the child's successful socialization with other speakers of her native tongue? Piaget admits that the child's utterances are made of words "acquired in relation to other people" (1959, 17). However, he hastens to add that the language-learning child is the victim of confusion between her own point of view and that of other people, which by definition precludes any talk of social relations during the language acquisition process. No amount of the child's factual engagement with others in play and speech can therefore rise to the level of *socialized* behavior as long as the thesis of original undifferentiation is upheld. Note however that Piaget's concept of understanding other points of view may make too high cognitive demands on the child. Consider the following example of an exchange between two children, which Piaget classifies as a mere "clash of assertions" devoid of sensitivity to the other's point of view (1959, 25):

> Lev looks to see what Hei is doing: "Two moons—No, two suns— Suns aren't like that, with a mouth. They're like this, suns up there— They're round—Yes they quite round, but they haven't got eyes and a mouth.—Yes they have, they can see—No they can't. It's only God who can see."

Even though this exchange belongs to the category of "adapted information," that is, socialized speech, Piaget comments that the two interlocutors fail to appreciate the other's point of view, or the reasons behind their claims, and give no explicit reasons for defending their own statements. Such explicit justification of one's view however would need to mobilize the cognitively advanced skills of rational demonstration that the child may not have mastered yet. That does not mean that the child is indifferent to the other's perspective in a cognitively lower, perceptual, and spatial manner. Piaget proposes a mentalistic construal of the difference in perspective in his hypothesis of egocentrism, which precludes the possibility of an embodied nonpropositional polycentric sense of perspective in the child.

Piaget identified two elements that belong to adult conversations and are missing in the case of verbal exchanges in children: (1) the distinction between interlocutors' perspectives (as opposed to the adualism of perspectives) and (2) an ability of both partners to exert a measure of influence upon the other (as opposed to the indifference about the other in egocentric speech) (1959, 265). Drawing on up-to-date research, I propose to show that young children's interactions with others may, contra Piaget, be credited with both factors, even in preverbal exchanges. This research defies the thesis of pervasive egocentrism in childhood; it also helps provide a more continuous story of person-deixis acquisition, which respects the cognition hypothesis mentioned above.

RECENT RESEARCH ON THE SOCIALITY OF CHILDREN

Experimental research post–Piaget has dealt a major blow to the well-established thesis of the child's initial adualism. Neonate imitation studies provide overwhelming evidence that a child is born with an ability to differentiate between the activity taking shape within her body proper and that perceived in others. Contra Piaget, imitation may not be a simple phenomenon of self–other fusion but rather of the self relating to the other in a way that affords both similarity and difference. Consider exactly why that is the case. Infants have been demonstrated to successfully imitate a range of facial and manual gestures performed by the adult, such as tongue and lip protrusion, lip opening, and finger movement.[3] These abilities are especially striking since the infants involved in the experiments were literal neonates; some of them have been tested no later than ten minutes after birth. Importantly, imitating infants do not directly produce fully fledged copies of the gesture that they see the adult perform. Imitation does not proceed in a reflexlike fashion (for example, neonate imitation can be postponed, while reflexes do not jump temporal gaps).[4] Instead, they first activate and experiment with the appropriate body part, such as the mouth or the tongue, gradually arriving at the closest possible match of the target gesture. The infants' ability to monitor and correct gestures through practice in order to attain the closest possible match of the gesture performed by the adult indicates that she relies on proprioceptive feedback from her own body while imitating others and has a sense of the body proper as distinct from the perceived body of the other from the start. Infantile imitation therefore provides evidence for the presence of an innate body schema and of a minimal sense of self gained through proprioception. One can therefore speak of rudiments of interpersonal relations being established in infancy, wherein the infant senses both a similarity and difference between her own and the other's bodily performance, rather than fusion. Furthermore, as Meltzoff and Gopnik (1993, 353) argue, imitation involves primitive motor-level *perspective-taking*, since one's own acts are experienced from a different viewpoint from those of the other. The sense of perspective appears on this approach as a perceptual ability rooted in the bodily organism of the neonate rather than a mentalizing act postulated by Piaget.

Other evidence for the infant's ability to differentiate between self and other comes from recent research supported by audio technology on "contagious crying" in nurseries. It has traditionally been reported that distress crying tends to spread among neonates; the prevailing interpretation of this phenomenon has been along the lines of transitivism, that is, the inability to set boundaries between the infant's own crying and the crying of others. Martin and Clark (1982) conducted an experiment to test this traditional interpretation. Calm and crying babies heard a tape recording of themselves or another baby crying. Babies who were initially calm cried more if they heard a tape recording of another baby cry than if they heard themselves cry, while babies who were crying initially cried less if they heard themselves rather than another baby cry. These findings provide evidence for discrimination between one's own and another's vocalization in the first hours of human life (average age of babies in this experiment was of less than thirty hours), and so challenge the previously held interpretation of distress crying as indicative of fusion between self and other.

The growing evidence for a minimal distinction between self and other undermines Piaget's claim that no socialized relations occur between infants. There is a growing consensus in the psychological community that humans socialize much earlier than was previously thought, even though disagreements remain as to when the social clock begins to tick. The proponents of the so-called theory of mind approach, which dominates the debates on social cognition, argue that children can be credited with knowledge of other minds only once they have passed the so-called false-belief test. The task typically involves a subject whose knowledge of a given state of affairs, for example, the contents of a Smarties box, surpasses that of a third party who is temporarily absent from the experimental situation and whose beliefs regarding the given state of affairs the subject is asked to predict.[5] Children under age four systematically fail to predict false beliefs. Having discovered upon inspection that the Smarties box contains a bunch of pencils, they predict that the absent child will believe likewise rather than attributing the appropriate albeit false belief to them (that the box contains Smarties)—the belief that they themselves held in the initial stages of the experiment. Insofar as their prediction fails to allow for beliefs other than their own present beliefs, the false-belief task has been regarded as proof that the young child does not yet possess a theory of mind. Note that the theory of mind construal of social cognition resonates with Piaget's mentalistic talk about understanding points of view: in both cases, the underlying process is rational thinking rather than embodied perceptual activity. Furthermore, there is not direct interaction in the first- to second-person mode between the child making predictions and the child whose beliefs are predicted; the relation is of a third-person type: theorizing *about* an absent nonparticipatory third party. Yet it is highly questionable that the de facto stance of detachment from the other captures the dynamics of social interaction.

Leading researchers in the field of language-acquisition studies like Michael Tomasello (for example, 2003) tend to view the nine-month birthday as a hallmark in the socialization process. It is around that time that children begin to systematically engage in the so-called acts of joint attention with others, notably following the gaze of another person and pointing at an object of interest in view of eliciting the other's attention. The onset of joint attention is viewed as indicative of the child's nascent understanding that other people have mental states wherein they intentionally relate to a perceivable element of the shared world, such as a colorful toy—the states that the child may share with them. It is indisputable that the so-called revolution of nine months is a major developmental breakthrough in the child's transactions with others and with the world and may serve as a condition sine qua non of uttering first words. Importantly, however, the joint attention mechanism recruits interpersonal abilities operative well before the nine-month turn, notably shared eye contact between the infant and the adult. Consider that in order to attend *jointly* an object located in their perceptual field, that is, to be not only attending to the object concurrently but to attend to the object with the accompanying awareness that the other is sharing her attentional state, the infant and the adult need to regularly "check" that each one is paying heed to the other's awareness (rather than simply to the object of interest). In other words, the two spectators must engage in an act of mutual attention if their looking is to be a *joint* perceptual act, rather than two independent, even though simultaneous, acts of looking at object

X.[6] This jointness is made possible by an attention check—establishing eye contact with the other during the shared looking event. Eye contact serves as a communicative base for the two perceivers, which connects the "rays" issuing from their eyes. To continue using geometrical metaphors, joint attention mechanism is not composed of two parallel lines but rather a triangle with the base established by mutual eye contact and the two other lines by the rays of regard terminating at the common object of interest. Now, importantly, eye contact predates joint attention properly so-called; it occurs as early as one month of age (Wolff 1963), and it has been documented as a basic trait of a normally developing mother-infant relation.[7] Joint attention mechanisms are therefore continuous with more primary social competence in the child; the important cognitive milestone reached around the age of nine months depends on and harnesses earlier socioperceptual abilities exercised in dyadic face-to-face relations; it does not therefore constitute a revolution in the absolute sense.

Note also that in the acts of joint attention the child typically engages the coperceiver differently from the object of perception. As Bates (1990, 173) notes, pointing is restricted almost exclusively to third-person reference at this stage, and the child does not refer explicitly either to herself or to the receiver of the message as an "object of contemplation." The child engages the adult insofar as she demands a response or acknowledgement from the adult (children will repeat or vary their performance until they obtain this response), but she engages the adult in a second-person manner, reserving pointing to what the message is about. The child appears therefore sensitive to the distinction between, in the terms taken from Martin Buber (see chapter 4) an *I–you* and an *I–it* type of relation. This sensitivity makes the child well equipped to master the grammatical distinction advocated by Benveniste between second-person relation to a coparticipant in perception and discourse coded in the interpersonal "I"–"you" pronouns *and* the third-person relation to a nonparticipatory third party coded in "he"/"she"/"it." The act of joint attention is a combination of these two nonidentical attentional acts. Importantly, it cannot therefore be theorized in terms of an observational or spectatorial stance toward the other person in view of inferring their mental states, which is favored by the defendants of the theory of mind.[8] It is therefore crucial, in my view, since they do not receive the requisite attention within the theory of mind debates, to emphasize the existence of first-to-second person relatedness within the empirical studies of infant and child sociality. Needless to say, some of the empirical research discussed in this chapter can be (and has been) characterized in terms of the theory of mind. However, that researchers (especially philosophically unschooled researchers) choose to interpret their findings in a particular way does not imply that the empirical data unambiguously favors such an interpretation.

PROTO-CONVERSATIONS IN INFANCY

Colwyn Trevarthen (1979, 1993) is one of the key defendants of the view that the infant is literally born into intersubjectivity. Basing his analysis on microanalysis of filmed interactions between infants and their mothers, he showed that the movements of eyes, hands, and mouth are rhythmically timed in a turn-taking form with the adult. These rhythmically timed nonverbal exchanges between infant and caregiver involving vocalizations, touch, and gaze, follow a give-and-take, address-and-reply pattern, with both partners attending to one another and mutually coordinating their acts. Even though the mother initiates and supports the exchange, the infant is actively involved in this conversationlike process of what Trevarthen calls *primary intersubjectivity*. This view is at furthest remove from the egocentric stance advocated by Piaget and his followers in that it argues for a degree of decentralization and attunement to other perspectives in the infant's interactions with others from birth on. Importantly, it demonstrates that the earliest interpersonal exchanges bear a number of structural similarities to adult conversations.

According to recent research, face-to-face interactions in infancy are timed following dialogic rhythms, which resemble the rhythmic patterns of verbalized conversations in adulthood. For example, infants and their mothers alternate between vocalization and silence, or looking and looking away, in face-to-face interactions in a recurrent and nonrandom manner (albeit not in a strictly regular or periodic—as in heartbeat or marching—beat). Furthermore, the participants in a dyadic exchange mutually influence each other's on-and-off cycle of activity and receptivity, either in a positive (matching) or negative (compensation) way. A dialogic or conversational competence of a nonsymbolic type, which precedes language-based dialogue, is therefore at work from the earliest moments of human life. Furthermore, some elements of the earliest nonsymbolic dialogic rhythms, like gaze patterns, remain operative within adult dialogue. Infants are therefore partially skilled in areas of communication that belong to adult-dialogic repertoire.

Consider the list of features uncovered in the dialogic exchanges of infancy.

The earliest interactions exhibit a degree of *mutual influence* between the infant and the adult. They are *context sensitive*. They follow a *turn-taking pattern*, wherein both participants occupy the *interchangeable roles* of agent and the recipient of action in a nonrandomly timed sequence. As such, they bear resemblance to the verbalized exchanges between two interlocutors who alternate between the active/speaking and the receptive/listening roles. They exhibit *a face-to-face orientation*, which is typically preserved within dialogue in adulthood. Combined, these factors provide strong evidence that verbalized interaction between speaker and addressee emerges out of the earliest prelinguistic self-other relations in infancy. This line of thought is in direct agreement with Lyons, who observes that deixis can be explained on the assumption that languages have "developed for communication in face-to-face interaction" (Lyons 1977, 637). The developmental perspective helps explicate in some detail how and why the earliest face-to-face interactions may set the stage for the mastery of person deixis.

Let me add that the emergence of dialogue and deixis from face-to-face interactions should be understood in two interrelated senses: (1) infancy may provide cognitive prerequisites of deixis and dialogue, which are necessary but not sufficient conditions of mastering linguistically coded dialogic roles; (2) key components of dialogic relations in infancy (context-dependence, face-to-face orientation, turn-taking character of interactions, interchangeable active and receptive roles, nonidentical perspectives) are preserved within verbalized adult interpersonal interactions. Both senses underscore a marked continuity between infancy and adulthood. Whereas the former provides a set of conditions that may have to be met for the child to acquire spoken language, the latter focuses on the gestural and temporal elements of interpersonal interactions that are found along the developmental curve and continue to typify face-to-face interactions in ontogenetically more advanced stages despite the fact that language has come on board. Following Gallagher's lead (2001), I believe that the second view has a greater explanatory force and is corroborated by both empirical evidence and phenomenological analysis of face-to-face interactions in infancy and adulthood. It suggests that the key features of Trevarthen's primary intersubjectivity are preserved in later life and so are primary throughout direct interpersonal interactions.

The notion of dialogic relations in infancy has become relatively well established in psychology. Spitz (1963) introduced the notion of *mother-infant dialogue* in the context of psychoanalytic theory. He argued that reciprocal exchanges between mother and infant were crucial to developing the feeling of being responded to and a sense of identity. Together with the spread of empirical developmental research in the 1970s, the study of infant's dialogic relations significantly increased. Numerous researchers studied mother-infant interaction in diverse-sense modalities, including gaze, vocalization, gesture, and characterized it as a conversation, protoconversation, or dialogue (for example, Bateson 1975; Beebe, Stern, and Jaffe 1979; Papousek and Papousek 1979; Stern 1974; Stern et al. 1977). Some researchers use dialogue as an all-inclusive metaphor for infant-mother temporally patterned transactions, including, for example, sucking (Kaye and Wells 1980).

In the face of such wealth of empirical data, it may be worthwhile to pause and ponder what the conceptual requirements for terming an interpersonal-transaction dialogic or conversational are. One critical requirement is the alternating turn structure between sound and silence. Consider that conversing adults can only speak one at a time for the dialogue to unfold smoothly and for the interlocutors to follow what the other is saying. We cannot emit speech and process speech emitted by our interlocutor simultaneously. To be sure, we hear ourselves as we speak. However, speaking and hearing is, so to speak, a single-track phenomenon in which only one vocal stream can flow within a given unit of time. That is why verbalized dialogue has a sequential rather than a simultaneous structure: it involves ongoing alternations between conversational turns held by the speakers in view of shared understanding. An interpersonal exchange involving infants will count as dialogic or conversational if it involves such an alternating turn-taking pattern between sound and silence. Infants who engage in such a turn-taking exchange can be said to partake in the fundamental temporal structure of dialogue, even though the vocalizations they emit and hear are of a presymbolic type. Their interactions with others can therefore count as instances of protoconversation—alternating vocal exchanges that may serve to create social bonds.

THE DIALOGIC MODEL OF JAFFE AND FELDSTEIN

Conversational abilities in infancy demonstrate that *the rhythms of dialogue* cut across preverbal and verbal stages in social development and characterize the temporal ordering of face-to-face interactions both in infancy and adulthood. Unsurprisingly then, the model of temporal coordination in adult dialogue has been successfully used in the study of infant communication (see examples below). This dialogic model was devised by Jaffe and Feldstein

(1970). The Jaffe–Feldstein model claims to provide an exhaustive classification of everything that can possibly happen in a two-person vocal exchange. Firstly, the temporal flow of a dialogue between two adult speakers can be parsed into five parameters, called *vocal states:* vocalization, pause, switching pause, and interruptive and noninterruptive simultaneous speech. Importantly, these vocal states, discernible in adult conversation, are also at work in mother-infant conversational exchanges (discussed below).

Consider the five vocal states in more detail.[9] A *vocalization* is a continuous utterance of one individual. It may contain a silence no greater than 250 milliseconds (silences less than 250 milliseconds are attributable to stop consonants in speech). A *pause* is a joint silence greater than or equal to 250 milliseconds, which occurs within the speaker's turn. (The turn begins at the moment either interlocutor vocalizes alone and is held until the other vocalizes alone, at which point the turn is exchanged.) A *switching pause* is a joint silence greater than or equal to 250 milliseconds initiated by the turn holder, but terminated by a unilateral vocalization of the partner, who thereby gains the turn. Jaffe and Feldstein assign the switching pause to the speaker whose turn it terminates. Finally, there are two types of simultaneous speech, both initiated by the partner who does not hold the turn (the listener or addressee). *Noninterruptive simultaneous speech* is what begins and ends while the partner who holds the turn continues to vocalize. *Interruptive simultaneous speech* is initiated by the listener or addressee while the turn holder is vocalizing, but then continues after the turn holder falls silent. It is the speech segment uttered coactively, while the trailing portion, which is a unilateral utterance, marks the beginning of the turn of the interlocutor who initiated the interruption, and is considered to be her vocalization and the beginning of her turn.

Note that the parsing of dialogue into the vocal states (vocalization, pauses, and simultaneous speech) is based not only on the on-and-off values of the vocal stream, that is, on whether either interlocutor is emitting sound or keeping silent. It also takes into account the turn-taking character of the dialogue, that is, it follows the so-called turn rule. The turn rule stipulates that a turn begins at the instant either interlocutor vocalizes alone and is held until the other vocalizes alone (the turn is then exchanged). The turn can therefore be a composite of some or most vocal states: for example a sequence of vocalizations and pauses, as well as instances of noninterruptive simultaneous speech. The switching pauses and the interruptive simultaneous-speech mark the end of the speaker's turn and her yielding the floor to her partner. A combination of two turns constitutes a cycle that is termed *the interpersonal turn rhythm* (45).

It goes without saying that the Jaffe–Feldstein model is limited by its focus on *recordable vocal behavior* (sound and silence). One could object that there is more to a human conversation than what this model is able to capture. For example, listening and paying attention to what is being said is a vital component of a well-jointed dialogic exchange. A dialogue is not simply a sequence of individual monologues that happen to be timed in an interlacing pattern. It is not just an on-and-off cycle of sound and silence, of activity on the speaker's side, and passivity on the listener's side. Listening is also a way of being active by attending to the speaker's words, and the speaker is typically aware of her interlocutor's attention (or lack thereof) to what she says. The Jaffe–Feldstein model, limited as it is to recording vocal behavior, cannot capture these mutual attentional states. Note also that due to its rigid turn rule, which consistently ascribes a piece of behavior to an individual interlocutor, the Jaffe–Feldstein model leaves out the elements of dialogic exchange that do not follow a strictly sequential order but afford simultaneity. For example, eye contact or a shared smile does not follow a turn-taking pattern but occurs at one time in vocal exchanges in the face-to-face mode. Such cases of simultaneous engagement through the gaze and facial expression testify to the interlocutors mutually attending to one another and are therefore an integral part of face-to-face communication. They are de facto a part of the turn-taking exchanges between interlocutors: both speaker and listener simultaneously attend to what is being said and to one another. It follows that there is simultaneous mutual attending within dialogue that is irreducible to the sequencing of individual conversational turns, even though undeniably the latter are a key component of dialogue.

Despite its confinement to recordable vocal behavior arranged in a sequence of individual turns, the Jaffe–Feldstein model offers clear advantages to dialogue researchers. Thanks to its logical rigor, it can be easily coded by a computer program and used in diverse experimental studies of vocalized dialogic relations. Consider the mechanics of this coding process. The experimenters begin by recording vocal behavior (sound or silence) of the interaction on two separate channels of a stereo tape recorder. The two audio signals provide input to a computer system called the Automatic Vocal Transition Analyzer (AVTA; Cassotta et al. 1967, quoted in Jaffe et al. 2001, 42). AVTA performs an analogue to digital conversion of the audio input. It also listens or samples simultaneously every 250 milliseconds to determine whether each of the participants in the interaction is vocalizing or silent (that is, whether the signal in each channel is on or off). No regard is paid to the semantic content recorded but only to the temporal pattern of sound and silence.

The time series thus obtained is converted into a sequence of binary numbers that represent the four observable dyadic states of the dialogue: 0 = partners A and B are both silent, 1 = A is vocalizing while B is silent, 2 = B is vocalizing while A remains silent, and 3 = A and B vocalize simultaneously. It is possible to switch back and forth between this dyadic code and the two-channel time series, so the identities of the two interlocutors are preserved. AVTA program converts the 0–3 numbers into the five vocal states composing the turn-taking sequence of the dialogue (vocalization, pause, switching pause, and interruptive and noninterruptive simultaneous speech) and averages their duration per time unit, typically a minute of interaction. These data are revealing in that they show whether or not the partners have a mutual effect on one another over the course of the conversation. In fact, Jaffe and Feldstein (1970) document a powerful phenomenon termed *vocal congruence,* in which interlocutors tend to match the time patterns of their speech. The major vocal states the researchers found to be congruent were *pauses* and *switching pauses.* The durations of vocalizations and turns were not generally found to match. The researchers did not examine whether simultaneous speech is matched since it occurs relatively rarely, especially in orderly or "polite" conversations among adults (such a conversational clash is typically associated with affectively charged exchanges, whether among distressed and angry partners or lovers).

There is general agreement among researchers that conversational congruence reflects the interlocutors' susceptibility to mutual influence, or their ability to accommodate the other person in one's own actions. Such rhythmic adjustment to the other may be a key factor in our emotional response and evaluation of the partner: speakers who tend to match their temporal speech patterns see each other as more attractive, warmer, and similar than those who do not; they are also found to be more interpersonally sensitive or empathic toward others (Feldstein and Welkowitz 1978). It may be that those perceptible "good vibrations" in the timing of our transactions with others help us to feel that we connect with them both emotionally and morally.

The Jaffe–Feldstein adult dialogue model of temporal coordination has been successfully applied to the studies of interpersonal interactions in infancy. For example, Bakeman and Brown (1977) examined "behavioral dialogues" in mother-infant interaction in neonates. Numerous researchers focused on gaze and kinesic interactions at the age of four months (for example, Beebe et al. 1979; Beebe, Jaffe, Feldstein, Mays, and Alson 1985; Stern 1974; Stern et al. 1977). Vocal interactions have been studied at the age of four months (Beebe, Alson, Jaffe, Feldstein, and Crown 1988) and nine months (Jasnow and Feldstein 1986). In these studies, researchers recorded spontaneous interactions between infants and their mothers. The recordings were fed into the AVTA described above, and the five basic vocal states and their patterns of mutual coordination were derived out of the sequences of sound and silence. As Jasnow and Feldstein (1986) observe, the turn-taking pattern was clearly visible in the infant-mother exchanges: "the[. . .] data make it plain that alternating vocalization was much more common than simultaneous vocalization and indicate that the vocal exchanges between these preverbal infants and their mothers partake of the same essential format that governs conversations between linguistically competent adults" (757). Together with the other existing data on reciprocal active and passive patterns in infant-mother interaction, these findings "lend support to a view of the mother-infant pair as a system that follows basic rules of dialogic exchange prior to the development of linguistic competence" (ibid.)

Another important finding of the vocal interaction studies is that *the switching pause* durations between infants and their mothers are positively correlated. Jasnow documents that this correlation occurrs due to mutual or bidirectional influence. The matching of switching pauses points to another similarity between dialogue in adulthood and infancy, since in both cases the switching pauses in vocal exchanges tend to match (Beebe et al. 1988, Beebe et al. 1985, Jasnow and Feldstein 1986). This positive correlation shows that both participants tend to adopt a uniform manner in which they regulate the exchange of conversational turns. Importantly, the switching pause is a saliently interpersonal element of the exchange—it is a shared silence that regulates the pace of the back-and-forth movement of the conversation in its passage from one speaker to another. It is therefore telling that it is the switching pauses (rather than the pauses within individual utterances) that are matched via bidirectional influence within infant-mother pairs.

Clearly, the analogy between adult-infant vocal exchange and a conversation among adult speakers is not complete. The pauses within utterances that show strong congruence in adult conversations do not match in mother-infant interactions. However, the differences are not limited to this specific finding. Needless to say, the infant's vocalizations are not structured linguistically. Nor is the mother "speaking" to the infant in the same manner she would to an adult interlocutor. In contrast to adult-directed speech, her vocalizations tend to be shorter, pauses longer, and pitch higher when addressing an infant (for example, Stern et al. 1977). Trevarthen (1993) notes a universal presence of "intuitive motherese" characterized by an adagio beat in the mothers' mode of address of their babies across cultures. These specificities of mother-infant interaction and the demonstrable differences between vocal congruence in infancy and adulthood do not, however, undermine the case for the primacy of dialogicity in human social relations as long as we view it along a continuous curve from birth to adulthood, without expectation of strict identity between the earliest and the subsequent developmental states. It would go against a genetically sensitive approach to expect a strict overlapping between the patterns found in adulthood and infancy. Nor is it necessary to locate identical structures in the early and later phases of ontogenesis to make a strong case for the consistently dialogic character of interpersonal transactions in a face-to-face mode. The argument for continuity between infancy and adulthood leaves room for both difference and similarity between them.

Few authors have studied the consequences of these early rhythmic patterns of coordination between infant and mother for later development. A notable exception to the rule is an extensive infancy study conducted recently by Jaffe, Beebe, Feldstein, Crown, and Jasnow (2001), which follows the Jaffe–Feldstein approach in the examination of vocal dialogues. The researchers looked into how the coordination of vocal rhythm at four months predicts the trajectory of social and cognitive development at twelve months of age. They found significant correlations between the degree of vocal matching in adult-infant pairs and the infants' performance on standard tests evaluating attachment and cognition (respectively, Ainsworth Strange Situation and Bayley Scales) around their first birthday. They were thus able to show that the degree of coordinated interpersonal timing in infancy has direct repercussions for the patterns of social relatedness and cognition in later years. As Rochat (2001) notes, this is especially remarkable considering that the assessment of cognition involves tasks that are not obviously social, such as stacking blocks or looking for hidden objects.

Jaffe and colleagues' research is innovative in that they studied not only the infant's rhythmic patterns in the interactions with the mother in the familiar home setting, but also looked into how a stranger and an unfamiliar setting of the lab affect the infant's interpersonal timing. Jaffe and colleagues' research confirms the earlier findings that infants are fully fledged participants in bidirectional turn-taking interactions with others. Notably, they reaffirmed the previous data showing that infants tend to match the switching pause duration just as the adult interlocutors tend to do. Thanks to the inclusion of an unfamiliar social partner in the lab setting, however, the researchers were also able to document another similarity between vocal interactions in infancy and adulthood. Like adults, infants discriminate between social partners (mother-stranger) and are sensitive to the context of the interaction (home-laboratory). They exhibit a greater level of temporal coordination in their interactions with an unfamiliar person in an unfamiliar environment than with the mother at home. As the researchers note, such tighter conversational rhythms are also typical of adults conversing with a novel as opposed to a familiar partner (Crown 1991). This similarity in the relative increase and decrease of social coordination, depending on the degree of familiarity, suggest that infants like adults may actively use the interactive exchange as a fertile ground for adjustment or "attunement" to the unfamiliar partner (in a way one would practice with an unfamiliar fellow musician), and make predictions about the infant's behavioral patterns (or, in the case of a musician, the playing style). A tightly knit vocal exchange suggests an increased level of vigilance and insecurity with regard to a novel interlocutor than in the case of a familiar partner like the mother, wherein the interaction may be less constrictive and the participants feel greater ease in being together. Such loosely interwoven temporal coordination may leave more room for play, variation, and creativity in interpersonal interaction, both in infancy and adulthood. Note finally that the sensitivity to both the context of the interaction and the partner demonstrated by Jaffe et al. suggest that the infant has the skills needed to acquire deictic terms whose meaning is consistently contextualized by the spatiotemporal environment and the existential relation to an interlocutor. It seems that the infant is anchored in both the physical and the personal context of interaction and so cognitively well placed to ultimately code these relations in appropriate linguistic terms.

FROM PROTO-CONVERSATION TO CONVERSATION

Despite the wealth of studies on dialogic relations in infancy, there are, to my knowledge, no current studies specifically investigating the relation between the congruence in vocal (and other presymbolic) interactions and subsequent linguistic competence in the child. However, if it is valid to call the rhythmic turn-taking exchanges in infancy proto-*conversations,* one can also advance the claim that the proto-*speaker* and proto-*addressee* roles are taking shape in the infant's face-to-face interactions with the caregiver. It is reasonable to assume that the bidirectional matching between the infant and the mother that provides one of the first instances of the self taking the other into account serves as a developmental foundation for the verbalized relation between interlocutors who take each other into account in speaking and listening to one another. If this hypothesis is correct, then the linguistically coded speaker and addressee roles can be said to emerge gradually from the earliest interchangeable turn-taking roles occupied by the infant during interpersonal interactions. It may be that the protospeaker and protoaddressee roles that take shape in synchronized face-to-face interactions in infancy serve as necessary (albeit by no means sufficient) preconditions of acquiring interpersonal deixis. Since "I"–"you" pronouns are canonically deployed in a turn-taking face-to-face interaction, it is reasonable to assume that they have their roots in the turn-taking face-to-face interactions of infancy. It is also reasonable to assume that the earliest exchanges of vocal turns between the infant and the adult provide an excellent practice field for the future transition to verbalized turns and for the acquisition of personal pronouns as linguistic markers of the coparticipants in the turn exchange. In agreement with Christine Tanz (1980, 163), the alternation of turns in conversation provides the *macrostructure*, while the alternation of the deictic "I"–"you" pronouns provides the *microstructure* of language. The alternating rhythm and role switching of protoconversations in infancy appears therefore to provide the macrostructure of conversations in which the speaker and addressee markers will eventually be embedded. The macrostructural level, together with its facial expressions, gaze patterns, and face-to-face orientation, survives from infancy to adulthood as much as it incorporates linguistic elements into the negotiation of the dialogic exchange.

My hypothesis finds support in larger claims that have been made about the relation between face-to-face interaction and gesture on the one hand, and language on the other. For example, Rochat (2001, 140) draws attention to the uniqueness of human infant-caregiver engagement in extended face-to-face exchanges. Even though nonhuman primates engage in grooming and display affectionate care for one another, they do not seem to engage in reciprocal dialogic exchanges to the same extent human primates tend to across cultures. The psychologist concludes that these uniquely human face-to-face dialogues "may be a partial mechanism for the developmental emergence of uniquely human co-cognitive adaptations such as language and explicit thinking in the form of real as well as virtual dialogues" (2001). To take that point further, face-to-face dialogues are the fertile ground for planting the seed of teaching and learning about the world via the Socratic Method, which is naturally the parents and children's own. After all, it is unclear in what manner other than a conversational exchange a child could ever learn about the world; it is only if we favor an adult-centered bias that we can support the view of solitary study as the doorway to gaining knowledge. In Rochat's view, however, the developmentally first conversational model of learning about the world gives way to internalized dialogues, as a way thinking about the world. Thinking is then debating mentally with oneself. Following the lead of Lev Vygotsky (1978) who argues that all higher mental functions are internalized forms of social interaction and that they retain this social-interactive character even when they are performed in solitude, Rochat calls for further empirical research that would capture the dialogic and social nature of cognition as it unfolds in development. For it is only by following the developmental trajectory from the external to the internalized (but still social) mind that we may overcome the attachment to the solitary ego as paradigm of what it means to be human.

My claim about the emergence of "I"–"you" from dialogic roles in face-to-face communication finds further support in larger hypothetical claims about the relation between gesture and language. Jaffe and Anderson (1979) put forward a brief proposal for a gestural communicative hypothesis of speech origin, according to which the evolution of language derives from the interpersonal matching of temporal patterns of gesture. In the authors' words: "Our view of language origins is in terms of social-emotional communication, conveyed by paralinguistic properties of dialogue, with their major locus in prelinguistic mother-infant interaction" (17). Vocal congruence is discussed in this chapter, as well as intersubjectively coordinated patterns of gaze and movement (Beebe et al. 1985, Stern 1974, Stern et al. 1977), which provide specific instances of socioemotional communication in infancy out of which verbalized communication emerges. The authors point notably to the similarities in the time patterns of gestures and the temporal course of vocalizations and pauses that occur during speech. The shared rhythm between the articulatory movements used in speech and the body movements in gesture helps to understand speech as an evolved type of communicative bodily gesture. On this hypothesis, speaking is primarily an activity carried out with our expressive and communicative bodies, and the movements of speech-making are correlated with the ones involved in gesturing. The authors argue further that skill in interpersonal matching of communication rhythms (protoconversation) is not only an important principle in the evolution of language, but continues to be operative in interpersonal communication among adults. After all, language does not displace nonverbal gesture and the latter continues to carry meaning in interpersonal communication once the language comes on board. Nonverbal communicative and rhythmic gesture operative from the first moments of human life appears therefore simultaneously as a prelinguistic condition and an irreducible paralinguistic component of verbalized dialogue.[10]

PERSPECTIVES FROM BLINDNESS AND AUTISM

Additional support for my claim may be found in the studies of atypical populations that exhibit abnormalities in personal-pronoun acquisition and profoundly impoverished social interaction. The groups in question are congenitally blind infants, as well as autistic individuals. Consider possible implications of the lack of vision in infancy for language acquisition, especially as far as person deixis is concerned. To master deictic terms, the child has to comprehend how their meaning is contextualized by the "here and now" of the interaction, that is, the spatiotemporal situation in which they are uttered. The child also needs to comprehend how the interrelated yet distinguishable points of view occupied by the interlocutors contribute to the meaning of deictic terms. Now, the child's access to this contextual anchoring and perspectival configuration of deictic terms is primarily via visual perception of the environment directly under her eyes and via face-to-face interaction with other seeing and visible persons. It seems therefore reasonable to assume that deprivation of this visual information about the spatiotemporal and personal context of communication may negatively affect the child's mastery of person deixis, especially in the early stages of the acquisition process. After all, nobody doubts that blind children become proficient language users; the key question, however, is whether their early language learning may show some significant differences, which when compared with their sighted peers can be traced to lack of visual input.

Selma Fraiberg was a psychoanalytically trained researcher who broke new ground in the understanding of developmental implications of blindness in infancy. Typically, developmental researchers work with sighted infants and apply their findings to the age group at large. Yet it is doubtful that blind infants engage in face-to-face interactions of a proto-conversational type discussed in this chapter. After all, face-to-face orientation supposes that the two parties may see one another or engage in mutual visual contact. As Fraiberg notes (1979, 155), however, with no eye-contact experience, the sense of mutual attention, of connecting with the other in a reciprocal way, is missing in one's interactions with a blind infant. Researchers have shown that this reciprocal connection is vital in forming social bonds and recognizing the infant as a person. The blind baby is deprived of the human face gestalt, which is a powerful stimulus that may not have an equivalent in other sense modalities. She tends also to be significantly less communicative in her own face than her sighted fellows. The absence of differentiated facial expressions is typically mirrored on the face of the observer and produces the insurmountable sense that "something vital is missing in the social exchange" (151). Specifically, "What we miss in the blind baby, apart from the eyes that do not see, is the vocabulary of signs and signals that provides *the most elementary and vital sense of discourse long before words have any meaning*" (152, emphasis added). The blind baby's face shows no signs of preference, discrimination, and recognition of others (164), making attachment difficult and giving the impression that the baby generally lacks interest in things and people. Furthermore, the channel of vocal dialogue that is in principle open to blind babies and their caregivers may be negatively affected by lack of vision. Fraiberg notes that blind babies rarely vocalize to greet and initiate dialogue with others, speculating that vision may be a potent elicitor of vocalizations.

Fraiberg did not find that blindness was an impediment to the acquisition of language. However, "the impediment of blindness revealed itself most cruelly in an impoverished dialogue and in the protracted delay in the constitution of a stable concept of 'I'" (1977, 283). In her study group, blind children started to use the so-called syncretic I roughly at the same time as sighted children usually do (around 2 to 2.6 years). "Syncretic I" is embedded in set phrases, typically verb forms of need or want, for example, *ahwanna*, and regarded as formulaic speech. The first-person pronoun use in the child becomes nonsyncretic once is it disengaged from set phrases and used inventively in new combinations. Fraiberg and Adelson observed a marked delay in the blind children's use of the nonsyncretic "I" in comparison to sighted children's norms. The blind children began using the pronoun "I" in different contexts and creative combinations with other words as late as between 2.11 and 4.10 years of age, despite their otherwise steadily advancing language abilities. Furthermore, they displayed frequent "I"–"you" reversal errors, apparently facing greater difficulties in mastering the speech role dependent on the shifting reference of personal pronouns than their sighted peers. Other researchers (for example, Andersen, Dunlea, and Kekelis 1984; Warren 1994; Webster and Roe 1998) also point out these specific difficulties that blind children encounter with personal-reference terms. Segal (1993) notes that children who are blind may be five years old before they accomplish the correct use of pronouns.

The abnormalities in the blind children's acquisition of personal pronouns have been given two basic explanatory accounts. Influenced by the psychoanalytic theory and the idea that the discovery and identification of the body image is formative of the child's sense of self, Fraiberg and Adelson trace back the pronominal difficulties to a missing self-representation resulting from the lack of visual information about oneself. Pronoun reversals and protracted syncretism of the pronoun "I" reveal the difficulties that the vision-deprived child encounters in forming a stable self-representation in language, as well as in symbolic pretend play. Support for this interpretation has been recently provided by the Lewis and Ramsay (2004) study into the relation of visual self-recognition to personal-pronoun use and pretend play. The authors found that at the ages when self-recognition was emerging (fifteen, eighteen, and twenty-one months), children showing self-recognition used more personal pronouns and demonstrated more advanced pretend play than did children not showing self-recognition. This study was, however, limited to examining the child's first-person pronoun use regarded in isolation from the second-person one and did not examine whether visual self-recognition relates to the full mastery of personal pronouns in dialogic setting. This limitation to the first-person viewpoint typifies Fraiberg's explanatory account as well, in which the focus lies on the emergence of the pronoun "I" out of the child's visual and symbolic self-representation rather than on the interrelation between self and other-representations as well as their linguistic coding in the reversible "I"–"you."

Another explanatory account of the blind children's difficulties with personal pronouns, particularly reversal errors, points to the problem with perspective taking. Andersen, Dunlea, and Kekelis (1984) performed a longitudinal study of a group of six children with varying degrees of vision, from total blindness to perfect sight, aged nine months to three years and four months. They performed a microanalysis of the children's utterances in view of comparing speech patterns in different groups. What is especially promising about this particular study is that the authors did not limit themselves to surface structural similarities in the differently visually able groups but examined linguistic competence in the context of use. Notably, they showed that on the surface blind children may be credited with the mastery of perspective-dependent reversible personal pronouns comparable to their sighted equivalents. For example, Urwin (1979, 1978) argues that blind children understand reciprocal verbal roles in interaction and have a grasp of how reversibility of perspective impacts the meaning of deictic terms. However, Adersen and colleagues respond, on the basis of a reinterpretation of Urwin's data as well as the material collected in their longitudinal study, with the claim that this understanding turns out to be incomplete upon inspection. The blind children fail to consistently make the appropriate adjustments in pronoun use necessitated by changes in perspective, typically by committing "I"–"you" reversal and using the pronoun *she* when talking about one's self. They appear to be buying language ready-made, that is, they incorporate utterances and entire dialogic exchanges from the speech of others via delayed imitation into their own speech without fully analyzing the components and understanding how perspective and speech role figures into the verbal meaning. The authors conclude that the reversal and other pronominal errors in the blind children's speech are a manifestation of a general lack of perspective-taking ability (660), resulting from the unavailability of relevant visual input (661). Importantly, this explanatory account regards visual experiences in the interactive context of the child's transactions with other perceivers rather than as an act of self-observation. It seems therefore better adapted to capture the interpersonal aspect of personal-pronoun acquisition than Fraiberg's psychoanalytic account ever could. In conclusion, the research on blind children underscores the importance of vision for establishing personal reference in language (see Perez-Pereira 1999 for criticism, however). On the one hand, vision provides a powerful stimulus for engaging in the protoconversational routines discussed earlier in this chapter and may be an indispensable condition for engaging in well synchronized turn-taking interactions with others, at least in the early stages of development. On the other hand, vision helps to appreciate perspective in spatial/perceptual terms, and may help with the subsequent mastery of perspective-dependent words. Vision thus seems to be an important element of getting a lived sense of being connected *and* distinguishable from others in the early years of human life. It is therefore reasonable to assume that it plays an important role in the acquisition of linguistic code for the complementary self and other roles in dialogue.

It is noteworthy that autistic children, whose difficulties in navigating the social space have been well documented, encounter severe challenges in managing first- and second-person pronouns correctly due to problems with grasping reciprocal relations involved in their use (Loveland, 1993). Furthermore, Hobson consistently argues that there are important parallels between autism and blindness as far as the failure to appreciate differing personal perspectives is concerned. In Hobson's theory of autism (1993), which departs from Baron-Cohen's influential mind-reading model (2001) by focusing on the embodied perceptual aspects of development rather than the mentalistic skills of inference, the ability to perceive and identify with another person's manifest attitudes toward things, events, and persons plays a key role in the development of self and the relations to others. Blind children are impoverished in this regard in that they lack the sensory access to other people's emotional expressions and attitudes toward the shared world. For example, they cannot read facial expressions of others as clues how to respond to an unfamiliar and potentially dangerous situation (the so-called social referencing skill, documented in the classic "visual cliff" experiment). Autistic children may have visual access to other persons' emotional expressions and attitudes toward the shared world. However, following Hobson, they lack the ability to identify with those manifest attitudes, and to relate as well as to disambiguate their own attitudes from those of others. Thus, even though for different reasons, autistic and congenitally blind children display similar difficulties in their understanding of the reciprocal and complementary relations between self and other.

POLYCENTRISM AND PERSONAL-PRONOUN ACQUISITION: LOVELAND AND OTHERS

These shared difficulties in the congenitally blind and autistic populations lend credence to the hypothesis that a perceptual/spatial appreciation of perspective plays an important role in self and other reference and its linguistic coding in first- and second-person pronouns. This hypothesis was taken up by Katharine Loveland (1984). The psychologist pioneered a series of studies, which demonstrate that the acquisition of first- and second-person pronouns and their possessive forms "my," "mine," "yours," taking place around the age of three, is correlated with the understanding of visually grasped spatial perspectives. Loveland tested this hypothesis in a series of cross-sectional and longitudinal experiments. In the former series, the experiments engaged a group of children in a variety of spatial tasks, such as conspicuously hiding a toy and requesting that the child retrieve it, conspicuously shifting the gaze in one direction to elicit gaze-following in the child, or requesting the child to show a picture to Mommy so that she can see it. These spatial tasks centered on understanding differing points of view were followed by language tasks, which tested pronominal competence in "I"–"you" comprehension and production. For example, the adult asked "What do 'I'/'you' have?" when both have a toy, but not the same one. In other examples, the adult asked "Who has the toy?" when either adult or child has it, and "Whose toy is it?" when it is either the adult's or child's. The results confirmed the hypothesis that only children who demonstrated understanding of differing points of view in the spatial tasks were able to produce and comprehend "I" and "you" pronouns correctly.

The longitudinal experiments studied how spatial point of view and reciprocal deixis interrelate over the course of development. In these experiments, the author also finds that progress in acquiring the "I"–"you" pronouns was correlated with increasing knowledge about points of view. She concludes that there is a clear link between the child's growing understanding of the visual/spatial relations among persons and the child's emerging ability to refer to persons pronominally. Loveland's results have since been confirmed and extended to cover the comprehension and production of the third-person pronouns by Ricard, Girouard, and Gouin Decarie (1999). The authors confirm that children's performance on perspective-taking tasks was requisite to full pronoun acquisition. Interestingly, they demonstrate that competence at coordinating two visual perspectives precede full mastery of the first- and second-person pronouns, and competence at coordinating three visual perspectives precede full mastery of the third-person pronouns in a nonaddressee context. As the researchers were careful to note, early perspective-taking skills alone are not sufficient to explain all aspects of personal-pronoun acquisition. Phonological and syntactical abilities must also be taken into account in the full story of pronominal competence. However, perspective-taking skills in a spatial context do contribute to the perspective-taking skills in the linguistic context of pronominal reference. It is therefore justified to posit continuity and gradual emergence of perspective-dependent "I"–"you" pronouns from the spatioperceptual grasp of coordinated viewpoints deployed by self and other in joint visual attention to the shared world.

Loveland's and Ricard et al.'s research on personal-pronoun acquisition demonstrates not only that spatial perspective figures into the acquisition of personal pronouns, but also, more generally, that cognitive nonegocentrism is a prerequisite of mastering personal deixis. This research substantiates theoretical reflections from chapter 2 about the presence of *polycentrism* in both spatial orientation and interpersonal communication. Additional support for polycentrism is found in earlier empirical work on young children's grasp of multiperspective in the understanding of deictic terms by, for example, De Villiers and De Villiers (1974). These authors demonstrated that children between their third and fourth birthday were adept at switching to the speaker's perspective for the comprehension of deictic terms such as "this"/"that," "here"/"there," and "my"/"your" in the context of a hide-and-seek game. These children exhibited a polycentric orientation in speech context. Furthermore, Tanz (1980) carried out an experiment on pronoun production that showed that children under three years old rarely make errors between different speakers' perspectives in their use of personal pronouns. The children were asked to relay indirect questions of the type "Ask Tom if I have blue eyes" from the experimenter to the person named in the question. The children averaged only five percent errors in their answers, thus proving remarkably proficient in their understanding of the dependence of personal pronouns on the corresponding speech role and perspective.

AN EGOCENTRIC MODEL OF PERSONAL-PRONOUN ACQUISITION: CHARNEY AND OTHERS

Given the empirical evidence for typically developing children's precocious grasp of multiple perspectives, as well as the sheer logical necessity of adopting a polycentric stance within the context of proficient personal-pronoun use, it comes as a surprise that the dominant model of personal-pronoun acquisition in developmental psychology postulates an initial mastery of personal pronouns in an egocentric mode, according to which the personal pronouns are produced and comprehended only if they indicate the child herself, but not others (Charney 1980). This egocentric grasp would only subsequently extend to encompass other speakers/hearers in a dialogic and adultlike conception of personal pronouns. Implicit in this hypothesis of personal-pronoun acquisition is Piaget's influential thesis of the child's initial cognitive egocentrism discussed at the opening of this chapter. Upon inspection however, the experimental data used in its favor does not provide persuasive evidence for an egocentric stance in the language-learning child.

Instead, as shown below, the data is interpreted along a preexisting bias, which belongs to the experimenter rather than to the children participating in the experiment. Furthermore, the egocentric interpretation encounters the logical aporia of how a speaker could ever acquire and deploy linguistically coded speaker and addressee roles within the narrow confines of an egocentric stance. This logical difficulty puts additional pressure on the interpretation of personal-pronoun acquisition in terms of initial egocentrism.

A word of caution is due when studying the emergence of personal pronouns in the child's talk. As Chiat (1986, 343) notes, "it is simply not possible to identify with certainty the point at which a particular pronoun is established as a separate, productively used form with a pronominal function." In other words, pronoun acquisition should not be understood according to a simple, exclusive on/off model, and pronouns occur sporadically before they are fully integrated into the child's linguistic repertoire. Note also that the child may use a pronoun without having full understanding of its cognitive value and application in diverse speech contexts. As discussed below, children initially use personal pronouns in unanalyzed word strings and in the service of a small set of speech acts compared to proficient speakers. They cannot therefore be credited with full pronominal competence from the moment they utter the pronoun. One needs to steer away from an adult bias that would credit the child with the mastery of a word just as soon as it issues from the child's lips. Consider in this regard the anecdote about the idealist philosopher I. G. Fichte who interpreted his son's use of "I" as the first sign of self-consciousness, and from then celebrated not his birthday, but the day on which he first spoke of himself as "I" (Jespersen 1922, 123). Importantly, this anecdote says more about the philosopher's unquestionable attachment to a mentalistic subject purportedly indicated by the word "I" than the meaning of this word as it was used by his child.

To be sure, empirical studies indicate that children tend to produce the word "I" and its possessives "my" and "mine" relatively early, typically around the second birthday, ahead of the remaining personal pronouns. Typically, the second-person pronoun is acquired second, while the third-person pronoun is acquired third (Loveland 1984). However, not all children follow this developmental pattern, and additional research on personal-pronoun acquisition relative to the child's exposure to conversations is needed to fine-tune and contextualize the existing models. For example, Goodz and Lightbown (1996) provide evidence of simultaneity of first- and second-person acquisition in observations of parent-child dyads. This finding is congruous with the expectation that children acquire personal pronouns in a conversational context and are exposed to "I"–"you" reversibility from the start. The complexity and diversity of the child's exposure to conversations may significantly impact whether or not she masters "I"–"you" reversibility at an earlier or later stage. As Oshima-Takane and colleagues showed, the mastery of "I"–"you" reversibility is correlated with the child's exposure to overheard speech and to interactions with a greater number of speakers. In other words, children learn correct semantic rules for first- and second-person pronouns by observing the shifting reference of these pronouns in nonaddressed speech. In addressed speech, the second-person pronoun refers to the child and the first-person pronoun refers to the person who is speaking. It follows, Oshima-Takane (1988) argues, that the dominant exposure to addressed speech is likely to lead the child to entertain incorrect semantic rules that second-person pronouns refer to themselves and first-person pronouns refer to the person speaking to them. The children exposed primarily to addressed speech would have difficulties mastering "I"–"you" reversibility and would tend to exhibit consistent "I"–"you" reversal in their language use. In line with this hypothesis, Oshima-Takene, Goodz, and Derevensky (1996) gathered evidence that second-born children acquire the correct usage of pronouns earlier than firstborns, arguably because they have relatively more opportunities to hear pronouns used in conversations between their parents and older sibling than the firstborn. To be sure, this modeling effect of overhearing the parents' and siblings' conversations does not per se exclude the importance of direct child-other interaction as a context for learning and practicing correct personal-pronoun use. It is likely that the combination of listening (in a nonaddressed fashion) and participating in dialogic exchanges provides the fertile ground for mastering the roles of speaker and addressee. In sum, children exposed to a rich and varied conversational context are likely to master "I"–"you" reversibility without errors. It may be that such exposure increases the child's ability to grasp "I" and "you" pronouns as interrelated entities rather than discrete labels for specific persons and so facilitates simultaneous (and correct) mastery of the first- and second-person pronouns by the child. If so, the order of personal-pronoun acquisition would turn out not to be a universal datum (proceeding uniformly from the first- to second- and third-person pronoun) but rather a context-dependent process that leaves open the possibility for the child to directly access the dialogic connection between "I" and "you" on the condition that the child is immersed in dialogue.

In addition to postulating a clear progression from the first- to second-

and third-person pronouns, some psychologists also concluded that the child produces the first-person pronoun (in limited contexts, as discussed below) ahead of comprehending this pronoun as it is used by others. This conclusion might at first sight suggest an egocentric slant in the child's acquisition of personal pronouns, with the child progressing from an ego-bound to an interpersonal conception of personal pronouns. The work of Rosalind Charney (1980) provides a clear example of this approach. She proposes that the child's acquisition can be broken down to a sequence involving at least two successive levels:

(1) the child is able to refer to herself as "I" and comprehends the pronoun "you" when it is addressed to her
(2) the child is able to comprehend "I" produced by another and to produce the pronoun "you" when addressing a conversational partner

Legerstee and Feider (1986) point to an apparent consensus among developmental psychologists that this model accounts for the bulk of the data on English-speaking children. Unsurprisingly, the authors used it as a working hypothesis in their study of personal-pronoun acquisition in French-speaking children. They claim to have found "the regular developmental sequence" within their study group (with some delays in the French-speaking children, when compared with English speakers). As shown below, however, the developmental model of personal-pronoun acquisition that postulates a passage from egocentrism to dialogicity is ridden with problems. I propose to expose them within the context of Charney's research.

Charney distinguishes between three possible hypotheses regarding the personal-pronoun acquisition. The child could begin with a correct reciprocal view of dialogue and the speech roles of speaker, addressee, and nonparticipant coded in personal pronouns. She would be unfazed by the shifting character of personal pronouns in discourse and possess an "adult" representation of personal pronouns from the start. The child would both use and understand each pronoun "I," "you," "s/he" in relation to any person, both herself and others, as long as the person occupies the appropriate speech role coded by the pronoun. This hypothesis is termed *speech-role-referring* (abbreviated as ROLE). It implies that the child is not enclosed in her own experiential viewpoint but rather is able to perceive others in the (speech) roles she plays, as well as play the roles of others. According to Charney, authors such as de Villiers and de Villiers (1974) would be sympathetic to this view.

Another hypothesis is that the child begins with no sensitivity to dialogic roles, even her own. In that case, one would expect "person-referring (PERSON)" pronouns. Here the pronoun always refers to the same person (or set of persons) regardless of which speech role that person is in. For example, the child would use "me" only in reference to her mother. She would also be prone to the so-called pronoun reversals, calling herself "you" and others "I," since she would then preserve the same pronoun-person pairing in utterance as experienced in hearing others that address per "you" and self-refer with "I." Some psychologists who observed a high rate of pronoun reversals in typically developing children (for instance, Clark 1978) would give partial credence to the PERSON hypothesis. However, pronoun reversals are rare among typically developing children (Chiat 1986, Tanz 1980). As discussed earlier, there is evidence that autistic as well as blind children consistently exhibit pronoun reversal, together with severe social impairments. One may therefore consider applying the PERSON hypothesis to these groups.

The third hypothesis defended by Charney stipulates that the child begins by learning the pronouns most relevant to the child as participant in dialogue. She would learn which pronoun refers to her as speaker, addressee, and nonparticipant, and only later expand to a more generalized conception of pronouns applicable beyond the egocentric position. The child would thus be aware of her own speech role only. She would understand the speaker, addressee as well as nonparticipant roles only when she herself occupies any of these roles. This would enable the child to produce "I" and understand "you" as well as "s/he" pronouns, apparently on a par with the "adult" understanding, albeit limited at first to her egocentric sphere, and only subsequently applied to other dialogic participants. Charney terms this conception of pronouns "person-in-speech-role-referring (PERSON-ROLE)." This conception leads to a counterintuitive notion that a child might master the dialogic role of speaker coded in the first-person pronoun without comprehending that other speakers might use the same word to indicate themselves. It also raises the problematic notion of the child locked in a private linguistic world, in which she apparently grasps the general rules applicable to personal pronouns, but only if these rules apply to her.

Charney tested a group of twenty-one children between the ages of one-and-a-half and two-and-a-half on both the comprehension and the production of personal pronouns. The children were tested on the comprehension of the possessives "my"/"your"/"her" (the nominative "I"/"you"/"she" forms were not used in this task) as addressees as well as nonaddressed listeners. The children's comprehension was evaluated using a Hiding Task. Three framed photographs of the child, the mother, and the experimenter were used. The experimenter showed the child one of a series of animal or doll cutouts, and then (under a cloth) slid the cutout onto the back of one of the photographs. The experimenter or mother then said to the child, "[Child's name], it's under my/your/her picture," or to the other adult, "Mommy/Roz [the experimenter's name], it's under my/your/her picture." In both cases, the child had to use the pronoun information contained in the possessives "my"/"your"/"her" to find the cutout.

Since some children encountered difficulties with the hiding task, a simpler task was used as well. In the Simple Task, "my"/"your"/"her" were used in three different procedures. In the Pointing procedure, the child was asked, "[Child's name], where's my/your/her X?" (X being either a body part or an article of clothing). In the Action procedure, the child was asked to extend the activity she was currently engaged in, such as brushing, combing, pouring tea in a cup, and so forth, to various people. For example, when the child was finished brushing but still had the brush in her hand, she was asked by the experimenter or the mother: "Brush my/your/her hair." Finally, in the Picture task mother and experimenter alternated randomly in asking, "[Child's name], where's my/your/her picture?"

The children were also tested in the speaker role on their *production* of pronouns. The children were engaged in a free-play situation. Their entire speech (outside of the comprehension tasks) was recorded and transcribed.

Charney reports that the results from comprehension and production tasks confirmed the PERSON-ROLE rather than the PERSON or ROLE hypothesis for the first- and second-person pronouns. Consider that each hypothesis makes a different prediction about

(1) the order of acquisition of the pronouns in each speech role the child takes
(2) the consistency and correctness with which the child comprehends and produces the pronouns in speaker, addressee, and nonaddressed listener conditions (performance patterns)

As far as the *order of acquisition* in each speech role is concerned, the predictions, in Charney's view, are as follows. Since ROLE pronouns are not dependent on any one person taking the speech role referred to, there is no reason to suppose that they should be acquired first with one particular person rather than another in that speech role. In contrast, the PERSON-ROLE hypothesis states that the pronoun indicating the child in each should be easiest. This means that the first-person pronoun should be easiest when the child is speaker, second person when the child is addressee, and third person when the child is a nonaddressed listener. Finally, for PERSON pronouns, as for ROLE pronouns, the order of acquisition of pronouns with consistent meaning should be the same in all three roles. In some roles, however, the consistent meaning would be an incorrect one.

As far as *performance patterns* are concerned, a PERSON pronoun should result in consistent errors in certain situations. For example, the PERSON conception would be shown if the child consistently produces "my" in reference to her mother instead of herself, even when someone other than the mother is speaking (and thus is the correct referent). A ROLE pronoun, on the other hand, should result in correct performance regardless of who the referent is. The child would correctly use or understand the pronoun in reference to at least two different people. For example "my," meaning "speaker," is shown if the child comprehends correctly when at least two different people alternate as speakers (that is, are indicated by the first-person pronoun). Finally, a pronoun that is PERSON-ROLE should not result in errors but in omissions: the child would associate the correct pronoun with the correct speech role but only when the child is indicated by the pronoun. In other situations the pronoun would not be understood. "My" meaning "child as speaker" predicts that the child could produce "my" correctly while still not understanding it correctly as addressee or nonaddressed listener.

Consider now the results obtained by Charney regarding *the order of acquisition,* based on the material from the spontaneous-production task (1980, 517). Only those pronoun forms were preserved in the study whose reference was clear (whether or not they were used correctly). The experimenter used a rating scheme to determine the order in which CONSISTENLY CORRECT first-, second-, and third-person pronouns appear in each child's speech. A pronoun form (for example, "my," "mine," "I") was considered to have a consistently correct use when (1) it was only used correctly or (2) it was used correctly and incorrectly but the correct uses passed certain INDEPENDENCE criteria and the incorrect uses did not. The independence criteria indicated that the pronoun function as an independent linguistic unit and not only in set rote phrases: the pronoun form had to appear in at least two different syntactic contexts, at least one of which also occurred in combination with a different word, either a noun or another pronoun. The consistent usage of at least some syntactic form of each pronoun (for instance, "mine") counted toward the final results in this study. The results show that the order of emergence of consistently correct pronouns (in any forms) was first person, and then second, followed by the third. At both visits, consistently correct first-person pronoun forms were produced by significantly more children than either second- or third- (nondeictic) pronoun forms (while consistently correct second- and nondeictic third-person pronoun forms were produced by significantly more children than deictic third-person pronoun forms). All children but one conformed to this first-, second-, and third-person pronoun production sequence.

Consider now the results with the child in the addressee role, based on the Simple and the Hiding tasks. In both tasks, "her" was more difficult than "my" and "your." No child passed "her" without also passing "my" and "your." "My" was more difficult than "your," and "your" was always prior to "my." The order of difficulty was thus: "your," then "my," then "her." (As nonaddressed listener, there was no consistent order across children between speaker/addressee roles).

In conclusion, Charney states that the order of acquisition depends on the child's speech role: *in each role the child initially learned the pronoun form that referred to her.* As speaker, first-person pronoun form precedes second person, whereas as addressee, second-person pronoun form precedes the first. This result is interpreted as clear evidence for the PERSON-ROLE hypothesis, which states that the pronoun indicating the child in each role should be easiest (1980, 520). However, it is unclear whether all the instances of the child using the first-person pronoun accumulated by Charney can be credited with full understanding of the speech role this pronoun carries in discourse. Recall that the experimenter rated the data from the child's spontaneous production according to which pronouns were *consistently correct*. If the first-person pronoun were used in a consistently correct manner, that is, in apparent reference to the child, it did not need to meet *independence criteria*. Now that means that the so-called syncretic use of the first-person pronoun would be regarded as indicative of the child's full mastery of the speaker role—a point that is highly contentious. Recall that the pronoun is used in a syncretic manner when it is consistently embedded in set phrases, with no variation in use and no ability to inventively combine the pronoun with other words in different contexts. These syncretisms would have counted as correct instances of first-person use on Charney's account. However, they do not display the child's grasp of the pronoun as individual lexeme and of its role in varied speech contexts. The child's early productions do not therefore provide clear evidence for the child's full mastery of the person deixis (in an egocentric realm only) and for the order of acquisition in line with the PERSON-ROLE hypothesis.

Charney finds additional evidence for the PERSON-ROLE hypothesis in the child's performance with respect to "my," "your," and "her." Following this hypothesis, "my" would be mastered but with respect to one person only—the child. In other words, "my" would be initially uttered by the child but not understood when used by others (PERSON-ROLE), before being understood when the child is in the nonspeaker position (ROLE). Individual children studied by Charney exhibited such progression (1980, 521). The author notes that it seems in fact *illogical* that the stage of "my" production should precede the stage where the pronoun "my" is comprehended. After all, children acquire words for personal reference from other speakers, rather than being their original producers. As discussed in chapter 2 in reference to Peirce and Jakobson, personal pronouns are not only indexical or deictic terms standing in an existential relation to speech participants but also symbols, which indicate their referent by means of a conventional rule specified by the given language. That is why the same meaning may be assigned to different words across languages and why children reared in an English-speaking environment use the possessives "my"/"mine," in German *mein/e,* in French *mien/mienne,* and so forth. The English-speaking child does not produce the word "my" ex nihilo, in the privacy of her mind, and subsequently extend it to others. It follows, as Chiat (1986, 348) observed already, that "the child's correct production of 'my' implies that she has understood 'my' as referring to other selves, which means it is not person-in-speech-role-referring." The logical impossibility of the child acquiring "my" in an egocentric manner translates therefore into a real-life impossibility that no amount of empirical data could overthrow. Furthermore, since the child has not yet segmented the pronoun as an independent linguistic unit (has not met the independence criteria), she could only be expected to understand others' use of the first-person pronoun in the same unanalyzed phrases she uses (Chiat 1986, 348). As Charney observes, every child whose production of "my" passed the criterion of independence also passed the comprehension test (1980, 526). In conclusion, the child's limited understanding of others' first-person pronoun use reflects a limited grasp of the pronoun *in general* rather than a complete albeit ego-bound mastery.

Consider also that in Charney's study the pronoun "my" was produced (in fourteen out of fifteen instances) by children while acting on an object in a specific way—searching for, grabbing, or claiming it (usually an object that was *not* the child's). In contrast to ROLE use, the early "my" does not express ownership but rather a claim to ownership. Children frequently use the possessive "mine! mine!" as a stereotyped form of making a request. This wishful possessive, so to speak, is thus narrowly bound to specific actions and differs from the way the possessive is used in discourse by competent speakers (to indicate what belongs to oneself). In fact, researchers have demonstrated that children initially use terms of self-reference, such as personal pronouns, primarily in just *two* communicative contexts: making requests/proposals (for example, "give me ball") and stating intended actions (for example, "I do it") (Imbens-Bailey and Pan 1998). Children engaged in spontaneous interactions with their parents used personal pronouns in far fewer contexts than their parents did. It follows that there are important discrepancies in the typical child and adult use of personal pronouns, despite surface similarities. Following Imbens-Bailey and Pan, the fact that children make explicit reference to self (and other) in the service of a relatively small subset of speech acts shows that the former is driven in part by pragmatic needs. "If control over linguistic factors alone determined the emergence of self- and other-reference, one would have expected use of first and second person pronouns to be distributed more uniformly across the full range of communicative functions that young children are able to express" (232). Importantly, this narrow pragmatic constraint of the children's early use of personal pronouns provides another reason why their early production of, for example, "my" does not fully map onto adult productions, which extend to dozens if not hundreds of existing speech acts and pragmatic contexts of personal pronoun use.[11] It also explains why the child's early production of "my" within the few communicative contexts does not go hand in hand with the comprehension of the same word as used with versatility by the adult. Production of a word may be accompanied by its limited understanding.[12] However, again, this limited use reflects the child's limited grasp of the personal pronouns *in general* rather than a complete albeit egocentric mastery.

In conclusion, the influential model of personal-pronoun acquisition, which posits a progression from an egocentric to a polycentric conception, is not supported by the evidence mounted in its favor. Charney hastily attributes a complete grasp of the pronoun to a child based exclusively on surface correctness, without taking into account the cognitive value of the child's productions and the pragmatic context of pronoun use. Her important and influential study lacks therefore the requisite depth and finesse in the analysis of empirical material. The hypothesis of egocentric mastery of personal pronouns appears less strongly founded on the data than on the preexisting intellectual tradition in psychology (and philosophy), which skews the interpretation of Charney's findings in the direction of the canonical conception of childhood originated by Piaget. It is because of such unexamined individualist bias that a philosopher needs to exercise a good deal of caution in the face of the conclusions drawn from empirical research and refrain from incorporating it wholesale into an interdisciplinary project in the name of respect for hard data.

I hope that my critical analysis of Charney's research illustrates that scientific work is necessarily, for better and for worse, informed by assumptions of a theoretical nature which a philosopher can help clarify and possibly challenge, as well as provide alternative ways of viewing. In my view, such an alternative conception of personal-pronoun acquisition is found in terms of gradual emergence of speech roles from presymbolic patterns of interpersonal interaction that exhibit alternating turns, interchangeable roles, and the grasp of multiple perspectives. This polycentric conception has the logical advantage over an egocentric one in that it avoids the perpetual puzzle of how the child locked in the first-person viewpoint could ever successfully acquire dialogic role markers. It also has empirical backing. Given that few children encounter problems mastering the shifting reference of personal pronouns in speech, it is reasonable to assume that they are equipped with a prelinguistic notion of role and perspective that translates relatively smoothly into a linguistic one. Personal-pronoun acquisition is therefore not a cognitive task requiring a painstaking process of understanding that some words may function differently from labels for things. (Such a process is predicated upon an objectivist conception of language that is, again, probably more likely to result from a preexisting intellectual tradition than the child's own initial view.) It may rather involve a process of grammaticalization of roles and perspectives that are firmly rooted in the earliest forms of embodied interpersonal interaction and in the shared attending and acting on the surrounding world. It may be that these presymbolic bodily patterns provide the *protogrammar* out of which symbolized communication develops. Following Chiat (1986, 355), the mystery lies then not in explaining how children acquire personal pronouns, since they seem to acquire them effortlessly, but rather in the prelinguistic construction of role and perspective which makes personal pronouns so accessible. The task remaining open to the psychologist is to continue probing those prelinguistic constructions and to document fully the polycentric and polyrhythmic orientation of the child's early experience. The task is also to explicate the transition from prelinguistic to linguistically coded conception of role and perspective in appropriate detail and to study the possible impact of the former not only on personal deixis acquisition but also on the acquisition of language in general. As discussed in chapter 2, spoken language is inescapably rooted in the perspectivally configured spatial context of interaction, and it deploys the interrelated speaker and addressee roles. To fully understand the emergence of spoken language we need therefore to account for the establishment of the connections to the spatial context and to the interacting participants in language.

PHILOSOPHICAL IMPLICATIONS AND DIRECTIONS FOR FUTURE RESEARCH

There is to my knowledge no existing longitudinal study that investigates the relation between the alternating protoconversational turns in infancy and language acquisition. If it is true, as hypothesized above, that the protoconversational turns provide a broader macrostructural pattern in which the person deixis becomes embedded, then these macro- and microstructural levels should be significantly correlated (even though other factors enter into play as well). For example, additional research on personal-pronoun acquisition by congenitally blind children could further illuminate this relation and help resolve the debate about the exact importance of visually mediated interpersonal interaction in infancy and early childhood for establishing personal reference in language. Furthermore, an exhaustive study of the evolving cognitive value of personal pronouns in the typically developing child's speech still remains to be completed. It is important to study not only what the child says but also the semantic range and illocutionary force of her utterances. Such a study would need to pay heed not only to the pragmatics of the child's speech but also to the degree of her exposure to addressed and overhead speech, the familiarity with the interlocutor, and the context of the interaction. It is only by paying due regard to the complexity of the language-acquisition process that one can hope to avoid forcing it into traditional explanatory models.

This brings me back to the philosophical point raised toward the end of the second chapter: What conditions need to be met in view of acquiring personal pronouns? Recall that according to Castañeda (and the philosophy of subjectivity), a mentalistic inner self is a necessary prerequisite of the first-person pronoun acquisition. This preexisting self is necessary insofar as the first-person pronoun expresses but does not constitute self-awareness. Recall also my response that had such a mentalistic self been in place, it would de facto have hindered rather than helped in the pronoun-acquisition process by forcing the language-learning child to perform a conceptual leap from an asocial self to a socialized speaker. To paraphrase Merleau-Ponty's comments quoted at the opening of this chapter, the child would fail to acquire the pronoun "I" in its fullest linguistic and grammatical meaning, for she would fail to understand that even though she uses "I" for self-reference, others address her as "you." In Benveniste's terms, the child would be incapable of mastering "I"–"you" reversibility, and so of mastering either of the interrelated first- and second-person pronouns. An inner private self is not a necessary condition of possibility of mastering the pronoun "I."

The empirical material discussed in this chapter further supports the argument against a mentalistic self. Recall that in Castañeda's view, this self is a cognitively sophisticated construction, which supposes the ability to cogitate privately à la Descartes—an ability that small children do not have. It would therefore postpone the personal-pronoun acquisition in ontogenetic time in a clear disregard of the actual time line of the child's linguistic development and of the fact that children master personal pronouns in conversational context before they can be credited with advanced intellectual skills. Such disregard can only be corrected by a deliberately interdisciplinary approach to the personal-pronoun acquisition that is not limited to a theoretical stance and overburdened by a preexisting attachment to transcendental subjectivity. The empirical data surveyed in this chapter demonstrates that cognitive prerequisites of personal-pronoun acquisition are not to be located in an egocentric stance. In fact, Piaget's influential thesis of the child's cognitive egocentrism turns out to be problematic in light of more recent research. This research suggests that cognitive prerequisites of personal-pronoun acquisition are to be found in (but not limited to) the child's innate attunement to the other, evidenced by the grasp of the temporal rhythms and turn-taking exchanges of dialogue. These early protoconversational exchanges via the voice, gesture, and gaze ground the child in the play of alternating reciprocal active and passive/receptive roles she will subsequently take up in verbalized dialogue.

Contemporary research points to other prerequisites, including the spatial grasp of multiple perspectives in the context of attending to the world with others and attending to one another, which readies the child for the linguistic mastery of interrelated yet discrete points of view in a conversational setting. It is in the interpersonal context of the child's (typical) early experience, with its rhythmic flow and its spatial context, that the child learns about persons, roles, and perspectives. As such, the child is cognitively primed to handle them in language and can acquire conversational competence with relative ease.

Importantly, the child's nascent sense of self is interconnected with that of the other. Proprioceptively, the child is aware of the contours and the animate mass of her body. She therefore has a sense of self, however primitive and subject to future elaborations. The child is also learning about others in a variety of interactive engagements, both face-to-face transactions and, subsequently, the navigations in the shared world. Her sense of self develops consistently in pace with the other; she is aware of her place within the world not only via the proprioceptive sense, but also via the type of address tailored specifically to the child's needs and abilities by the caregivers who hold her in the cradle of their bodies, vocalize in a high-pitched sound that accommodates the child's hearing range, make the "exaggerated" facial expressions of emotion the child can easily register, and selectively shadow the child's own facial expressions. The child's sense of self is thus simultaneously fed by her living body, via muscle, joint, and skin sensations; the happy gurgle of a full stomach; the discomfort of a soiled diaper; *and* is shaped by the attentions received from others, who not only satisfy her physiological needs but enculturate her to the practices of the society she is born into by promoting certain types of expressions and gestures and disregarding others, as in the parents typically echoing the syllabic sounds made by the infant but not the involuntary physiological sounds associated with the digestive process (the so-called social scaffolding). Her sense of self does not therefore belong to the province of inner sensation alone; it is consistently monitored, interpreted, and influenced by the others. It is a site in which organic *self-awareness* and *being addressed* by others in the context of the shared world intersect and intertwine with such promiscuity that no inner private realm could be neatly separated from the outer public world, and no purely mental self could be effectively severed from the mundane materiality of communication. No basis for a purely mentalistic self as the locus of internal awareness remains in the perspective that takes embodiment and interpersonal address seriously. Consequently, no basis for a mentalistic construal of the first-person stance remains either. Insofar as self-awareness and addressability interrelate in the child's early experience, a copresence of the first- and second-person stances is evidenced from the start. This copresence accounts for what otherwise remains a perennial puzzle: the child's entry into the social field of language.

CHAPTER 4

PHILOSOPHY OF DIALOGUE

Some ideas impose themselves with a sense of urgency on more than one thinker, regardless of whether these thinkers know or influence one another directly. Such was the case with the dialogical principle of I–you connectedness that found expression, most famously, in the writings of Martin Buber, but also Hermann Cohen, Franz Rosenzweig, Ferdinand Ebner, Eugen Rosenstock-Huessy, Gabriel Marcel, Karl Jaspers, and others.[1] This urgency of a renewed consideration of dialogue arises in part as a response to the gaping class divisions within Europe at the turn of the 19th century, as well as to profound disarray produced by World War I. As Buber put it, "Out of the experience of the Vesuvian hour, a strange longing awakens for thinking to do justice to existence itself" (2002, 252). This urgency of dialogue is also of a profoundly philosophical nature, and it responds to the limitations of the philosophical worldview of modernity and idealism, which is predicated on the sufficiency and sovereignty of the universal subject, who builds all-encompassing systems of knowledge and neglects the ethically and politically pregnant questions of mutual coexistence between individuals in peaceful communities. This critique and the urgency to reformulate the question of sociality in a nonsubjectivist manner applies equally well to the egocentric tradition in philosophy and psychology. I propose, therefore, to offer in this chapter a renewed account of sociality along the lines of dialogic tradition, in view of providing powerful resources for the multidiscipline of dialogical phenomenology.

Specifically, I propose to examine the principle of I–you connectedness with a focus on the better-known representative of the dialogic tradition, Martin Buber. This choice is motivated by my contention that Buber's philosophy offers particularly helpful resources for shedding the individualist bias of classical phenomenology and resituating phenomenological research within the social sphere. Buber's philosophy is phenomenological insofar as it is rooted in the lived experience of dialogue as it unfolds between social partners, but it refrains from stripping that experience of its speech-dependent and sustained character. It is a phenomenological philosophy immersed in direct experience that avoids the transcendental turn to the ego and the difficulties associated with it. At the same time, Buber's philosophy builds upon a slightly earlier initiative, one to turn philosophy away from its traditionally sanctioned domain of speechless thought back to the practice of living speech, which was undertaken by Eugen Rosenstock-Huessy and continued by Franz Rosenzweig. To appreciate fully the scope of the dialogic project and its ambitious program to reform the philosophical method it is appropriate to begin with the lesser-known Rosenstock-Huessy, and then turn to Rosenzweig, and, finally, Buber.

ROSENSTOCK-HUESSY'S GRAMMATICAL METHOD OF SOCIAL RESEARCH

Rosenstock-Huessy's relatively unknown but groundbreaking work was inspired by two interrelated needs. The former was the pervasive sense of decay in the social fabric of the Germany of 1920s, the stratification of the people into a class society, and the growing professional and economical rifts between different groups. This practical concern was echoed in another sense of crisis, the latter of a more scholarly type. The existing academic methods modeled on mathematical sciences, notably physics, proved inadequate to address the complexities and particularities of the social world. Consider Euclidian geometry in this regard. The geometrical categories and principles are used to map out and organize three-dimensional space, but they have little bearing on the sense of space an animate organism that inhabits a spatial environment may have. The spatial categories like high/low, near/far, left/right arise within a spatial world as it is negotiated by embodied locomoting creatures, and they have no place within the geometrical universe of points in space. The Euclidian categories, however helpful they may be in the province of geometry, are therefore not derived from the lived experience of space but rather logical projections. A similar point could be made about the social world. The logical categories used in scientific sociology do not capture the lived experience of sociality but are projections imposed on it from outside by an external observer who has no foothold in the very phenomenon being investigated. To enter the social world, the scholar requires therefore more apt methods than those offered by the exact science. She needs a revised *Discours de la methode*—a discourse that challenges the universal validity of logical and mathematical methods in science, and provides an alternative methodology tailored to the specificity of the social world. Such an alternative *Discours de la methode* is developed in Rosenstock-Huessy's *Speech and Reality* (1970), as well as in an earlier study, a revised version of a *Sprachbrief* Rosenstock-Huessy addressed to Franz Rosenzweig in 1916, titled *Practical Knowledge of the Soul I* (1988 [1924]).

The new method is, in Rosenstock-Huessy's view, of a *grammatical* kind. As phrased in the famous motto, "Grammar is the future organon of social research" (1970, 9). It is the sole method appropriate for the study of language, this "lifeblood" of the society (1970, 10), a connective tissue that holds human beings together in a web of relational processes. For Rosenstock-Huessy, language is not a code used for manipulating symbols but rather the living medium of social unity and coexistence. The social scientist needs therefore to be able to diagnose language in order both to unveil the principles organizing interpersonal interaction in spoken communication *and* point to the ways in which these principles may have been partially distorted in the course of Western history. The grammatical method is therefore directly engaged in its subject matter. It does not serve merely to categorize linguistic rules from a detached viewpoint of external observer sanctioned in exact science. Insofar as it is a method deployed by a social and speaking being who has a participatory understanding of spoken discourse, it serves also to raise the question of whether the dominant grammatical system upheld by the academics and inculcated in schoolchildren is rooted in language as *speech* or a projection of categories derived from *thought* onto language. Grammatical systems are after all not sets of brute natural facts operative out there in the world but rather organizational principles of social and cultural phenomena that are shaped and interpreted by language users. The methods employed in social science are therefore themselves social in nature; the study of language is itself a linguistic enterprise. This apparent circularity of method proposed by Rosenstock-Huessy is not its shortcoming but its advantage; it maintains the scientist's firm foothold in the phenomenon under investigation.

Unsurprisingly, the conception of grammar propounded by Rosenstock-Huessy is not "a dry-as-dust textbook obsession" (1970, 9), the received set of rules and principles memorized in elementary school. In fact, Rosenstock-Huessy was critical of the dominant grammatical models like the conjugation table to which we subject schoolchildren. Nor should the grammar be understood in the restricted sense of a set of principles used to combine symbols in order to produce more complex unities. Grammar is not to be located primarily in the province of symbol manipulation but rather spoken communication, which includes direct interpersonal address in the I–you mode, but extends to the entire domain of discourse, such as literature, history, laws, contracts, policies, and any other verbalized means of expression that serve, in part at least, to maintain and organize communal life. On Rosenstock-Huessy's reading, grammar is the modus operandi of the society in that it both reflects and enables interpersonal relations, notably by establishing an order of persons within the system of personal pronouns. Importantly, the dominant grammatical system circulated in textbook grammar is not rooted in "the grammar of the soul"—the deep grammar organizing human speech as a felt corporal necessity of standing in relation, but rather in a superficial notion of language as an expedient means for conveying ready-made insights, a "rational and informative" notion of language derived from a disembodied mind. The latter notion of language contains a bias toward a lone *cogito*, and needs to be corrected in ways that make the primacy of interpersonal connectedness apparent.

It was Rosenstock-Huessy's contention that the received textbook grammar reflects the individualist bias of thought-based philosophy—this "nightmare of a speechless thinker who computes a speechless universe" in which the reality of speaking and listening people fails to be preserved (1970, 111). The grammar sanctioned by public schools uncritically assumes the primacy of mute inward-directed thought while it claims to retrieve the regulating principles of spoken discourse. Consider an example of why this may be the case. Like Benveniste (discussed in chapter 2), Rosenstock-Huessy charges the prevalent conjugation table for failing to represent the reality of spoken discourse and for imposing a uniform model of purportedly interchangeable first, second, and third persons. Rosenstock-Huessy provides however additional philosophical insights and clues for how to revise the existing grammatical system in view of capturing the primacy of interpersonal connectedness. First of all, he challenges the primacy of the first person sanctified by the traditional conjugation table, which sets up the "I" as the first person, the grammatical notion mirrored in the academic attachment to a "doubting and discerning thinker's I," a "purely inward-oriented, mental and reasonable" agency posited as starting point of inquiry (1988, 13).

The primacy of *I* is not a datum derived from speech and so cannot be used to regulate speech and sociality. Rosenstock-Huessy adopts an expressly genetic and phenomenological perspective to make that point.

> Out of a thousand cares, impressions, and influences which surround, flow around, and beset it, a child gradually stakes out its borders as an independent entity.... The first thing that happens to the child—to every person—is that it is spoken to. It is smiled at, entreated, rocked, comforted, punished, given presents, or nourished. *It is first a "you"* to a powerful being outside itself—above all to its parents. (1988, 16)

From a genetic phenomenological perspective of a socialized human being, the primary existential stance is of *being addressed by others*—being a focus of parental care, the terminus of multiple overtures and imperatives issuing from the caregiver, who attends to the child's needs but also engages the child directly as a person with her own desires and temperaments and as a possible companion who responds to the ministrations and attentions by returning or avoiding the gaze, smiling or frowning back, vocalizing in return. This experience of being addressed helps, in Rosenstock-Huessy's view, to establish the child's *I* as both a point of focus and a response to a command. From the genetic point of view, and against the formalism of thought-based grammar, "you" indicates the primary personal stance, whereas "I" is the secondary one. This sequence from address to response is furthermore preserved throughout human life in our responsiveness to the multiple voices whose calling does not necessarily issue from visible mouths and that command us to act in determinate ways, whether by adopting a political stance or following a specific professional *vocation* (1988, 26). By postulating the primacy of the calling, Rosenstock-Huessy is in agreement with another dialogic philosopher, Ferdinand Ebner, who notes that "The true I in man is his innermost ear which admits the Word."[2] Contrary to the ocularcentric tradition, which regards the eye and the *I* as primary, with the mental acts issuing out of the subjective agency like visual rays, it is the ear that receives a command from the other that is primary in the philosophical discourse situated in the domain of speech.

The grammatical revision of personal stances proposed by Rosenstock-Huessy is not limited to the reversal of priorities from the first to the second person. Consider the received conjugation table again.

> I love
> You love
> He/she/it loves
> We love
> You love
> They love

What is striking about this table is the persistent use of the *declarative or indicative mode,* coupled with *the present tense.* Each statement is pronounced in a similarly flat voice, as a declaration of fact, without personal involvement (1970, 111). All statements appear therefore to have a minimal degree of emphasis and equivalent social character (1970, 100). However, Rosenstock-Huessy notes, in agreement with Benveniste, there are nonnegligible differences in emphasis between the persons. A third-person statement "He loves" lacks emphasis, but "I love" and "you love" have "grave social consequences" (1970, 100). Saying "I love" is a promise and a commitment. In terms of Austin's "old view," entertained initially in *How to Do Things with Words* (1962), it is a speech act belonging to performative rather than constatative utterances. And, as Rosenstock-Huessy observes, only the third-person statement may function as a nonparticipatory *compte rendu* of an occurrence situated outside the field of mutual influence established by the speaker and the addressee.

> Amatur—he is loved, is an objective statement. Some fact is reported of somebody who is neither the speaker or writer nor the listener or reader. He usually does not know that people speak of him. On the other hand, it is equally noticeable that neither the speaker nor the listener has any stake in the sentence "amatur." In "amatur," the process of love has been made powerless. This is no small achievement. Of love we can only speak in fear and trembling if we speak of it in the first or second person. The third person neutralizes the power of love. The objects of science are made powerless. (1970, 101)

The reader of this passage may wonder whether Rosenstock-Huessy does not overemphasize the separation between dialogic and declarative discourse in this passage, that is, whether he does not overlook the first-to-second person connectedness that may continue to bind the interlocutors who speak and hear "amatur." For even though the lover under discussion is dialogically disengaged, the interlocutors do not issue pure declarative statements, they address each other while talking about a third. Their discourse is not therefore simply purged of a dialogic dimension, if such a purging could ever be realized without a total loss of meaning and communicability in language. As discussed in further detail in reference to Buber, it may be that the dialogic dimension can never be simply lost but it can be and has been partially effaced within the pervasive attachment to "objective" language, forgetful of its indebtedness and service to communicative praxis, and devoted primarily to labeling entities in the world. Rosenstock-Huessy's deprecating comments about third-person discourse may therefore themselves be marked by partial oblivion of the inescapably communicative character of language that never splits neatly into blocks of purely declarative and dialogical discourse. In fact, following Austin's later view (1962), we cannot make a neat distinction between constative and performative utterances. Rather, all utterances have some performative speech element—and may therefore have an intrinsic dialogic dimension. Even though the statement "he is loved" is a perfect example of a declarative sentence, it may have the illocutionary force of a warning (to not pursue him as a romantic possibility), as well as perlocutionary effects (the interlocutor may decide not to court him). Rosenstock-Huessy may not have fully appreciated this inherent illocutionary force (and perlocutionary effects) of grammatically declarative utterances. Although his comments provide a much-needed critique of the illusory belief in the possibility of pure constatation, and outline the dangers inherent in the forgetting that language is inescapably rooted in I–you connectedness, they may inadvertently suppose the possibility of a real rather than only ideal separation between (purely) declarative and (overtly) dialogic discourse.

Turning back to Rosenstock-Huessy's critique of third-person discourse, he argues that even though an indicative statement (such as *amat*—he loves) is typically cast as objective—a positive mark of the subject's impartial take on the world, it is in fact objectifying and reductive. It disempowers the event of love as a personal act by converting it into an indifferent-classified *factum,* abstracted from both the interlocutors involved in the conversation and from the third party spoken about. Consider the dangers involved in applying this disempowering mode to statements made in the first and second person. Construing "I love" as an indicative "omits one half of the sentence's significance: *amo* [I love] has a double emphasis compared to *amat* [he loves]." "I love" is an act of disclosure—the speaker makes herself vulnerable to interference from the listener, not the least because the latter coparticipates in the speech—a relational act whose meaning is coconstituted by the interlocutors. Hence, Rosenstock-Huessy insists that listening is an act—it is not a passive reception of stimuli but rather an attentive directedness toward the speaker, who must be held in esteem if she is to be heard at all (1970, 106). Stating one's love is therefore a risky act—an act divulged can be interfered with (1970, 102).

As a performative rather than a declarative statement, "I love" bears the stamp of personal involvement and responsibility that is easily overseen if we move it from the domain of speech to mute thought. Consider Descartes' use of the first person in that regard. *Ego cogito* is an impersonal statement that has lost its original power of a confession and disclosure. It is rather a report of mental processing that any thinking substance could in principle be an exemplar of, and which can therefore be cast equally well in the first- as in the third-person statement.

Consider Valery's apt remark in this regard (1948, p. 17):

> Never before [Descartes] had any philosopher so deliberately displayed himself upon the stage of his own thought, showing himself off, daring to use the first personal pronoun throughout whole pages. And never. . . had any philosopher so gone out of his way to convey to us the details of his mental debates and the inward workings. . . that least personal of *Me*'s which must be the same in all men, the universal in each of us.

Descartes' use of the first person as a subject of universally valid truths has anesthetized the "I," making us oblivious of the generalized indiscretion and the exhibitionist aura of the pervasive first-person pronoun use initiated in modern philosophy. The "I" has been deprived of its usual emphatic form, emotional charge, and personal involvement, which carry some of the weight of its meaning in spoken discourse. By assuming the primacy of muted ego over the resounding "I," thought-based philosophy adopted the primacy of the deflated indicative mode from the traditional grammatical ordering of persons without raising the question of whether or not indication may be derived and made dependent upon performative personal discourse.

For Rosenstock-Huessy, the modern disconnect between the emphatic "I" of speech and the deemphasized ego of speechless thought is facilitated by the disregard for proper names. The ego of speechless thought is *anonymous* or without a name—it does not belong to René Descartes, the white European male born to Jeanne Brochard and Joachim Descartes on March 31, 1596. It is a purportedly *universal* rather than a *personal* marker because it loosened the connection ordinarily maintained in discourse between proper names and pronouns. For Rosenstock-Huessy, unlike Buber, the proper name is integral to personal address since it individuates the speaker and the addressee, picking them out of the crowd of possible interlocutors as this unique person. Furthermore, it adds a broader historical framework to the interaction that would be missing in a purely pronominal discourse. Proper names predate and postdate the use of personal pronouns; their existence is not confined to the actual event of being uttered by the parties involved in dialogue but extends into the past and continues into the future. The name unlike the pronoun has a multigenerational component missing in the pronoun; one may be spoken about as a specific individual, the referent of one's proper name in one's absence and after one's death, whereas pronouns live a momentary existence confined by the flesh-and-blood presence of the interlocutors. As argued below, however, in reference to Buber, this limitation of personal pronominal discourse is an asset from a phenomenological point of view insofar as it taps directly into the lived event of the interpersonal relation in a way that may not be possible in discourse involving proper names.

As a performative rather than declarative statement, the first-person utterance is not cast in the indicative but rather in the subjunctive mode. It is the hopeful "that I may love!" that opens up the future of possibilities for the speaker. Its rightful tense is therefore not the present but rather the future. It is the tense of commitments, responsibilities, and promises made. Rosenstock-Huessy's "I" is a forward-looking "I," the "I" that serves as the mouthpiece of free will, and could therefore also be called *voluntative* (1988, 19).

Consider now the deep grammar of a statement made in the second-person mode. The address *amas* (you love) presupposes that a social relation is in place (Rosenstock Huessy 1970, 105), such as between a mother and a child or a doctor and a patient. "The speaker's right to say 'amas' is derived from a covenant under which a certain degree of authority was granted him!" (ibid.). The speaker wields certain authority over the listener—as previously noted, the significance of the sentence is not only its objective content, but also the regard of the listener to the speaker. *Amas* is said with emphasis, for the interlocutor must lend her ear to receive the utterance. Furthermore, in line with the genetic phenomenological account of speech provided above, the direct address should be cast originally not as a declarative "you love" but rather as the imperative "love!" (100). The imperative to love received by a willing ear is the origin of what is traditionally termed the second person. "Love transforms. It implores and commands... the 'you' is virtually discovered for the first time in the imperative which arises from the transformation love creates" (Rosenstock-Huessy 1988, 21). In a conjugation table representative of the grammar of the soul, "you" as recipient of the imperative would be the primary or the first person, followed by "I."

The imperative is a unique personal statement whose temporal frame is the present tense. Even though in the traditional conjugation table, all three persons are cast in the generic present of matters of fact, the lived present occurs exclusively in the startling moment of being directly addressed in a face-to-face situation by another who speaks to *you*—and nobody else. "The second person in amas is not somebody or anybody, but is you in particular for who I have become in some degree responsible" (Rosenstock-Huessey 1970, 106). The utterance that connects to a specific noninterchangeable listener when it travels through the air from the mouth to the ear generates the lived sense of the present as the now-and-at-no-other-time of being addressed in a face-to-face situation. For Rosenstock-Huessy, and subsequently for Buber, the present is not an abstract point on the string of elapsed and the forthcoming events; the present has a phenomenological aspect of a lived encounter with another. As Buber puts it, "the actual and fulfilled present—exists only insofar as presentness, encounter, and relation exist. Only as the You becomes present does presence come into being" (1970, 93).

The assignment of the present tense to all grammatical persons is therefore an unfounded usurpation of this unique relational process by the pervasive indicative mode in the superficial grammar. Yet properly speaking, the indicative mode is bound with what has been, even though it may be cast superficially in the present-tense form. The indicative mode "recounts things which have come to be, which have been, or things which have passed or are passing in the universe outside the speaker" (Rosenstock-Huessy 1988, 21). Insofar as the indicative reports the already established so-and-so of events immune to the influence of the speaker and addressee, it narrates about an already-congealed world and fails to enter into a relational present with it. In ontological terms employed by Buber, the declarative statement that professes that something is thus-and-so (*Sosein*) fails to touch its being (*Sein*), for it has suspended the living relation to the reality it proclaims to dispense knowledge about (Buber 1970, 113).

In conclusion, the superficial grammar based on logical categories of thought rather than the living reality of speech assumes the primacy of the first person. This *cogito*-based assumption is historically coupled with a "philosophy of worldview," a discourse about the world, grammatically cast as an *it*. Traditionally, then, the philosophers' grammar has privileged the first and the third persons and left the second person out of account. A revised grammar must bring You back into the center of debate, and establish its primacy with regard to the remaining personal stances.[3]

Furthermore, it is crucial to correct the second pervasive misconception embedded in the traditional grammar's across-the-board adoption of the indicative mode for all persons. As Rosenstock-Huessy notes, the pervasive indicative of textbook grammar creates the illusory impression of all statements made by human beings as neutral statements of fact (1970, 108), and this devalues human relations. "Human relations thrive where we attribute secretes of communication and loyalties of listening. Human relations die where all our statements only contribute facts" (1970, 109). The pervasive indicative is thus by no means neutral, but it anesthetizes and deflates speech of social significance and so it may lead to the degeneration of social relations by prescribing a disengaged matter-of-fact discourse devoid of personal involvement and emphasis. Rosenstock-Huessy was troubled by the spread of such flat impersonal discourse, its "brazen objectivity" leading to social malaise (1970, 114). His call for a grammatical reform is therefore a response to the growing sense that society is losing its personhood, that social life is being drained of the juices needed to keep it alive. For social life happens only when speech is excitable—when it carries emphatic qualities, enables and renews personal involvements, leads to exposures and risks, and may in moments of heightened involvement raise its voice to a shout or flounder in whispering shyness, erupt in bouts of stuttering and stammering, be tainted by blushing and punctured by the silence of forgetting the right words. These latter cases count as failure only from the perspective of the rational and informative discourse of a pure mind. Yet the speech of social life is impure by design, without being thoughtless. It may be heavy with affect; it carries and causes pleasure and pain, it can hurt and heal others, like the talking cure Anna O. discovered with Freud. It is the speech of what Rosenstock-Huessy terms "emphatic living" (1970, 114), which preserves the usual emphasis of the first and second persons, in a revised grammar beginning with "you" in relation to "I," together with the tenses and moods/modes peculiar to them. It is the grammar of speech and speech-based philosophy, the new organon of social research, which strives to deliver a diagnostic of social malaise *and* initiates a concrete therapeutic mission of bringing life back to language.

ROSENZWEIG'S SPEECH-THINKING

Rosenstock-Huessy's grammatical method had a profound impact on another representative of the dialogic tradition, Franz Rosenzweig. Rosenzweig (2000, 127) declared that the *Practical Knowledge of the Soul* had "the decisive influence" on his own book, *The Star of Redemption* (1921). Furthermore, Rosenstock-Huessy played a key role in Rosenzweig's rejection of the Greek-based system of European philosophy, including Hegel's philosophy, which Rosenzweig devoted his doctoral dissertation to, in favor of his native Judaism, with its focus on revelation and the word (Stahmer, 1968, 151–3). *The Star of Redemption* is a monumental witness to this turn away from the Hellenistic to the Judaic worldview. It is for good reasons that Rosenzweig (2000, 91) referred to it as "my armor, the dangerous book." This study deliberately resists being read as a linear argument and grasped in a momentary flash of insight. Grand philosophical narratives such as Hegel's *Phenomenology of Spirit* or Schopenhauer's *The World as Will and Representation,* which fall under the regime of thought-based philosophy, can be grasped by thought with one blow even though the thought may take a thousand pages to develop. These books are meant to be conquered Napoleonic style, "in a bold advance on the enemy's main force, after whose defeat the small border fortresses will fall on their own" (2000, 113). That is why the best advice one can give to perplexed students is to soldier on through the vast terrain of text-covered pages, to not slip into the trenches between the dark lines of text, and to head for the principal idea, which will eventually shine through and help organize the entire book into a neat conceptual system the multiple relations of which can be grasped in one blow.

Compared to such systematic philosophies, Rosenzweig's *Star* appears as an antibook by design. It refuses to yield one idea graspable in a single blow. Its methods and aims are not derived from the laws of thought but rather anchored in the lived process of speaking and listening. They follow the relation inherent in the German language between the word (*Wort*) and answer (*Antwort*); "the word is only a beginning until it reaches the ear that re-ceives it and the mouth that re-sponds to it" (1985, 119). This eliciting of response is captured in the indissoluble relation between speaker and respondent: to the *I* there answers (*antwortet*) a *you* (1985, 188). This connectedness between a speaking mouth and a receptive ear is situated in the *Star* within a larger commentary on the book of Genesis and the Day Six, when God created man. The Creator spoke: let us make a man. In this "let us," the *I* addresses a *you* to itself (166). Yet this *I* of divine monologue is a hidden one. It only becomes audible with the discovery of the *You*, once divine solitude is broken with the creation of man to whom God can ask "Where are you?" "The I discovers itself at the moment where it affirms the existence of the You, through the question about where it is" (189).

Consider Rosenzweig's precise exposition of his speech-based method:

> Into the place of the method of thinking, as all previous philosophy developed it, steps the method of speaking. Thinking is timeless and wants to be. . . the ultimate, the goal is for it the first. Speaking is time-bound, time nourished. . . . it does not know in advance where it will arrive; it lets its cues be given by others. It lives in general from the life of the other, whether the audience of the narration or the respondent in the dialogue or the cospeaker in a chorus; whereas thinking is always solitary, even if it is happening among several "symphilosophizing" partners: even then, the other merely raises objections which I myself would really have to raise—which is the reason why most philosophical dialogues, including Plato's, are so boring. In actual conversation something happens; I do not know in advance what the other will say to me because I myself do not even know what I am going to say. . . . Language thinker—for of course the new, speaking thinking is thinking, just as much as the old, thinking thinking did not occur without inner speech; the difference between old and new, logical and grammatical thinking does not rest on loud versus quiet, but rather on needing the other and, what amounts to the same, on taking time seriously. . . ." (2000, 125)

Speaking thinking philosophy liberates us from the system-based philosophy and its concomitant desire for closure and finiteness of the *one* by preserving rather than absorbing the alterity of difference. Recall from the opening of chapter 1 that according to Rosenzweig, Western philosophers consistently strove to provide a single explanatory principle of reality, whether in terms of the Greek naturalistic philosophy and its focus on the cosmos, the theological Middle Ages and their exclusive attachment to God, or most recently and lastingly, the anthropological modernity (and idealism) with its reduction to "the I" (2000, 115). It was Rosenzweig's conviction that by replanting philosophy in the soil of the Judaic tradition this totalizing impulse of Greek-based philosophy and the drive for a unitary principle or category can be diverted and a philosophy of radical difference can begin to take root. The Judaic tradition does not collapse humanity, the world and God, and it does not raise one to the status of "the real essence" of the others. In grammatical terms, this philosophy preserves the difference between the God spoken about in the capitalized third person (He), the world spoken of as an impersonal "it," and humanity subsumed traditionally under the heading of the "I." Yet it does more than merely allocate these three defining grammatical categories of antiquity, Middle Ages, and modernity and idealism, in a multifarious tripartite universe. It is a *speech-based* philosophy, and as such it a unique position to reinsert the grammatical category of the second person into philosophical discourse, which was covered over in the traditional trio I-He-It. Better still, it is a philosophy in a unique position to recover the relation unfolding between dialogic partners as a unique site of interpersonal difference.

Unsurprisingly, it was Levinas who was most attentive to the revelation of difference in dialogue—even though he was also the most outspoken critic of the purported difficulties to give full justice to the separation between self and other in Buber's philosophy. Consider his comments:

> Dialogue is. . . not merely a way of speaking. Its significance has a general reach. It is transcendence. The saying involved in dialogue would not be one of the possible forms of transcendence but its original mode. Better again, transcendence has not meaning except by way of an I saying You. It is the *dia* [*across*] of the dialogue. (1998, 147)

Rosenzweig was well aware of this revelation of difference within dialogue. After all,

> If the other were "in its deepest ground" the same as I, as Schopenhauer wants it, I could not love him to any degree, for I would be loving only myself. Or if God were "in me" or merely "my loftier self". . . this would constitute not merely an unnecessary linguistic obfuscation of an otherwise clear relation, but above all this God would hardly have anything to say to me, for what my loftier self has to say to me, I already know." (2000, 124–5)

The very event of dialogue is therefore a concrete site of nonidentity between *I* and *you*. To speak and to listen to another is to recognize the underivable singularity and novelty of the other who may always surprise me with her perspective, objection, or silence. The other of dialogue is not an a priori category of knowledge, which I already possess, but rather a mystery that continually dispossesses me in the direction of the unknown and the unknowable. Contra the illusion of thought knowing itself with the uncompromised intimacy of instantaneous intuitive insight, I do not know myself fully in the open-ended temporality of dialogue. I cannot anticipate where the dialogic adventure will lead and what will be discovered in the process. I play by ear—literally.

BUBER'S I AND YOU

As Levinas was correct to stress, this dialogic difference is compatible with proximity—it is the non-in-difference toward one another of dialogic partners, the distance of proximity, this "marvel of social relations" (1999, 93). Buber termed this marvelous opening of concern for without confusion with the other "the between" (*das Zwischen*) (for example, 1999). *The between* is the relational sphere common to both dialogic partners yet reaching beyond them. It is the surplus of significance engendered by people engaged in dialogue, which is irreducible to the special sphere of each. Importantly then, for Buber, the I-you relation is not reducible to the polarity of two isolated terms confronting one another, but contains an ambiguous nonsubstantial element of connectedness surging in the encounter between them. Consider again Levinas's insightful comments on the uniqueness of this notion:

> Buber shall insist upon the novel and primordial pattern of the relation that one cannot close up within the psyche of the I or the You. It is the between (*Zwischen*), an origin that disposes the I as I and the You as You, and which evidently could not be understood anew as a third instance, a subject, or a substance that would here lay a mediating role. This signifies a break not only with psychology but also with the ontological notions of both substance and subject, in order to assert a new modality of the between-the-two, itself signifying the ontology and the psyche of co-presence and of sociality. (1998, 148)

As Levinas rightly suggests, the modality of *the between* should not be construed as a mediating term, like a screen placed at midpoint of the dialogic exchange, but rather the field of force generated by their mutual engagement. This field can, but need not, be verbalized. Buber frequently refers to a shared gaze as an instance of I–you connectedness, where two individuals meet in the space circulated by their reciprocal regard, without uttering a word (for example, 1970, 79). The meeting can therefore be both an event of saying received by the other who lends me her ear, turning my vocal productions into speech, and of looking in a nonobservational manner, in which I am not a spectator looking *at* you but a coparticipant in the event of vision lighting up between us as mutual regard, without objectification. In *the between*, the dialogic partners share a sphere of speech and regard generated and unique to their encounter—hence the profound intimacy of the I–you moment, an intimacy underscored by Buber's persistent use of the familiar German *Du* and not the formal mode of address *Sie* reserved for strangers and nonequals.

The category of the between helps to emphasize the crucial point regarding Buber's principle of I–you connectedness: it is not an additive unity composed of isolated individuals or substances but a relational process. This relational process will be developed in this chapter under the heading of *a primordial duality*—a philosophical and grammatical category fit to capture interpersonal relatedness in its distinction from both a singular individual and a numerically impartial multiplicity. The category of duality applies both to the order of speech/grammar, regarded in the pragmatic context of use, and embodied existence, regarded in a dynamic and developmental context. I propose to develop this category in reference to Buber, with additional insights from Humboldt and Plato.

In Buber's philosophy, I–you indicates a basic posture or stance (*Haltung*) adopted by a human being. It is basic not only because it is developmentally first, but also because it provides a manner of standing in relation (*Beziehung*) with others that is filled with meaning. Adopting the I–you stance signifies an openness to the other with one's whole being and receiving the other in their singularity, not as a species of a genus but as an underivable and unique being. The I–you stance needs therefore to be distinguished from the objectivating, spectatorial, and instrumental I–it stance, where there is no relation but rather experience (*Erfahrung*) of the other from a detached nonparticipatory standpoint in a one-sided manner. While in the I–you relation the other is encountered in the lived present (*Gegegwart*), the objectivating experience freezes the other into a vestige from the past (*Vergangenheit*). It is important to highlight that the present of Buber's philosophy does not map onto the punctual now-moment cutting between the past and the future moments on a linear representation of time. The present is the extended lived process of being fully present to the other in the event of the encounter, such that the other "fills the firmament" rather than being one of multiple mundane entities competing for my attention. Being present (*Gegenwart*) designates therefore the temporal frame of ontological revelation in that I do not encounter an object amount other objects (*Gegenstand*) but being as such (1970, 113). Once the other gets objectified as being so-and-so, her being gets mediated by a set of relationally neutral, generally applicable categories of genus and species, which push the other out of the relational present to the disengaged past. Now, it is important to note that even though Buber introduces I–you and I–it stances in one breath in the opening sections of *I and Thou*, the latter is a derived notion that signifies a loss of the original connectedness and relational meaning, and marks the point of detachment and alienation from otherness into the solitude of the ego. The I–you and I–it stances are therefore not coprimordial, even though it may be that they are deployed together throughout human life and belong together to the dynamic of speech, this privileged (even though not exclusive) perspective on human life.

Consider how speech is the privileged site of I–you connectedness. Speech is a communicative practice that evidences the primacy of relational processes over against the detached stance of observation. To be sure, a formalist take on language would regard individual words as basic units of meaning, as in the classic "cat is on the mat" statement, where the two nouns designate entities in the world, connected by means of the existential copula "is." Buber's take on language departs from such a formalist standpoint and looks into how meaning arises in the practice of speaking. Focusing on examples from the so-called primitive languages, Buber points out that complex phrases rather than single words are basic units of meaning. The so-called primitives use entire sentence–words to convey emotionally pregnant meaning; for example the Zulu expression, "Where one cries, 'mother, I am lost,'" is a relationally rich equivalent of the analytic European "far away" (1970, 70). In such sentence–words, the wholeness of interpersonal connectedness is made fully manifest—here persons have not yet achieved "the fully rounded independence of nouns and pronouns" (ibid.), but stand in an affectively charged relation to others and to the world. This original wholeness of the relation is underscored in Buber's own terminology, where "I"–"you" signifies the basic word—neither a single word nor a sum of two discrete words but an indissoluble word–*pair* (1970, 53), an original coupling of speaking partners that is neither a fusion nor an impartial multiplicity. This coupling is evidenced by the event of greeting (70)—a basic speech act in Buber's philosophy, which initiates discourse before any declarative statements about a third can be made.

In accordance with the indissoluble unity of the basic word, there is no "I" as such (54) and "I" and "you" are coprimary. "I require a you to become, becoming I, I say you" (62). ("*Ich werde am Du; Ich werdend spreche ich Du.*" Buber 2005, 18.) *I* is a consciousness of the constant partner (1970, 80) rather than a lone ego. To be sure, the Buber of *I and Thou* does not thematize the I–you stance as a permanent condition of the human lot but rather as an event erupting in our life on occasion, inevitably succeeded by detachment from the other and adoption of the I–it stance. This inevitability of I–you connectedness being succeeded by the I–it posture represents "the sublime melancholy of our lot" (68). At the same time, and notwithstanding their separation, the two modes do not necessarily take turns in neat separation: "often it is an intricately entangled series of events that is torturously dual" (69). This entanglement underscores, in my view, the inherently dialogic dynamic of language qua speech, which does not cease to address an at-least potential interlocutor even when it supplies statements about a nonparticipatory third party or an *it*. Put differently, speech about a third does not cease to be an event of *saying* oriented to the other, and so the I–it moment perpetuates rather than annulling the I–you relation. As Levinas aptly puts it, "The *Grundwort* I–Thou is ultimately the opening condition of all language, even the language that states the relation of pure knowledge expressed by the *Grundwort Ich–Es* (I–That) [I–it]; for the I–That [I–it], precisely because it is language, also addresses an interlocutor, and is already dialogue, or residue of dialogue" (1993, 41). To be sure, it is easy to forget about this dialogic dimension of language qua speech and elevate impersonal discourse above interpersonal connectedness in the pursuit of neutrality and objectivity. It may even be that Buber's own radical dichotomy between I–you and I–it stances is a mark of the forgetting that even the most objectivating discourse retains at least a residue of dialogue, and so is never at an absolute remove from I–you. Alternatively, it may be that the forgetting does not lie on the side of Buber but of the very I–it stance he describes; the forgetting of being rooted in communicative practice and dependent on the other by the detached ego adopting the I–it stance. It also needs to be added that in the texts postdating *I and Thou*, notably "Dialogue" (2002), Buber expands the notion of dialogue beyond the relatively constrictive notion of punctual encounters inevitably succeeded by alienation and detachment to the broader notion of the life of dialogue—a style of being in the world, marked by readiness and preparedness for engaging in dialogue whose temporality extends beyond the momentary presence of encounter and becomes coextensive with the temporality of life. This broader notion of dialogue exhibits, in my view, Buber's recognition that I–you connectedness is intrinsic to language qua speech and to life.

THE PRIMORDIAL DUALITY: BUBER, HUMBOLDT, PLATO

I–you connectedness can be fruitfully fleshed out by means of the principle of primordial duality (*Zweiheit*), a grammatical and philosophical notion irreducible to either fusional oneness or impartial multiplicity. Buber introduces the notion of duality in the context of his discussion of religion, especially in his criticism of the mystical striving for fusion with God and the Hindu notion that the one is more primary than the individuated self (1970, 132). However, the notion of duality is applicable beyond religious discourse; it underscores the primal actuality of dialogue (*Zwiesprache*, literally *two-speech*) as a relational engagement between nonidentical partners whose personhood would be annulled if the *two* were fused into *one* (133). It is likely that Buber's notion of duality was influenced by Humboldt's groundbreaking though little-known study on the "Dual Number." Buber cites this "significant treatise" in his "Dialogue" essay (2002, 31) and refers to Karl Loewith's book *The Individual in the Role of Fellowman*, which contains "a competent structural analysis, especially penetrating in its evaluation of Wilhelm von Humboldt's great findings in the philosophy of language" (2002, 258–9). However, Buber himself does not inquire into the direct relevance and explanatory potential of Humboldt's duality for the principle of I–you connectedness. In what follows, I propose to show how this notion helps to provide both grammatical and philosophical backing to Buber's dialogic principle.

Humboldt presented the lecture "Ueber den Dualis" to the Academy of Science in Berlin on April 26, 1827. This relatively remote date is of significance if only because this influential study has not yet been translated into English (the citations are my own translation). In this study, Humboldt makes the case for a dual number or duality (*Zweiheit*), which is irreducible to the traditional plural number. The duality in question is not simply a diminutive case of the plural number but a category that stands on its own. Between the *one* and the *many* Humboldt inserts therefore the category of twin-hood, rarely heard of in Western metaphysics but evidenced by the grammar of natural languages. An example of this duality can be found in ancient Greek, where *ho pais* stands for the child, *hoi paides* for children, but a separate grammatical category *tō paide* is used to indicate twins. Importantly, we find evidence of this dual number use in Plato's *Symposium* (189c ff.), in Aristophanes' celebrated speech on the twin nature of humanity. Aristophanes tells the story of the natural human form being originally that of congenitally conjoined twins. These twins were roundly shaped, two-faced, four-legged, and four-armed creatures, and could walk in any direction—or spin rapidly like cartwheels if they wanted to locomote fast. They were equipped with two sets of genitals, male–male, female–female, and mixed. These powerful beings "made attempts on the gods," and were severely punished by Zeus by being torn asunder. From that time on, each severed being longed for its other half, and desired intimacy with a man or a woman, depending on the nature of its original form. Men desired men, women desired women, and either desired the opposite sex, in accord with the composite character of the conjoined twin they previously formed a part.

It is easy to read Aristophanes' speech as a folk tale of nostalgia for original unity and indistinction. Notably Levinas reads Aristophanes' speech in *Totality and Infinity* as a clear expression of such a reduction of alterity to unity (1969, 254). Yet Levinas's reading is guilty of a double oversight. Firstly, he overlooks the multifarious nature of Eros celebrated in Aristophanes' speech, with its trinity of male–male, female–female, and female–male manifestations of desire. Levinas opts to read Eros exclusively in terms of heterosexual orientation as an attraction based on the difference between the sexes (1990, 85–6), and thus excludes homoeroticism from the economy of being. Secondly, he interprets the speech as a case of unambiguous desire for being one with the other, which reduces her alterity to sameness. The sexual duality of terms in the relation presupposes a preexisting whole, and thus posits love as fusion (1990, 86). This interpretation overlooks, however, the philosophical and grammatical category of duality operative in Aristophanes' speech, which does not translate into fusion and sameness, and does not project a totalizing oneness onto erotic partners. This latter oversight can be rectified with Humboldt's notion of duality, which supports my alternative reading of the myth.

I believe that the twinlike human form does not represent unequivocal sameness of the one but indicates rather the complex nonidentity of the dual number that refuses to be construed as either singular or plural. Plato's use of the dual rather than singular or plural number is grammatical and philosophical evidence that the original human form should not be read as a straightforward case of identity and sameness. Nor should we construe the separated twins in terms of sheer plurality of the many. Consider that plurality can be produced by multiplying instances of the same, as in adding apples to apples and oranges to oranges. Such a plurality is typified by numerical impartiality—items are added up to form aggregates with no internal relation binding multiple members. In the case of duality, however, the relational bond is integral to their numeric form, for a couple is not constituted by means of external additions but rather by a lived attraction and reciprocal attachment of the two who are not one. Aristophanes' story is, after all, the story of desire, not an impartial treatise on additions, and the question of the dual number cannot be settled by multiplication tables. It needs rather to be addressed phenomenologically as a lived mutuality, as a first- to second-person circularity of emotion experienced within the couplet.

This lived reciprocity within a pair is best exemplified by what Humboldt takes to be a key duality: the "I" and "you" pronouns. "I" and "you" are markers of interrelated speech roles of speaker and addressee that are integral and indispensable to language (*Sprache*) and grammar. The de facto existence of the dual number is therefore not only of philological and historico-philosophical but also of systematic interest; it provides us with deep insight into what constitutes speech. Humboldt insists that the function of speech does not consist only in the transmission of information; speech is the very fabric and medium of sociality (*Gesselligkeit*). Due to its social and dialogic nature, duality (*Zweiheit*) is built into speech qua speech. "There lies in the primordial essence of language an unalterable duality (*Dualismus*), and the possibility of speech itself is determined by addressing and replying (*Anrede und Erwiderung*)" (Humboldt 1907). The spoken word is in essential need of extention (*Erweiterung*) by the hearer and the respondent. This necessity of extention belongs to the archetype of all languages (*Urtypus aller Sprachen*), regardless of whether they dispose of personal pronouns of the "I" and "you" type. Language as such, language as speech (*Sprache*), deploys and marks speakers and hearers as coprimordial coparticipants in discourse. It may do so by means of semantically poor person deixis we are familiar with in Indo-European languages (I–you, *ich–Du, Je–Tu*), in which self and other are not marked for gender, race, social status. It may use more complex and content-laden forms of self and other reference that are infused with meanings related to the individual's role and position in the society. It may adopt self-deprecatory and honorific forms such as "your humble servant" and "your highness" to construe the relation in vertical rather than horizontal terms. Regardless of the weight of its semantic load and the nature of the relation established between the interlocutors, the mutual relation of address and response must obtain to form the key duality of speaker and hearer within which the speech unfolds.

Note that Humboldt's conception of speech differs profoundly from the received view of speech as *facultas repraesentandi* of ready-made concepts. For Humboldt, speech (or language) helps to fashion concepts and is a generative rather than reproductive faculty. In agreement with Schelling (1990, 40), who regards speech as imprint of the inner type of understanding, Humboldt (1999, 54) considers speech to be a veritable "organ of thought"—a corporeal source and generator of meanings. The corporeality of meaning-making must, needless to say, be construed in social terms as an inter-bodily process of vociferating to the other who receives and responds to the speaker's vibrations. Both share the aerial element in which their communications travel, and both are firmly supported by the back of the earth. Now, if speech is an organic element of thought and meaning-making, then its inherent duality of speaker and addressee must be inserted into the deepest levels of selfhood rather than regarded as secondary and derived. On this account, I–you connectedness is foundational and primary, whereas the lone ego appears as the philosopher's abstraction, a ghost settlement built on the ruins of communication. In this perspective, the muted subject of solitary thought can only be posited as primary if the philosopher becomes oblivious of the ways in which meanings are grounded and dependent on the community of speakers from which the philosopher learned to formulate and articulate her insights in the first place. The philosopher was after all a child who received the gift of language from her elders, and carries this gift around to even the most deserted parts of the world and to the loftiest regions of the mind. That is why Humboldt (1907) insists that the primordial duality of *I* and *you* is preserved even in solitary thinking: "Human thought is by nature accompanied by an inclination toward social existence. Apart from all relations based in the body and sensations, the human being longs, for the sake of thought, for a you corresponding to the I. The concept will acquire its clarity and certainty only through a reflection from a foreign intellect."

Humboldt's notion of duality, fleshed out in Plato's mythical account of the inescapably twinlike character of the human being, is a conceptual resource that underscores the uniqueness and irreducibility of interpersonal connectedness in Buber. It helps to transcend the usual paradigm of selfhood as a lone individual and sociality as a collective thereof, and embrace the primacy of person-in-relation. The notion of duality finds additional reinforcement in Buber's developmentally sensitive account of human embodiment. In a highly unusual move in Western philosophy, Buber does not privilege the viewpoint of an adult but begins with a child, and, even more uncharacteristically, with prenatal life. It is in these early stages of human development that the primacy of the I–you relation is clearly evident, even to an untrained observer:

> Now, whoever has observed children, especially in their first year, will have noticed that, both in the manner of looking and in the manner of certain motions. . . there exists a very specific kind of. . . relationship to a Thou. . . . The essential life of the child fulfills itself in relationships with a Thou. . . . the I begins in this relationship to a Thou. . . the I at first lifts itself out as one that confronts a Thou, and only afterwards. . . a plurality of He, She, It, of things. (1988, 66–67)

This developmental priority of interpersonal engagement in the I–you mode over manipulation of objects explains why some trained observers of childhood, notably ecological psychologists, turned to Buber's dialogic philosophy as a helpful conceptual resource in the effort to provide alternatives to the cognitivist perspectives on "the problem of other minds."[4] Buber helps to thematize relatedness to others as an original rather than derived state of human life. Buber is a radical thinker in that he situates I–you relatedness already in prenatal life. The life in utero is for Buber an instance of the natural bond (*Verbundenheit*) with the mother, where there is a "flowing toward each other, a bodily reciprocity" (1970, 76).[5] This intimate bond developed in utero remains pervasive throughout postpartum life, not in the naive sense of a craving to crawl back in but rather as an undying longing for one's true You. At birth, the child breaks off from the primary bond and enters the domain of elemental relations sustained by the shared medium of air and subsumed in Buber's ontology under the notion of the spirit (*Geist*) (1970, 76; 2005, 33). For Buber, it is a delusion of thought-based philosophy that spirit is inward; on the contrary, spirit should be thematized as the relational element of interpersonal life (1970, 141). In this way Buber returns the term *spirit* to the etymologically original meaning of breathing (*spirare*), but he avoids the usual individualist/internalist move of Western philosophy by restoring the elemental air, shared with others, to the breath. Buber's spirit does not therefore belong to purified consciousness and nothingness but to the animate life of the flesh, situated in its natural environment.

Returning to the question of the innate You, it is significant that the newly born child, separated from the mother's inner environment and emergent out of the elemental fluids it bathed in, retains the intimately relational nature of the earliest stages of its prenatal life. The mother and the newborn laid on her belly are not, after all, strangers introduced for the first time but long-time intimates; she is familiar with the child's unique style of movement, her patterns of rest and activity; the child is familiar with the mother's heartbeat, unique style of speaking, and with her touch. Their shared life extends and concretizes therefore what Buber terms the a priori of relation, the yearning for an innate You, which predates the separation of birth (1970, 78). In another atypical statement in Western philosophy, Buber regards this corporeal relational a priori as a precondition of speech. He terms it a "wordless anticipation of saying You" (1970, 78), an original orientation to the other that precedes and conditions the verbalized second-person address in the subsequent stages of human life.

I would like to suggest that Buber's remarks concerning the prenatal bond with the mother and its further elaboration in a longing for an innate You resonate profoundly with Aristophanes' speech about the originally twinlike nature of humanity and the desire for the other with whom one was originally organically connected. Buber, like Plato's Aristophanes, situates the original human form in the complex duality of a congenitally conjoined being that is neither *one* nor *many*. After all, it is only from the standpoint of a disinterested observer that a pregnant woman appears as an unambiguous *one;* the other enveloped by her belly is hidden from sight, and so, it would seem, from the mind. From her own standpoint, however, the pregnant woman exists in a complex relational nonidentity with the child, whose inalienable stirrings she may experience as the presence of a parasite feeding off her body and sapping her energy, as an intruder in the house refusing to go away, as a burden but also a joy, as a companion and playmate. This relational nonidentity is therefore on a par with the woman's host of attachments to the separated intimate others with its wide and often ambivalent spectrum of emotional colorings and with their entangled interests and destinies. After all, it is an illusion that the relations of dependency terminate or wane in the postpartum life and that the borders of the skin contain fully autonomous and sovereign selves; it seems more correct to say that relations of interdependency typify human life in its ongoing quest for meaning and value.

I believe that the experience of relational nonidentity with an intimate other is reflected in Buber's genetically accurate story of human life. In that narrative, we begin as unequal twins, growing in and off the nurturing and supportive body of the mother, in a relation too enveloping and intimate to be captured in rigorous phenomenological description. Only mythical discourse, like that preferred by Aristophanes, can serve to retrieve this ambiguous dawn of human life in its vital attachment to the other. Aristophanes' myth provides indirect insight into this living bond of an originally conjoined being, the profound intimacy within the relation, as well as the eventual breaking off and the eternal longing for the intimate other. Needless to say, to point to the similarity between Buber's narrative of pregnant relationality and Plato's/Aristophanes' twinhood is not to oversee the differences. Buber's child is of woman born, while Plato's twin is separated from either a male or female body. The child and the mother stand in a bigenerational relation, while the twins span a single generation. The focus in Plato's myth on the origins of human desire in its multifarious forms, while the focus in Buber's account, is on the primordial connectedness to the You in the developmental and ontological primacy of relation. Buber's child is an internal and invisible twin, bathing in elemental fluids, the environing world muffled by the cushions of the mother's womb. It is the maternal body that serves as the primary environment, even though the child is not cut off from the larger "life horizon" of mother nature, Buber tells us (1970, 76). Plato's twin is neither internal nor external but contiguous, and both are steeped in the elemental air; still, the intimate other of the conjoined twin provides also a grown-in filter of the environing world such that each side experiences the environment with and through the other.

I conclude that despite the nonnegligible differences, Plato's and Buber's stories of twinlike nature of humanity share the grammatical and philosophical notion of unsurpassable duality as the vehicle of relation in desire and speech. Combined with Humboldt's linguistic insights, they help us to venture beyond the limits of thought-based philosophy and its muted singular subjects into the world of interconnected excitable, vociferating, and sensitive bodies, bathing in the elements and supported by the back of the earth.

They enable us to overcome the traditional metaphysical numerology of the one and the many, wherein the self can only be thematized as an individual one and sociality as an impartial aggregate of the many. Instead, they make it possible for us to get at the heart of I–you connectedness as the primary relational bond inscribed in our living flesh and enacted in speech, which founds communal living with others in society. As argued in chapter 2, a vibrant I–you relation is indispensable for founding, preserving, and restoring the living *we* of a community. Or as Buber put it, "the word always arises only between an I and a Thou, and the element from which the We receives its life is speech, the communal speaking that begins in the midst of speaking to one another" (1999, 106). We can thematize communities and nations, these communities of communities, only if we begin with the "immediacy of relation" (Rome, 1964, 68; 71). I believe therefore that Buber's as well as Humboldt's and Plato's narratives discussed in this chapter provide rich resources for developing an experientially rooted theory of sociality, and that the principle of primordial duality should be adopted as a starting point in a genetically accurate description of being with others within the multidiscipline of dialogical phenomenology.

CHAPTER 5

BUBER AND HIS CRITICS

In this chapter, I propose to engage Buber in dialogue with some of his most eloquent critics, Rosenstock-Huessy and Levinas. Engaging Rosenstock-Huessy's critique will help to appreciate the *phenomenological* character of Buber's speech-based philosophy. Even more important however is it to engage Levinas's influential but also tendentious and ultimately harmful critique of Buber. Levinas's critique of Buber's ethics of fellowship, oriented by an ethics of the responsibility to the face of the other, has received a certain notoriety within the contemporary Continental scholarship, but it may be based on an uncharitable and ultimately distorting reading of the dialogic philosopher. It is therefore urgent to examine this critique in a critical light, and reconsider the position of Buber in particular and the dialogical tradition in general within the contemporary Continental philosophical canon.

ROSENSTOCK-HUESSY: NAMES AND PRONOUNS

In the direct exchange with Buber (*Philosophical Interrogations*), Rosenstock-Huessy critiqued the philosophy of I–you connectedness for privileging personalist pronominal discourse at the expense of discourse involving names, and, concomitantly, for privileging the present time at the expense of history. In Rosenstock-Huessy's words, "*ich* (I) and *Du* (Thou) are fictitious abbreviations for the real pluri-aged, named, 'nationalized,' and century-bound real person. To me, pronouns are *omissions*. . . . You are Mr. Friedman and Maurice Friedman long before you are I or Thou" (Rome, 1964, 32). Following Rosenstock-Huessy, Buber *omitted* the larger historical and futural dimensions of personhood from his account ("pronouns are *omissions*") by focusing on the personal pronouns of direct address employed in the actual encounters between flesh-and-blood beings rather than on the usage of the personal name that precedes and exceeds these encounters. Buber thus excluded the past and the future from his philosophy of dialogue, and confined it narrowly to the present within which interpersonal relations take place. In his response, Buber conceded that "memory and promise are mingled in language, and both extend immeasurably beyond the birth and death of the speaker." However, Buber observes that historicity does not capture the radical novelty of the "eternally new event" of "the saying," which is irreducible to the historical sedimentation of "the said," that is, the informational content of the utterance. Now, the saying as an event stands in the personal present, which cannot be derived from the past. It captures the untraceable being of each person, best witnessed in the welcoming of a newborn child. "What addresses you, not in the said but in the saying, is the underivable person, the now living new creature. The person becomes known in the I-Thou relation" (34).

This relational quality of being a person is captured in the personal pronouns and is missing in the case of proper names. Buber notes that the act of name-giving need not place the giver and the recipient of the name in a personal relation. The name might be assigned to the child by a "superintendent of an orphanage" with no genuine Thou being exchanged in the process (35). Hence names can (though do not have to) bypass the personal dynamic of living relations in ways that pronouns, with their inextricable invocative mode enacted in their utterance, never could. I conclude therefore that by privileging the personalist pronominal discourse over discourse involving names, Buber follows the phenomenological directive of description rooted in the very phenomenon it describes. His focus is on personal life as it is lived from birth to death, in dialogic engagement with others, and not the impersonal records of life generated in third-person documentation. His methods are therefore applicable to the descriptive task historically undertaken by phenomenology, with the added benefit of retrieving I–you connectedness in the process.

LEVINAS: RECIPROCITY AND RESPONSIBILITY

I now turn to Buber's most famous and accomplished critic, Emmanuel Levinas. Levinas is the most insightful ambassador of the dialogic tradition in that he fully recognized and articulated the original and revolutionary nature of Buber's notion of dialogue within the western philosophical tradition, in its potential to transcend the subjectivism of both modern and idealist traditions. At the same time, Levinas is the most tendentious and ultimately harmful caricaturist of the dialogic tradition, which he profoundly misconstrues in part to promote his own ethical philosophy of radical alterity. The harm produced thereby is all the more disturbing in that Levinas's philosophy has gained ascendance and notoriety within the Continental tradition, whereas the dialogic tradition in general, and Buber's philosophy in particular, suffers a partial if not a total eclipse within Continental circles. It is unfortunate that Levinas's misreading of Buber is, with some notable exceptions, given full credit by experts in the area, with the end result being that the philosophy of the face succeeded in partially effacing the very tradition it is inspired and informed by. In what follows, I would like to point to ways of reversing this overwhelmingly critical tide by subjecting Levinas's key objections to Buber to critical analysis.

Levinas's marked difference from Buber lies in the construal of interpersonal relations. For Buber, the other is a partner engaged in the egalitarian and reciprocal relation of dialogue. This dialogue follows the inherent dynamic of the pronominal discourse, in which the interlocutors adopt the reversible speaker and addressee roles typically marked by "I" and "you" pronouns. The reversibility of speaker and addressee roles shapes the interpersonal relations in reciprocal terms, in the sense that both partners can play these two speech roles and that the roles are interrelated (there is not speaking without listening). Reciprocity is therefore evidenced even before the listener speaks back, for active listening is already a mark of coparticipation in dialogue via mutual attentiveness, which unfolds in the elemental *between*.

Levinas, like Buber, locates sociality in the domain of spoken discourse (1969, 204–7). He shares the notion that direct face-to-face relation is the primordial site of signification, which every recourse to language as a system of signs already presupposes. Levinas agrees therefore on assigning primacy to the word that is spoken. However, he insists that the speaking to the other should not be cast in the informal pronominal "I"–"you" discourse, if the absolute alterity of the other necessary for establishing ethics is to be preserved. To preserve the alterity of the other, it is necessary to account for the inherent elevation of the other with regard to the self, as evidenced in the formal mode of address directed to a stranger that is captured in the second-person pronoun *Vous* and missing in the informal *Tu* (and Buber's *Du*) (1993, 44). Following Levinas, only the formal address to a stranger can capture the ethical nature of acts of generosity without reciprocity; when I give to the other in need because of ethical obligations and without the expectation that the other gives back. The "I"–"you" discourse, is however inescapably committed to reciprocity since, "To Buber, the *Thou* that the *I* solicits is already, in that appeal, heard as an *I* who says *thou* to me. The appeal to the *Thou* by the *I* would thus be, for the *I*, the institution of a reciprocity, an equality or equity from the start" (1993, 43). Or as Buber himself put it: "Relation is reciprocity. My You acts on me as I act on it" (1970, 67).

This inherent reciprocity and ethical equality of I–you relations in principle excludes selfless generous acts in Levinas's view. Since I suppose that you will answer in the first person, I expect you to act in similar ways, to give as I have given. The I–you relation thus inadvertently turns into a "commercial relation," an "exchange of good behavior" predicated on the supposed symmetry of I and you (1999, 101). What must be put forward, as a precondition of ethics, is therefore a different reading of the basic "I"–"you" word in terms of a compulsion to service in the I and as a valorization of the other in a capitalized You (1998, 150). What is originary is a responsibility for the other in the ethical inequality of my subordination to the other in the "first person accusative," which precedes speaking in the "first person nominative" (1993, 43–4).

In response, Levinas's construal of reciprocity in pronominal discourse in terms of a quid pro quo is unjustified. As noted above, reciprocity of I–you relations does not stipulate that you do as I have done but first and foremost that you receive my gift. When I speak to you, you receive my gift by attending to what I am saying. If you do not receive, I have not been generous; if you do not listen, I have not said anything. It is this participatory *receptivity* of generous acts that counts as *reciprocity* in I–you relations; as such, it is far removed from the expectations of the commercial exchange of goods postulated by Levinas. Generosity is therefore reconcilable with the reciprocal dynamic of I–you relations, or, put more strongly, reciprocity (as the relation of giving and receiving) is itself a manifestation of generosity. This point remains true even though Buber occasionally uses the German term *Wechselwirkung* for reciprocity, and this term may have commercial connotations of exchange of goods and money. However, the term *Gegenseitigkeit* also used by Buber is free of commercial connotations, and focuses rather on the oppositionality in the facing orientation and the mutual turning of the partners in dialogue. This latter term underscores the shared attentiveness of the partners in face-to-face relations that is as much evidenced by the act of speaking as that of listening to the other, and that leaves room for the "accusatory" address directed at me by the other in the interplay of "I" and "you" pronouns. Consider also that the German *Du* employed by Buber is consistently capitalized, in accordance with the usual practice of respectful address in the German language, thus denoting the kind valorization of the other Levinas advocates. It is therefore unnecessary to resort to the formal *Sie* mode of address to valorize the other. It is also to be noted that the German *ich* is always in the lower case, contrary to the English capitalized "I." For Buber, respectful address may therefore be fully consistent with the intimacy of reciprocal relations cast in informal pronominal discourse, and the elevation of the other with regard to the self is manifest already in the grammar of *ich* and *Du*. Finally, as Levinas himself acknowledged in a later essay, the dimension of response to the other inherent in the I–you relation exhibits the ethical dimension of responsibility "of the one for the other" (1984, 317).

Levinas's critique of reciprocity extends however beyond the charge of purported commercialism implicated by the symmetry of self and other in I–you relations. As charged in probably the most caustic piece of criticism Levinas devoted to Buber ("Martin Buber and the Theory of Knowledge"), interpersonal relations can be deemed reciprocal only if regarded from the standpoint of an external observer who surveys and compares the two poles of the relation (1991, 147). Only a disengaged spectator is in the position to note that the other acts on the self as the self acts on the other, or that the two terms in the relation are interchangeable and play analogous roles. Levinas thus deliberately frames reciprocity in physicalistic terms, as if it were deployed by two polarities that produce a field of force between them. Sociality is predicated, however, upon the distancing of the radical other who commands me from above as a magisterial height (Rome 1964, 24–26). Buber's construal of interpersonal relation in terms of reciprocity would fatally overlook this elevation of the other above mundane being and confine the other to the universe of observable phenomena, thus enacting yet another totalizing gesture typical of ontology, which precludes the possibility of ethics. We need a radical separation between self and other in order to avoid such totalizing impulses. This separation acknowledges not only the irreducible height of the other with regard to the self, but also the "ineluctable character of isolated subjectivity," which Buber is said to have underestimated (Rome 1969, 94). Importantly, unlike Buber, and despite the emphasis on otherness, Levinas champions therefore a nonrelational notion of the self as enclosed monadic subjectivity, purportedly in view of safeguarding the radical separation between the self and the other necessary for a nontotalizing account of sociality. This "substantiality and independent reality of the self" is said to reside in the egoism and happiness of enjoyment (Rome 1969, 23; see also Levinas 1969, 109–52). For Buber, on the other hand, being an *I* outside of relations or egoism would not produce happiness but rather "the deepest suffering of which we are capable" (Rome 1969, 28). These differing notions of selfhood will have profound implications as far as the validity of Levinas's critique of Buber is concerned.

Consider first that the reciprocity of the bipolar relation construed by Levinas is again out of line with Buber's own characterization of I–you relations. Reciprocity does not amount to an externally manifest system of relations, akin to the recordable mutual physical impact of billiard balls. Reciprocity is a phenomenological datum of the relation, the lived sense of mutual attending in the relation, rather than a behaviorist record. Furthermore, reciprocity is a unique event generated within the meeting that cannot be derived or predicted based on the qualities of individual beings. As Buber argued, the meeting takes place thanks to grace, and cannot be willfully put into practice. That is why Gabriel Marcel (1991, 45) insisted that rather than talk of the field of forces generated in the I–you encounter, it may be more appropriate to talk about a creative milieu opening up between them. Such deliberately nonphysicalist language is better equipped to preserve the element of mystery in I–you connectedness, which does not fit the causally determined relational field obtaining between, for example, two magnetic poles. In the latter case, we are still talking of a "neutral unity" encompassing the two poles (Marcel 1991, 43), rather than a unique semantically charged encounter between singular beings. That is why Marcel ultimately wavered at using the term *relation (Beziehung)* in the discourse about I and You, opting instead for the unmistakably personal term *meeting* or *encounter (Begegnung)* (1991, 45). Marcel granted, however, that Buber consistently thematized I–you connectedness as such an unambiguously personal event, and the unique sphere of the *between* as a dimension accessible to the participants alone, despite his adoption of the term *relation*, with its possible connotations of impersonal neutrality. The spirit of Buber's philosophy definitely resists therefore the physicalist construal Levinas subjects I–you connectedness to, even if Buber's lack of rigor in the choice of vocabulary may have partially betrayed his intent. Furthermore, by reading reciprocity as a physical rather than a personal relation, Levinas deliberately misrepresents Buber's distinction between I–you and

I–it stances. Buber grants reciprocity exclusively to the engaged personal I–you stance and not to the disengaged I–it attitude of observation from a distance. It is therefore a gross oversight on Levinas's part to read reciprocity as an observable physical phenomenon attributable to the domain of the impersonal *it*-world.

Consider also that Buber was careful to note that reciprocal interpersonal relations do not involve interchangeable partners. The relation between the teacher and the student is a classic example of reciprocity for Buber (1970, 178), but that does not mean that the two partners play equivalent roles. To be sure, Buber notes that the teacher learns from the student, and the parent is, to a degree, reared by the child (1970, 67). Such unequal relations, however, "by their very nature may never unfold into complete mutuality if they are to remain faithful to their nature" (1970, 177). Buber concludes that mutuality is never complete (1970, 179), and there are degrees of mutuality in interpersonal relations (Rome 1969, 28). Buber's I–you relations, with their broad spectrum of mutual involvement that ranges from requited love to the necessarily unequal relation between the teacher and the student or the therapist and the client, are therefore quite different from, for example, Aristotle's model of perfect friendship. Buber's intent is to preserve the diversity and singularity of human relations, without devising a single universally applicable model to be projected onto them with the aim of preserving an ethically purified stance. As he puts it in response to Levinas, "The 'asymmetry' is only one of the possibilities of the I-Thou relation, not its rule, just as mutuality in all its gradations cannot be regarded as the rule" (Rome 1969, 28). Furthermore, Buber notes "Even as the foundation of an ethic, I cannot acknowledge 'asymmetry.' I live 'ethically' when I confirm and further my Thou in the right of his existence and the goal of his becoming, in all his otherness. I am not ethically bidden to regard and treat him as superior to me through his otherness" (ibid.)

It turns out therefore that Buber has a much broader conception of ethically pregnant relations to otherness than does Levinas, for whom the relation to the other figures ethically as a stranger commanding me from a magisterial height, while situated at an economic "low" (the other is inherently "poor, hungry, widowed, orphaned"), making it difficult to thematize the ethical in intimate and proximal situations of familial and familiar relations. Levinas's thinking appears rigidly constrained by the holy books in ways that make it difficult to thematize ethical action outside of the externally specified ethical comportment. In fact, Strasser pointed to the

Talmudic-rabbinical inspiration of his philosophy, contrasted with Buber's pietistic orientation informed by Hasidism, which lets the situation rather than the book determine the course of action (2004, 39). Buber's dialogic philosophy thus helps to envisage the possibility of ethical action in more varied and complex social contexts. This is in no way to deny the urgency of assisting the ones in need, and it is not to promote a purely spiritual friendship oblivious of the harsh reality of material life, as Levinas accuses Buber of doing (1991, 148 and 723). But it is to extend ethical responsibility to situations in which we continue to coexist even though the state of urgent need does not. As Buber puts it to Levinas, "when all are fed and clothed the real ethical problem will have just begun" (1991, 723). Furthermore, it is to explicitly acknowledge that the dispensation of aid constitutes an ethical action only if it recognizes the humanity of the other through respectful attentiveness and does not reduce the other to a suffering body in need. This latter relation would lack in reciprocity and equality.

Still more needs to be said regarding Levinas's critique predicated upon his misconstrual of reciprocity as the interchangeability of actions in the bipolar relation. To use one of Buber's canonical examples of I–you relations, consider that learning, like listening, is a mode of participatory reciprocity. If students learn, they reciprocate the teacher's efforts. Yet, learning is not teaching "in reverse"; learning is retroactive to teaching because it *takes time* for the student to receive the teaching. This temporal deferral inherent in I–you relations already manifests that teaching and learning (or speaking and listening) are interrelated but not interchangeable or equivalent. Only a static representation of reciprocity as two parallel lines that could be traversed indifferently in either direction can lend support to Levinas's model of equivalence/interchangeability. Yet this model is undone by the temporal process of reciprocity in teaching and speaking, wherein learning and listening are at an irreducible distance from the act they receive. As Levinas (1969; 1987) himself argues, in the context of his own ethical philosophy and not in his discussions of Buber, sociality is the domain of temporality par excellence, and the open-endedness of time supposes a relation to the other. The other is, inescapably, at a temporal "ahead" from oneself, and one is caught in the trail of perpetual tardiness when engaging another dialogically. It would be a generous act indeed to grant Buber such an overtly temporal understanding of I–you relations, which defies any project of fixing self and other in comparative quantifiable equivalencies of physical force at time X. After all, an overtly temporal understanding of interpersonal relations is fundamental to the dialogic tradition, as exemplified by the thought of Rosenzweig discussed above, where the open-ended temporality of dialogue means "being able to anticipate nothing, having to wait for everything, being dependent on the other for one's own" (cited above). Since Levinas's own conception of temporality in terms of the movement of transcendence instituted by an in-principle unpredictable other draws on these insights from the dialogic tradition, it is shortsighted at best to force the philosophy of sociality developed by one of the major dialogic thinkers into the static rendition of time as a tic-tac sequence of self-contained and nontranscendent temporal units that can be calculated with precision in physical science.

Fortunately, there are some resources in Buber's philosophy for fleshing out this temporal dynamic of I–you reciprocity that does not map onto two parallel lines that could be traversed indifferently in either direction. As Buber repeatedly notes in *I and Thou*, the lines of relation between *I* and *you*, though parallel, intersect (for example, 1970, 84). Reciprocity does not therefore suggest that my experience is the obverse of the other's, but rather, to use the term preferred by Merleau-Ponty, that there is a chiasm in interpersonal relations, that is, a crossing without coincidence. This crossing or intertwining of speaking and listening, teaching and learning, in interpersonal relations helps to represent both the irreducible dehiscence *and* the intimate interrelation of the dialogic partners; it captures the temporal nonidentity of speaking and listening *and* their interdependency. Yet a schema of two crossing currents does not on its own suffice to make the temporality of the dialogic process alive. Schemas live a spatial life, and need to be reanimated with a renewed investigation of the temporality of dialogue. To be sure, Buber consistently thematized the temporal dimension of dialogue as the present (*Gegenwart*), which may suggest that he privileged an unmediated now, and was wedded to the metaphysics of the present of which Derrida accused Husserl. And yet I contend that Buber's notion of a primary duality carries an implicit dimension of a *dual time* as the temporality peculiar and inextricable from the dynamics of dialogue. Levinas's critique of *synchronous time* as incompatible with a relation respectful of the alterity of the other, and his notion of *diachrony* as openness toward the authentic future that is not a derivation and projection of the present (Levinas 1990a), would read then as a much-needed elaboration rather than an external critique of the dialogic relation thematized by Buber. The *dia* of diachrony is after all the same as the *dia* of dialogue, that is, it is the across or *between* dimension of speech (*logos*) opened up within the irrecuperable transcendence of time (*chronos*). It is as if the space of dialogue could only open up in temporality, as if the difference between interlocutors was never a neutral spatial separation but inescapably a relationally charged and temporal nonidentity as well. We would then need to speak *dia-chrono-logue* in one breath to capture the temporalizing spacing of the across/between in interpersonal relation. On this *dia-chrono-logical* reading, the intersecting currents of I–you connectedness envisaged by Buber flow and meet (or cross) and remain two rather than one. The chiasm of I–you connectedness appears therefore as a complex nonidentity of both spatial and temporal kind, a situated transcendence that does not need to leap out of the body and the world to attain a purely ethical character. If such a reading of a spatiotemporal chiasm can be granted to Buber, then his notion of reciprocity is free of the charges of equivalence and symmetry within a purportedly synchronous relation between self and other.

Consider also how Buber's notion of chiasm differs from Merleau-Ponty's. Contrary to Merleau-Ponty's notion of chiasm as the reversibility of the senses which, in agreement with the individualist commitments of phenomenology, is derived from the dynamics of a singular body and subsequently projected onto intercorporeity, the chiasmatic structure of reciprocity in Buber's philosophy is situated originarily within the primordial duality of social relations. From Buber's point of view, the interrelation of seeing and being seen, of touching and being touched, is not simply a phenomenon of meaning-neutral sensibility of an animate organism but a site of meaning and value. As such it belongs from the start to the world shared with others whose touch and gaze *speaks* to me in multiple ways even before I begin to speak, and it is more primary than the reflexive situation of one of my own hands touching the other, or me contemplating my body reflection in the mirror. Within the genetically sensitive viewpoint adopted by Buber and other dialogic philosophers, the living human receives and responds to multiple sensory overtures from environing others well before she may engage in self-directed exercises of sensibility that routinely serve as the starting point of analysis in Merleau-Ponty's ontology of the flesh. These cases of auto-sensibility are only subsequently extended onto the realm of corporeal relations to the other, as in the reversibility of my own hands touching one another being also exemplified by the handshake. "The hand of the other that I shake is to be understood on the mode of the touching-touched hand" (Merleau-Ponty 2003, 109 [French]); "The handshake too is reversible, I can feel myself touched as well and at the same time as touching" (1968, 142). Both self-touch and other-touch are believed therefore to exemplify the anonymous reversible dynamic of activity and passivity that runs in multiple vectors throughout the flesh of the world. Unsurprisingly on this account, the other is consistently construed as a replica of the self, and interpersonal relations are devalued in favor of impersonal corporeality, of which the self and the other are exemplars.[1] Notwithstanding its groundbreaking contributions to the phenomenology of the body, Merleau-Ponty's philosophy remains therefore tributary of the ego–alter ego schema underpinning Husserl's transcendental theory of subjectivity. Buber's philosophy of embodied reciprocity, on the other hand, provides the means of conclusively breaking away with the egocentric tradition. Within Buber's philosophy, the corporeal reversibility of the senses is predicated upon the reciprocity of I–you relations rather than derived from the individual body; it therefore has an intrinsic communicative import; it is laden with meaning and value from the start.

In conclusion, a philosophy of the body can shed the individualist bias only if it founds reversibility on reciprocity, not the other way round. The starting point of inquiry for such a philosophy is situated within the primordial duality of relation rather than anonymous ontological principle of reversibility exemplified indifferently within *and* between bodies.

Returning to Levinas's critique that Buber adopted the stance of an external observer in his construal of I–you relations in terms of reciprocity, consider that it is rather the case that Levinas himself adopts such an external stance. Recall that reciprocity unfolds in the elemental *between* generated within the dialogic relation, and this interspace of dialogue is a dimension accessible to the participants alone, not to an external observer. The reciprocity of the relation does not therefore translate into the relative degree of symmetry in the distribution of power, knowledge, experience, and so on, between the participants in the relation. The teacher is, one hopes, more knowledgeable and experienced than the student, and does typically wield a greater amount of power within the relation (even though no standard measuring unit exists to quantify and compare these elements). However, to focus exclusively on these externally determinable elements is precisely to lose the focus on the relational dynamic within the relation and to adopt the point of an external observer who compares the two parties from afar, the stance that Buber does not adopt in his talk about mutuality. (It is rather a stance forced upon Buber's analysis by Levinas, who subsequently accuses Buber of adopting this very stance.) For Buber, mutuality is generated by the relational Thou-saying and not by an indifferent comparative assessment of the two parties regarded as discrete individuals. As Buber notes, the statement "I become in the Thou; becoming I, I say Thou" (1970, 62) is to be interpreted as "My I—by which here the I of the I-Thou relation is to be understood—I owe to saying thou, not to the person to whom I say Thou" (1991, 697). In other words my identity is constituted in the speech-sustained relation to the other and not via a usurpation of the identity of the other. The conflict between Buber and Levinas arises precisely because they talk about different things when they talk about sociality—for Buber it is the relational *between* opened up by the interlocutors in dialogue that exceeds the two individuals (even though it does not dissolve them into some mystical fusion), whereas for Levinas it is a "relation without relation" (1969, 60 and 295) in which the self and other are regarded as monadic entities. Levinas's charge of symmetry supposes that Buber employs an analogous nonrelational understanding of selfhood that Levinas himself promoted, and that Buber made the mistake of regarding the self and the other as ontologically similar rather than radically different, thus abolishing the distance between the two. However, Levinas's critique projects the notion of selfhood devised in his own philosophy and is inapplicable to Buber's; paradoxically then, it is guilty of a totalizing gesture that fails to respect the difference between Buber's dialogic philosophy and his own.

Before concluding, consider one final charge repeatedly raised by Levinas against Buber. It concerns the purported formalism of the I–you relation, that is, its emptiness of content. Levinas claims that since Buber does not consistently confine the I–you relation to human sociality alone, but extends it to nature, as well as works of art, he effectively voids I–you connectedness of any specific meaning (for example, 1991). As is well known, Levinas's ethical philosophy applies solely to the human face, at the exclusion of nonhuman life, and some have wondered just how this prerequisite of shared humanity can be reconciled with the stress on the radical mystery of the other, irreducible to any specific content. Following that criticism, it would be Buber rather than Levinas who has the means of welcoming the other, any other, into an ethically pregnant universe, without setting up preconditions for ethical standing along the lines of humanism. As Buber put it to Levinas, "I find. . . that our relationship to the domestic animals with whom we live, and even that to the plants in our gardens, is properly included as the lowest floor of the ethical building" (Rome 1964, 28). The ethics of Buber's philosophy of dialogue may therefore be characterized by a far greater openness that Levinas's ethics of the human face. Buber's ethics does not, however, conflate between humanity and the nonhuman others; there are gradations of reciprocity within ethically pregnant relations, and our life with nonhuman animals is situated at the threshold of mutuality and language (1970, 150 and 173). The relation between humans, on the other hand, is distinguished by its access to language in the mutuality of speech and reply (1970, 151). The interhuman relation remains, therefore, the privileged locus of dialogue in Buber's philosophy, in accordance with its speech orientation and preoccupation with sociality.

EPILOGUE

The studies conducted in this book have the explicit purpose of unsettling the egocentric tradition and proposing an alternative polycentric view, supported by renewed phenomenological description as well as the relevant contributions from sociolinguistics, developmental psychology, and the philosophy of dialogue. I challenge the individualist bias clearly apparent in the transcendental phenomenology of subjectivity, in which the first-person stance, typically deployed in overtly or covertly interpersonal contexts, gets internalized and mentalized, and thus stripped of its originary connectedness to the second person. I locate such an individualistic sense of personhood primarily in the transcendental phenomenology of Husserl, and I leave open the question of the extent of its influence on post-Husserlian phenomenology. I advocate the need for a dialogical phenomenology that resists the subjective turn, and preserves the primacy of I–you connectedness in personhood. Needless to say, this project is profoundly indebted to the developments in existential phenomenology, notably to the ontological categories of inescapably mundane and corporeal existence. In line with existential phenomenologists, I think of persons as embodied and embedded in the shared elemental world. However, I believe that these ontological categories are more helpful when thematized within a social rather than an individualist space. I hope to have shown how meaning and value, within mundane embodiment and perception, are enabled and constrained by first- to second-person relatedness in ways that have not been adequately captured by the phenomenological accounts of first-person experience. Even though I thematize I–you relatedness at length within speech, I argue also that it extends to the phenomenology of human experience at large, and captures its inherently dialogic dimension.

The relatively wide disciplinary focus of my inquiry helped to provide multiple perspectives on this central question of interpersonal connectedness. Contributions from sociolinguistics helped to develop the interrelated notions of personal and spatial deixis, whose polycentric perspectival configuration lends evidence to the coprimacy of the first and second person in situated perceptual experience of the world, as well as in speech. These empirical contributions enable me to dispel the interrelated transcendental phenomenological notions of an egological subject and the absolute *here*, as well as to flesh out the alternative notion of a situated viewpoint for spatial orientation and self-reference in discourse, which reverses, without objectification, into a *you* and a *there* within social and spatial deixis. Contributions from developmental psychology help develop the temporal aspects of first- to second-person interaction, notably the shifting addressor/addressee role and the turn-taking pattern of dialogue, whose manifestations are found already within the protoconversational exchanges with the caregiver in infancy. I have hypothesized that these temporally and rhythmically patterned interactions provide the cognitive scaffolding for acquiring personal deictic markers, and that young children are typically well primed for the acquisition of first- and second-person reference in language since they have already been familiarized with its prelinguistic forms in face-to-face interactions via gesture, gaze, and touch. The developmental empirical material provides support for the view that we are immersed in I–you connectedness long before the "I" and "you" markers are fully mastered in complex and varied conversational contexts.

Contributions from the dialogic tradition in philosophy helped to further develop a nonegocentric vision of interpersonal connectedness in terms of the primordial duality, irreducible to the usual metaphysical categories such as the singularity of the one and an impartial multiplicity of the many. I argue that duality is an irreducible, intrinsically relational category, and that it finds support both in the grammatical/philosophical category of the dual number, captured by Buber's "I"–"you" word-pair as well as the mythical accounts of original twin-hood of the human form. I therefore provide additional theoretical evidence for the primacy of I–you connectedness, understood as an indissoluble nonunitary dimension of personhood, and therefore as a direct challenge to the thesis of the primacy of an isolated nonrelational self.

I hope to have demonstrated in the course of my pluridisciplinary studies that there are direct benefits to a line of inquiry that creatively combines contributions from theoretical and empirical disciplines. For one, empirical studies validate and give extra weight to reflective insights. However, theoretical disciplines can also have a direct impact on empirical research by offering a nonindividualist frame of reference for the scientist to employ in her design of the experiments and the interpretation of the data. As shown in this book, some empirical psychologists would well benefit from an alternative conception of personhood in their lab work, and might thus be able to resist, for example, the impulse to construe the process of language acquisition in incomprehensibly subjectivist terms. I therefore employ the method of mutual constraint and illumination of interdisciplinary study by enriching phenomenological description with empirical material, but also by exposing and correcting the theoretical frameworks within which empirical research is conducted.

DIALOGICAL PHENOMENOLOGY

Interesting methodological conclusions follow from a deliberately interdisciplinary take on personhood. For one, they open the door for the multidiscipline of *dialogical phenomenology,* a method of descriptive analysis of human life that is emancipated from the transcendental heritage of classical phenomenology and able to speak to the lived human experience itself, rather than the abstract conditions of possibility of that experience located in isolated intellect. Dialogical phenomenology thus breaks to an extent with its historical tradition, but at the same time preserves the radical spirit of phenomenology in its attempt to retrieve human experience in all its existential complexity and concreteness. Rather than enact a reduction of the natural world and a retreat to first-person transcendental subjectivity, which constitutes the domain of third-person objectivities that other first-person transcendental subjects may validate, proponents of dialogic phenomenology advocate a reappraisal of the phenomenological method in terms of *wonder,* while insisting that wonder need not be spelled out as a subjective exercise but can be both shared *and* spurred by one's engagement with others in the first- to second-person mode. Within that mode, systems of sedimented meanings may become unsettled, lose their aura of intuitive certainty, and regain their status of an open, socially constituted practice rather than a pregiven fact. Dialogic engagement with others may produce such a "bracketing" effect of sedimented meanings, but it does not serve as a mere means to the end of enacting an epistemically motivated reduction. Instead, it enables a communal process of performing the reduction, in which the search for the truth inextricably intertwines with the communicative praxis of ethically pregnant relations to flesh-and-blood others. It is with others that one raises the question of meaning and value in speech, as well as in dialogic thought and nonphonophobic writing, which preserves connectedness between *logos* and *phone*.

Construed in this way, the phenomenological method appears as an open-ended process, a task that may be *infinite* (as Husserl noted) not simply because mighty intellectual efforts are required to reconstitute all the layers of meaning within the transcendentally constituted world, but because of the interpersonal temporality of the phenomenological practice, which consists of mapping out the network of objectivities populating the world *and* continuously renegotiating the applicability of these maps with one's guides and fellow travelers. The phenomenological reduction is *reductive* in a problematic, if possibly unintentional, sense when it limits the scope of inquiry to the first and third modes at the exclusion of the first-to-second mode of interrelatedness. It may therefore be more appropriate to shed the rhetoric of reduction, since it reduces too much, and opt for a naturalized inquiry that recovers its vital connectedness to the other as it makes pronouncements about the world.

From the dialogical point of view, the phenomenological method is not exhausted by the intentional relation of a collective of *I*-subjects to the objective *it*-world, but is enmeshed with the engagement to a *you*, my interlocutor, reader, and fellow practitioner of phenomenology. The philosophy of dialogue, as it turns out, inescapably depends on the practice of the dialogue of philosophy. That means that it coinvolves first- to second- as well as third-person stances; for as argued above, the I–you and I–it can be opposed only as long as one adheres to the illusion of purely declarative discourse, which could step out of the dialogic dimension of language and meaning and enact an I-it type of inquiry with no foundation in the I-you. We owe it to Kant that he prefixed declarative matter-of-fact statements with the transcendental "I think," grounding objective discourse in subjective thought. This transcendental prefix is located by some philosophers of personhood, like Castañeda, within the spoken language and posited as the mentalistic condition of possibility of enacting personal reference by means of the "I" pronoun. The multidisciplinary contributions discussed in this monograph challenge this transcendental move to the "I think" and its subjectivist construal of the first person. They suggest rather the primacy of first- to second-person address, and find this complex duality at work within the ordinary use of the pronoun "I," even in those instances where the relation of interpersonal address is not readily apparent and the pronoun "I" appears to operate in exclusion of others. In response to Kant, we need to prefix declarative sentences not with a transcendental *I*, enclosed within the subjectivist first-personal stance, but rather with the "I"–"you" couplet, which enacts interpersonal relatedness in speaking to an interlocutor, writing to a reader, and thinking to a potential addressee. "I think to you" (in silent thought, as well as in speaking and writing) would then be a more basic prefix than the abstracted "I think." The former prefix does not appear as the pole of pure reason, whose very possibility is challenged in this monograph, but rather as intrinsic to the "impure" reason practiced in the communities of embodied beings situated in a shared world. This impure reason is ridden with ambiguity without being meaningless, thick with the flesh without being resistant to thought, open-ended without being empty, dependent on others without compromising the autonomy of the self.

One could fret that the project of dialogic philosophy is endangered, and ultimately undone, by the fact that as soon as one speaks *about* dialogue, one has entered the *it*-discourse and left the dialogic dimension behind. Dialogue can be enacted and captured only *in actu*, the objection would continue, and resists the grasp of a philosopher who focuses on dialogue as the basic theme of inquiry. To dispel this objection, consider that within the perspective of I–you connectedness advocated here, dialogue appears both as the "subjective" and the "objective" end of philosophical inquiry, for it is the theme that is in question for the philosopher, but it is also the mode of engagement as she practices philosophy. It is only on the supposition of a disengaged thought, caught in a spectatorial rather than participatory stance, opposing a subject to the object of thinking, that one would worry about losing one's foothold in the dialogic dimension by speaking/thinking/writing about it. Once the dialogic dimension is recovered within the practice of philosophy, however, the risk of the objectification and concomitant loss of dialogue within the philosophy of dialogue dissipates.

THE DIALOGIC DIMENSION OF MEANING AND EXPERIENCE

Dialogical phenomenology proposes to thematize the dialogic dimension of meaning and experience in the deep sense, which extends beyond the overt instances of verbalized face-to-face communication, and includes also the cases of address to a potential, past, and future addressee in thinking and writing. The dialogic dimension thus gets broadly construed both to include and transcend surface instances of interpersonal interaction with a dialogic form, whether practiced in speech or utilized as a literary form in writing (for example, the form of dialogue used in philosophy by Plato, Boethius, Hume, or Berkeley). This deep sense of dialogue can be captured by an organic metaphor of a tree whose surface growth is enrooted in the deeper ground layers that may not be readily apparent to an observer but that sustain and enable the surface growth. This organic metaphor undercuts the usual transcendental/natural distinction, thought of in terms of two distinct layers of mute meanings/values *and* communicative acts, and thus helps to think of communicativeness and connectedness as intrinsic rather than extrinsic to meaning and value at both the surface and the deep level. This organic metaphor has the added benefit of enabling us to take the surface phenomena seriously, that is, not simply as enactments of already-constituted meanings, but rather as coconstituents of meaning, just as the surface growth and its interaction with the elements sustains the roots hidden in the ground. There can be an intrinsic dialogic dimension to speech, thought, and text because *there are* concrete "empirical" instances of speaking, thinking, and writing, some of which assume the overt dialogic form of interpersonal address (the relation between the surface and the depth of the ground is therefore bidirectional rather than unidirectional). And yet the dialogicity of these specific instances has not always been recognized as intrinsic to them, especially when no overt dialogic form is discernible in the thinking or writing style, and no flesh-and-blood interlocutor confronts the philosopher locked in the office or lost in one's own mind. Dialogue then gets construed narrowly in terms of the overt dialogic form, and the intrinsic dialogicity of speech, thought, and writing gets overshadowed by the dominant focus on the self.

It is my hope that this intrinsic dialogic dimension of speech as well as thinking and writing has been brought into relief in this monograph. I also hope that the sociolinguistic lens applied here helps to make a strong case for the deep sense of I–you connectedness as the deep grammar of speech, thought, and text.

Consider that the dialogic dimension in the sense developed in this monograph not only extends to the nonvisible roots of dialogic instances, but also includes the genetic dimension of dialogue, which harkens back to preverbal communication in infancy and childhood, and the intimate conjoinment with the body of the other during in utero existence. Thematized in such genetically sensitive, as well as beyond-the surface manner, the dialogic dimension resists being read narrowly as a string of rare moments of interpersonal connection, and the philosopher is therefore less tempted to fear its melancholic loss just as soon as the connection loosens. The philosopher's quest for meaning and value thus gets firmly situated in the ground of dialogue and is mindful of its genetic structure. The philosopher is therefore empowered to speak, write, and think dialogically. She can speak, write, and think *about* dialogue without objectification.

THE PRACTICE OF PHENOMENOLOGY

It is my contention that the vital I–you connectedness has been overshadowed in the model of subject-object intentionality, just as much as the dialogic dimension of language has been covered over within the account of language that privileges declarative third-person statements. The central objective of this book has been to restore the primacy of this dialogic dimension of language and thought, relying on contributions from both reflective and empirical disciplines. These contributions have helped to highlight the dramatic importance of first- to second-person engagement for personal development, especially the acquisition of language, but also they helped to clarify how first- to second-person relatedness shapes personhood and language in ways that reach beyond development, and capture some inescapable aspects of what we are and why we speak, write, and think. I believe that articulating the importance of this interpersonal relatedness has concrete implications for how we practice phenomenology and how we live as human beings. For one, it shifts the emphasis from the competitive to the collaborative dimension of human activity, and as such invites us to situate philosophical practice in the domain lying *between* the self and the other, wherein new meanings lighten up. This can be enacted practically in the dialogic style of education, in which *the meeting* between the teachers and the students is recognized as equally important to the learning/teaching process as is the acquisition of knowledge, refinement of oral and writing skills, and future success on the job market. Furthermore, since academics typically share their work at conferences, it is also worth pondering whether the traditional conference format, consisting of reading technical papers to a nonparticipatory audience, which gets a chance at some questions and answers in the final minutes of the presentation, could be challenged on the grounds that such institutional formatting tends to foreclose the possibility of communal thinking and lays greater focus on the speaker having to defend her views against the accusations and challenges leveled by peers, and lesser on the unique opportunity both the speaker and the auditors may have to advance their thinking in hitherto unthought-of ways. A smaller seminar-style roundtable discussion may provide a better setting for opening new meanings and unsettling the habitual ones than the court-of-justice format some academic gatherings call to mind.

IMPLICATIONS FOR POLITICS AND FEMINISM

There is a strong focus on speech in my monograph, since it helps to flesh out the participatory character of meaning-making. Contrary to the egocentric tradition, the meaning of a speech act is not a solitary accomplishment but is rather coconstituted by the interlocutors. This point can be fruitfully developed, as well as extended to the political arena those in classical phenomenology are hesitant to enter, in terms of Austin's speech-act theory and its contemporary applications in feminist theory, notably the work of Jennifer Hornsby and Rae Langton (1998). The authors draw on Austin's distinctions between the locutionary act, that is, the saying of certain words with a certain meaning or content; the illocutionary act, that is, performing an act *in* saying these words; and the perlocutionary act, namely, that *by* saying these words, certain effects follow. Consider an example. A woman says to a man who is making advances toward her: "I do not want to have sex with you." The locutionary act consists in the meaningful content of the woman's utterance, that is, in the fact that she does not produce mere noise but conveys meaning. The illocutionary act in this case is the woman's refusal to engage in sexual intercourse. The perlocutionary act includes the effects and consequences of the woman's utterance, and if she is successful, the withdrawal of the man. As Hornsby and Langton point out, the latter two acts cannot in fact be neatly disentangled in Austin's speech-act theory, since the illocutionary act itself supposes a response or an "uptake" by the hearer, which can be interpreted as a sort of effect of her utterance. The effect of the speaker on the hearer is found therefore within the illocutionary act itself, insofar as the hearer needs to recognize the speaker's intention (in this case, refusal), for the illocutionary act to carry force. The authors therefore propose a background condition of illocutionary acts, termed *reciprocity*.

> Reciprocity between speakers provides for someone's making of some noises being not merely her expression of a meaningful thought

(which is a locutionary act) but also, for instance, her stating something (which is an illocutionary act). . . . Normally when a speaker tells someone something, for instance, the hearer takes herself to have been told something—she knows what the speaker was up to. This is "uptake" in Austin's sense. Uptake consists in the speaker being taken to be performing the very illocutionary act that, in being so taken, she (the speaker) is performing. Language use then relies on a mutual capacity for uptake, which involves a minimal receptiveness on the part of language users in the role of hearers. This minimal receptiveness does not mean that a hearer will agree, or is even capable of agreeing, with what a speaker is saying; but it does mean that a hearer has a capacity to grasp what communicative act a speaker might be intending to perform. When reciprocity is present, the speaker's utterance works as she means it to. Its working so appears to depend on nothing more than speaker and hearer being parties of a normal linguistic exchange, in which a speaker's attempt to communicate is successful. A speaker tries to do an illocutionary thing; a hearer recognizing that the speaker is trying to do that thing is then sufficient for the speaker to actually do it. (Hornsby and Langton, 25)

The important conclusion following Hornsby and Langton's insightful analysis is that a speech act depends on the hearer's recognition of the speaker's intention to carry meaning, and is therefore not an individual accomplishment. The act of doing something with words, such as refusing to have sex, can be successful only if the hearer participates in the production of meaning, and the illocutionary act can get off the ground only if it is, to extend the term "interlocutive" previously used in the context of "I"–"you" pronouns (chapter 2), an interlocutionary act coinvolving the speaker and the hearer. The illocution would appear as a case of interlocution, and the speaker's connectedness to the hearer would be made fully apparent. This line of thought does not probably come as a surprise to the reader of this study. However, its political implications have not yet been developed, and I propose to shed some light on them in what follows.

Consider a speech act that fails. A woman says "No" to a man, using an appropriate locution for an act of refusal (the example is from Hornsby and Langton, 27, but the discussion is my own). However, the man refuses to recognize her illocution and grant her the right to refuse intercourse. The man rapes the woman. When charged with rape, the man might say something to the effect that the woman did not really mean *No*. She may have said it (locutionary act), but not with the intention of refusal (illocutionary act). Maybe her intention was to titillate and arouse him by saying *No*. He could hear the intention to have sex in the tone of her voice, and her provocative clothing had suggested consent rather than refusal. He had read her nonverbal intentions correctly, he might say. The perlocutionary effects of her locution are thus consistent with the illocutionary force of her perceived "body language" and appearance.

Needless to say, the man's defense only serves to confirm the crucial point that the woman is here deprived of the ability to make a successful speech act. The act of refusal is refused to her, and so the speaker fails to utter a *no* that means *No*, that is, a locution accompanied by the hearer's uptake and recognition of refusal. This specific speech act becomes impossible for her because of the hearer's refusal to regard her as a being with an inherent right to self-determination. Hornsby and Langton aptly term this deliberate absence of the hearer's uptake a case of "illocutionary disablement" (28) that makes certain speech acts unspeakable for women. They make the case that the illocutionary disablement of refusal is due, perhaps in part, to pornography, insofar as "pornographic speech acts help create a communicative climate in which the felicity conditions for some of women's speech are not met" (27). It is not my intention to address the question of whether or not pornographic speech contributes to illocutionary disablement within the limits of this epilogue. If it does, I would view it as a de facto effect that results from certain types of pornographic speech, themselves tributary of the larger history of oppression and discrimination of women in patriarchal society, rather than a de jure effect of pornographic speech in general. In other words, I do not think that pornography necessarily fuels illocutionary disablement of women. At the same time, I strongly believe that there are real cases of illocutionary disablement of women's speech, whether by blatant refusal to grant the woman the right to perform certain types of speech acts while allowing others, or by a more diffuse refusal to grant women's speech the weight and gravitas typically attributed to men's speech. I therefore strongly agree with Hornsby and Langton that speech acts bear on one's freedom as a speaker, and that the capacity for free speech depends on the hearer's recognition of the speaker as communicating what they mean to be doing when they make certain types of noise, which cannot be captured by regarding the speaker in isolation and by regarding speech acts as exclusively locutionary rather than illocutionary (and I would add, interlocutionary) acts. I agree therefore with the connection the authors establish between free speech and illocution.

This connection helps to bring into relief the ethical and political ramifications of speech. Speech is to be sure a natural capacity enabled by the typical bodily architecture and neurophysiology of the human organism. To speak, an animate being needs to be equipped with a mouth, a vocal box, an ear, and an efficient neural wiring. Phenomenological as well as cognitive psychological discourses typically limit themselves to viewing speech as such an embodied capacity. However, speaking is not limited to bodily givens, nor does the possession of the right vocalizing equipment guarantee one's ability to take up an active role in the domain of public discourse, or to perform certain types of speech acts successfully. In Christianity, St. Paul admonishes women to keep silent in the churches, and this silencing continues up to the present day with the refusal to grant women the right of representation in the Catholic clergy. In Islam, a woman attempting to employ the *talak* illocution to divorce her husband (by saying, "Divorced, divorced, divorced") necessarily fails because she is not a man. These examples demonstrate that speech is simultaneously a natural ability and a political right, which may or may not be granted. As in the rape example discussed above, the women's speech may be devalued and disempowered, and women face the real risk and/or are aware of the potential threat of such devaluing at some point or other in their professional and personal lives. Confronted by students with a strong sense of white-male entitlement, compounded with commitment to stereotypical gender norms, I experience their attempts of diffuse illocutionary disablement based on my gender and perceived age with regularity. My illocutionary acts associated with authority in the classroom, such as a *request* (to be in class on time, to contribute to classroom discussion, not to chat when class is in session), are at the risk of being undone by the absence of uptake and minimal receptiveness on these students' part (expressed in hostile and confrontational gaze, enacted bewilderment that punctuality and classroom participation are in fact expected, continued chatting). Some female colleagues of mine report a strong sense of the threat of physical violence from some of the students, especially if they are perceived as undermining the patriarchal society by their political views or sexual orientation. In those cases, the rape threat would and sometimes does transform illocutionary disablement from its diffuse state to a highly focused one, in that it attempts to undo the woman's authority by targeting her bodily integrity. The woman's response in such cases may here vary from a tense and defensive speech to a speech that fails and falters, and feels significantly inferior compared to her usual communicative and cognitive abilities.

The discussion of the speaker's dependence on the hearer's uptake for successful performance of speech acts echoes the thesis of I–you connectedness developed in this book, and it makes salient the inescapable ethical and political dimension of interpersonal relatedness in speech. The reciprocity of I–you typifies speech as a communicative practice coinvolving the speaker and the hearer, but it is in the contexts of presumed recognition of the speaker's ability and right to perform speech acts that the I–you reciprocity does in fact occur. Due in part to the masculine privilege exercised within the Western tradition, the philosophers of dialogue may have not fully appreciated that this recognition is never guaranteed, and that certain social groups are at a greater risk than others of being excluded from I–you reciprocity. This oversight can be corrected by emphasizing that I–you reciprocity is not a value-neutral sociolinguistic datum but a politically significant indicator of nonviolent mutual coexistence and participatory involvement in a nonhierarchical society, whose right may be refused or challenged to the members of various social groups at certain times. Pronominal discourse employing "I" and "you" may be a close-to-universal linguistic fact, with the speaker and addressee marking in discourse an inherent trait of spoken language. Yet, it is also an instrument of political representation in that it facilitates egalitarian relations and peaceful ways of engaging one another in the public arena. To deny certain groups the right to free speech, and to the recognition of the illocutionary force of their speech acts, is to deny them the right to participate fully in I–you relations.

It turns out, therefore, that an inquiry into the practice and experience of speech within society undoes the traditional distinction between descriptive science that focuses on matters of facts and the prescriptive or normative science that addresses rights and responsibilities in social and political life. Speech resists being cast in terms of value-neutral description of phenomena, whether the latter are approached from the point of view of a constituting consciousness or the structures of being. Speech inescapably spills over into the domain of the ethical and the political since it circumscribes the domain of personal rights of autodetermination and autonomy, which are never guaranteed by the individual alone but depend upon the active recognition by the other who lends me her ear and grants me the right to assert my rights in the course of our entangled lives. Without this interpersonal recognition rights are but empty words, hollow shells devoid of meaning. The implication of this necessary intertwining of the descriptive and normative layers in speech is that phenomenology itself must admit questions of ethical and political import into its regions, and shed the pretension of providing a disengaged documentary on human life. This pretension can only be preserved if human life is viewed along the individualist lines of inquiry as a predominantly private affair, hence politically neutral, and if political rights are assumed and henceforth concealed. The social understanding of selfhood in terms of originary I–you connectedness and interdependency promoted in this monograph exposes such an individualistic notion as a mentalistic construction of thought-based philosophy, traditionally practiced by those privileged enough not to fear for their rights. It challenges therefore the purported political and ethical neutrality of phenomenological description, and opens the possibility of providing a richer account of human life than is possible within a narrowly construed descriptive analysis. Political awareness exercised within phenomenology does, in my view, ultimately help to restore human existence in its complexity and speaks to the inextricable entanglement of the questions of what *is* and what *ought to be* the case in our interdependent lives.

Such a phenomenology is well benefited by contemporary research in feminist theory. It is striking in this regard that feminist authors such as Adriana Cavarero and Judith Butler actively adopt the principle of I–you connectedness in their recent work. In *Relating Narratives: Storytelling and Selfhood*, Cavarero expresses suspicion in the face of the 20th century philosophical rhetoric of alterity insofar as it is caught between the individualist and the collective notions of selfhood, captured by the first-person singular and plural but forgetful of the second person.

> Symptomatically, the you [*tu*] is a term that is not at home in modern and contemporary developments of ethics and politics. The "you" is ignored by the individualistic doctrines, which are too preoccupied with praising the rights of the *I*, and the "you" is masked by a Kantian form of ethics that is only capable of staging an I that addresses itself as a familiar "you" [*un "io" che si da solamente del "tu"*]. Neither does the "you" find a home in the schools of thought to which individualism is opposed—these schools reveal themselves for the most part to be affected by a moralistic vice, which, in order to avoid falling into the decadence of the *I*, avoids the contiguity of the *you*, and privileges collective, plural pronouns. Indeed, many "revolutionary" movements (which range from traditional communism

> to the feminism of sisterhood) seem to share a curious linguistic code based on the intrinsic morality of pronouns. The *we* is always positive, the *plural you* [*voi*] is a possible ally, the *they* has the face of an antagonist, the *I* is unseemly, and the *you* [*tu*] is, of course, superfluous. (90)

It is in the empathetic theory of literature, discussed in the context of autobiography, which reveals the fundamental dependency of the one who narrates her life on the *you* who enables her to develop a narratable self, that Cavarero locates a useful resource for feminist politics. She shows that the ability to tell one's life story is inescapably relational, enacted through the narrative engagement with an insuperable *you*. Such an empathetic theory of literature would, in her view, be in a position to subvert the dominant "curious morality of pronouns," and model the plural "we" on the relationship between "I" and "you" as it unfolds within literary practices, but also within our ethically pregnant lives.

In *Precarious Life*, Judith Butler explored the heightened vulnerability and exposure following the attacks of 9/11. Rather than construing this sense of "insecurity," deliberately enflamed and exploited by the US government, as an excuse to engage in acts of retaliation against the Arab other, and yet another opportunity to play out the fantasies of a sovereign state immune to external influence, she proposes to turn the sense of loss into a political resource for enacting a political community based on a renewed awareness of relational ties and ethical responsibility for one another. In a language strikingly resonant with Buber (whom she does not cite, even though she draws extensively on Levinas), Butler invites us to let the state of mourning and melancholia, following the World Trade Center and Pentagon attacks, serve as a sort of phenomenological reduction, unveiling profound interpersonal interconnectedness:

> When we lose certain people, or when we are dispossessed from a place, or a community, we may simply feel that we are undergoing something temporary, that mourning will be over and some restoration of prior order will be achieved. But maybe when we undergo what we do, something about who we are is revealed, something that delineates the ties we have to others, that shows us that these ties constitute what we are, ties or bonds that compose us. It is not as if an "I" exists independently over here and then simply loses a "you"

over there, especially if the attachment to "you" is part of what composes who "I" am. If I lose you, under these conditions, then I not only mourn the loss, but I become inscrutable to myself. Who "am" I, without you? When we lose some of these ties by which we are constituted, we do not know who we are or what to do. On one level, I think I have lost "you" only to discover that "I" have gone missing as well. At another level, perhaps what I have lost "in" you, that for which I have no ready vocabulary, is a relationality that is composed neither exclusively of myself nor you, but is to be conceived as *the tie* by which those terms are differentiated and related. (2004, 22)

Butler incites us to recover this relational tie and to transform the profound personal feeling of connectedness into a political resource for change. She believes a renewed political community can be founded on the experience of living inescapably with one another and depending on the other for one's own. She tells us to think together constitution and dispossession by one another, in the intertwined pleasures showered upon us by Eros and the threats posed by Thanatos. She offers a striking narrative of embodiment as vulnerability and exposure that cannot be confined to private subjectivity but underscores our situatedness within the shared world. She proposes that we envisage a community that "affirms relationality not only as a descriptive or historical fact of our formation, but also as an ongoing normative dimension of our social and political lives, one in which we are compelled to take stock of our interdependence" (2004, 27). I believe that this politics of bodily ties Butler advocates provides the best example within 20th century philosophy of how to practice with force and precision a politically responsible phenomenological inquiry into human life. I agree therefore with Bonnie Mann that Butler's recent thought exemplifies a phenomenological turn, and I believe that it shows also how to enact a much-needed political turn in phenomenology, aptly termed *liberation phenomenology* by John Murungi. It is my hope that this monograph helps to shed light on why this political turn is urgently needed, and why phenomenology risks stagnation if it fails *to raise* consciousness by aiming merely to describe it.

NOTES

CHAPTER 1: THE TRANSCENDENTAL TRADITION

1. The word "I" appears in quotation marks whenever it serves to mention the word/pronoun I. The word I is italicized whenever it is referring to more than just the part of speech, but rather to the entity/referent, such as the transcendental subject or a dialogical interlocutor acting in the first-person mode. Thus *I* should be read I-as-a-subject (in transcendental phenomenology) or I-as-addresser (in dialogical phenomenology), whereas "I" should be read I-as-a-word. Needless to say, the distinction is in emphasis, and not an absolute one.

2. An analogous point is made by, for instance, Castañeda (1999, ch. 10), discussed in chapter 2.

3. "Pure expression will be the pure active intention (spirit, *psyche,* life, will) of an act of meaning (*bedeuten*) that animates a speech whose content (*Bedeutung*) is present. It is present not in nature, since only indication takes place in nature and across space, but in consciousness." (Derrida, 1973, 40).

4. These insights are developed in the works of Vygotsky (1978).

5. A similar idea is articulated in *Thing and Space* (1997 [1907]), wherein Husserl stresses that pure consciousness arrived at after the phenomenological reduction does not belong to anybody or is impersonal.

6. Due to this import of a natural psychological concept into the pure transcendental domain, "in the foundation-laying reflections of the *Meditations*—those in which the epoche and its ego are introduced—a break of consistency occurs when this ego is identified with the pure soul." (1970 [1938], 79, 80). Descartes "persists in pure objectivism in spite of its subjective grounding [which] was possible only through the fact that the *mens,* which at first stood by itself in the epoche and functioned as the absolute ground of knowledge, grounding the objective sciences. . . appeared at the same time to *be* grounded along with everything else as a legitimate subject matter *within* the sciences, i.e. in psychology" (ibid.).

7. It needs to be added that Husserl did not regard the so-called Cartesian way as the only manner of performing the phenomenological reduction. In the *Crisis*, he outlined two alternative ways: through psychology, and through the lived world. (See discussion of the three ways in R. Bernet, I. Kern, E. Marbach. 1993. *An Introduction to Husserlian Phenomenology.* Evanston: Northwestern University Press, 1993, 66–75).

The English translator of the *Crisis* notes also that Husserl did not permit the German version of *Cartesian Meditations* to be published, and that he "had given up the project of a final version of the *Meditations* in favor of the *Crisis* as the definitive introduction to phenomenology" (155).

The redefinition of the phenomenological reduction in the *Crisis* does not however affect the egological conception of transcendental consciousness. The change of method fully preserves the contents yielded by the Cartesian way, notably the pure ego. I therefore view Husserl's conception of consciousness from the *Crisis* as continuous with the one developed in the *Cartesian Meditations,* insofar as the attachment to the Cartesian conception of consciousness remains intact.

8. For further discussion, see Stawarska. 2002. "Memory and Subjectivity: Sartre in Dialogue with Husserl." *Sartre Studies International,* vol. 8, no. 2, 94–111.

9. For further discussion of this point, see Stawarska (2004a).

10. On that question, see N. Depraz (1995).

11. Pol Vandevelde notes "En ce qui concerne autrui, l'imagination me permet d'avoir accès aux experiences d'autrui en me transposant, en une reproduction fictive, dans ce que je pourrais éprouver si j'étais à la place de l'autre. Le 'comme si' me permet d'élargir les frontières de mon expérience originale" (1996, 94).

12. See Bernet et al., 1993, 207.

13. Appendix 1 in Theunissen (1986): "Transcendental Philosophy and the Illusion of Dialogue: Alfred Schutz's Illusion of Dialogue."

14. See especially the "Postscript: The Transcendental Project of Social Ontology and the Philosophy of Dialogue" in Theunissen (1986).

CHAPTER 2: SOCIOLINGUISTICS

1. Definitions are from *The Oxford English Dictionary* online.

2. *Oxford English Dicti*onary online.

3. "Über die Verwandtschaft der Orts adverbien mit dem Pronomen in einigen Sprachen," *Gesammelte Schriften,* Band VI (Berlin: Preußische Akademie der Wissenschaften,) 304–30.

4. For example, Ryle (2000, 189) makes this point.

5. Incidentally, this narrative quality of personal identity may throw light on the staggering difficulty to retrieve the earliest childhood experiences, preceding the ability to tell and comprehend life stories.

6. Thanks to Bonnie Mann for sharing this example.

7. Wilhelm von Humboldt (1907), *Über den Dualis.*

8. Ibid.

9. I expand on Sartre's analysis of the effect of another person's gaze in Stawarska (2004b).

10. From G. Evans (1994).

11. For additional similarities and differences between Castañeda and Husserl, see J. G. Hart (1999).

CHAPTER 3: DEVELOPMENTAL PERSPECTIVES

1. *The Onion,* May 21, 1997.

2. "Piaget's bias is clear: the child will be an adult when she accepts that thinking is: (a) a matter of brain anatomy, (b) an internal event, (c) a subjective event, and (d)

disconnected from the material world. . . . our children are on the way to becoming little Cartesians who learn to stem the tide of subjectivity, animism, participation and magical thinking."

3. Meltzoff and Moore, 1977, 1989, 1994.

4. Infants can also differentially imitate facial gestures after a twenty-four-hour delay, with the adult who displayed the gesture on day one assuming a neutral face on day two. Meltzoff and Moore, 1994.

5. False-belief tasks were originally designed by Wimmer and Perner (1983).

6. For a further discussion of that point, see Gomez (1994).

7. See further discussion, Stawarska (2006).

8. See Stawarska (2007).

9. As presented in Jaffe et al. (2001). There may be slight differences in the parsing models used by the researchers in the field.

10. The idea that gesture and speech are inextricably interrelated has recently received substantial reinforcement from the leading researcher in the field, David McNeill (2005).

11. Austin (1962) noted that there may be as many as thousands of possible speech acts.

12. See Budwig (1990) for a study on personal-pronoun acquisition, which responds to Chiat's criticism of Charney's research and pays careful attention to the pragmatic context of personal-pronoun production in children, as well as to individual differences. For example, one child studied by Budwig (1990, 129) typically used *I* in utterances describing states and actions while she used a verbless *My* in control acts that attempt to bring about a change in the world. There is therefore a clear functional distinction in the child's use of these two forms of the first-personal pronoun.

CHAPTER 4: PHILOSOPHY OF DIALOGUE

1. See Buber "The History of the Dialogical Principle," in *Between Man and Man* (2002).

2. Diary entry, quoted in Stahmer (1968), 218.

3. For Rosenstock-Huessy, this primacy of the You is semantically complex in that it reads not only as a grammatical and social category, but also as a liturgical one (*Liturgical Thinking*, Stahmer 130). It designates the primacy of the divine figure of the Thou over against the human self, and thus introduces a steep hierarchy into the domain of I–you relations, wherein the self is embedded in a nonegalitarian relation with a higher being. It ultimately establishes the primacy of religious revelation over philosophical discourse in Rosenstock-Huessy's thinking, in accordance with the prologue to St. John's Gospel, which thematizes the eternal word (*logos*) as the originary word turned to flesh through divine creation. The status of the spoken word in Rosenstock-Huessy is thus not only sensuous and elemental (the lived sound traveling from the mouth to the ear and supported by the elemental air) but also sacramental—the word is granted a divine origin.

4. Jopling, D. 1993. *The Philosophy of Dialogue*. In *The Perceived Self: Ecological and Interpersonal Sources of Self-knowledge*, ed. U. Neisser. Cambridge: Cambridge University Press.

5. *Verbundenheit* is translated by Kaufmann as "association," but we know that Buber was weary of using abstract academic terminology in his writings and opted for more concrete and common terms. I therefore render *Verbundenheit* as "bond."

CHAPTER 5: BUBER AND HIS CRITICS

1. See Stawarska (2006) for further discussion.

REFERENCES

Austin, J. L. 1962. *How to Do Things with Words.* Cambridge: Harvard University Press.
Andersen, E. S., A. Dunlea, and L. S. Kekelis. 1984. "Blind Children's Language: Resolving Some Differences." *Journal of Child Language* 2:645–64.
Anscombe, G. E. M. 1991 [1975]. "The First Person." In *The Nature of Mind*, ed. D. M. Rosenthal. New York: Oxford University Press.
Atterton, P., M. Calarco, and M. Friedman. 2004. *Levinas and Buber: Dialogue and Difference.* Duquesne: Duquesne University Press.
Bakeman, R., and J. Brown. 1977. "Behavioral Dialogues: An Approach to the Assessment of Mother–Infant Interaction." *Child Development* 48:195–203.
Bakhtin, M. M. 1982. *The Dialogic Imagination: Four Essays.* Ed. M. Holquist. Trans. V. Liapunov and K. Brostrom. Austin: University of Texas.
Baron-Cohen, S. 2001. *Mindblindness: An Essay on Autism and Theory of Mind.* Cambridge: MIT Press.
Bates, E. 1990. "Language about Me and You: Pronominal Reference and the Emerging Concept of Self." In *The Self in Transition: Infancy to Childhood*, ed. S. Cicchetti and M. Beeghly, 165–82. Chicago: University of Chicago Press.
Bateson, M. C. 1975. "Mother–Infant Exchanges: The Epigenesist of Conversational Interaction." In *Developmental Psycholinguistics and Communication Disorders: Annals of the New York Academy of Sciences, vol. 263*, ed. D. Aaronson and R. W. Rieber. New York: New York Academy of Sciences.
Beebe, B., D. Stern, and J. Jaffe. 1979. "The Kinesic Rhythm of Mother–Infant interactions." In *Of Speech and Time: Temporal Patterns in Interpersonal Contexts*, ed. A. W. Siegman and S. Feldstein. Hillsdale, NJ: Erlbaum.
———, et al. 1985. "Interpersonal Timing: The Application of an Adult Dialogue Model to Mother–Infant Vocal and Kinesic Interactions." In *Social Perception in Infants*, ed. T. M. Field and N. A. Fox. Norwood, NJ: Ablex.
———, et al. 1988. "Vocal Congruence in Mother–Infant Play." *Journal of Psycholinguistic Research* 17 (3): 245–59.
Benveniste, E. 1971. *Problems in General Linguistics.* Coral Gables: University of Miami Press.
Bernet, R., I. Kern, and E. Marbach. 1993. *An Introduction to Husserlian Phenomenology.* Evanston: Northwestern University Press.
Bhat, D. N. S. 2004. *Pronouns.* Oxford: Oxford University Press.
Buber, M. 1970. *I and Thou.* New York: Free Press.
———. 1999. *Martin Buber on Psychology and Psychotherapy: Essays, Letters, and Dialogues.* Ed. J. Buber Agassi. Syracuse: Syracuse University Press.
———. 2002. *Between Man and Man.* New York: Routledge.
———. 2005. *Ich und Du.* Gütersloh: Gütersloher Verlagshaus.

Budwig, N. 1990. "A Functional Approach to the Acquisition of Personal Pronouns." *Children's Language*, 7. Ed. G. Conti-Ramsden and C. E. Snow, 121–46. Hillsdale, NJ: Lawrence Erlbaum Associates.

Butler, J. 2004. *Precarious Life: The Power of Mourning and Violence*. New York: Verso.

Cassotta, L., S. Feldstein, and J. Jaffe. 1967. "The Stability and Modifiability of Individual Vocal Characteristics in Stress and Nonstress Interviews." *Research Bulletin, no. 2*. New York: William Alanson White Institute.

Castañeda, H-N. 1999. *The Phenomeno-logic of the I: Essays on Self-consciousness*. Bloomington: Indiana University Press.

Cavarero, A. 2000. *Relating Narratives: Storytelling and Selfhood*. London: Routledge.

Clark, E. V. 1978. "From Gesture to Word: On the Natural History of Deixis in Language Acquisition." In *Human Growth and Development: Wolfson College Lectures 1976*, ed. J. S. Bruner and A. Garton, 85–120. London: Oxford University Press.

Charney, R. 1980. "Speech-roles and the Development of Personal Pronouns." *Journal of Child Language* 7:509–28.

Chiat, S. 1986. "Personal Pronouns." In *Language Acquisition: Studies in First Language Development*, eds. P. Fletcher and M. Garman, 339–55. Cambridge: Cambridge University Press.

Cromer, R. F. 1974. "The Development of Language and Cognition: The Cognition Hypothesis." In *New Perspectives in Child Development*, ed. B. Foss, 184–252. Harmondsworth: Penguin.

Crown, C. 1991. "Coordinated Interpersonal Timing of Vision and Voice as a Function of Interpersonal Attraction." *Journal of Language and Social Psychology* 10 (1): 29–46.

Depraz, N. 1995. *Transcendance et incarnation—Le statut de l'intersubjectivité comme altérité à soi chez Husserl*. Paris: Vrin.

Derrida, J. 1973. *Speech and Phenomena and Other Essays on Husserl's Theory of Signs*. Evanston, IL: Northwestern University Press.

De Villiers, P. A. and J. G. De Villiers. 1974. "On This, That and the Other: Nonegocentrism in Very Young Children." *Journal of Experimental Child Psychology* 18:438–47.

Evans, G. 1994. "Self-identification." In *Self-Knowledge*, ed. Q. Cassam. Oxford: Oxford University Press.

Feldstein, S. and J. Welkowitz. 1978. "A Chronography of Conversation: In Defense of an Objective Approach." In *Nonverbal Behavior and Communication*, ed. A. W. Siegman and S. Feldstein, 329–72. Hillsdale, NJ: Erlbaum.

Fink, E. 1995. *Sixth Cartesian Meditation: The Idea of a Transcendental Theory of Method with Textual Notations by Edmund Husserl*. Trans. R. Bruzina. Bloomington: Indiana University Press.

Fraiberg, S. 1979. "Blind Infants and Their Mothers: An Examination of the Sign System." In *Before Speech: The Beginning of Human Communication*, ed. M. Bullowa, 149–70. Cambridge: Cambridge University Press.

———. and E. Adelson. 1979. "Self-representation in Language and Play." In *Insights from the Blind*. New York: Basic Books.

Gallagher, S. 2001. "The Practice of Mind: Theory, Simulation of Primary Interaction?" *Journal of Consciousness Studies* 8 (5–7): 83–108.
Goodz, N. S. and Lightbown, P. M. 1996. "The Use of Personal Pronouns by Parents and Children in Bilingual Families." Poster presented at Tenth Biennial International Conference on Infant Studies, April 18–21, 1996, in Providence, RI.
Gomez, J. C. 1994. "Mutual Awareness: A Gricean Approach." In *Self-Awareness in Animals and Humans*, ed. S. T. Parker, R. W. Mietchell, and M. L. Boccia, 61–80. Cambridge: Cambridge University Press.
Gurwitsch, A. 1977 [1950]. *Outlines of a Theory of "Essentially Occasional Expressions": Readings on Husserl's Logical Investigations.* The Hague: Martinus Nijhoff.
———. 1979. *Human Encounters in the Social World.* Duquesne: Duquesne University Press.
Hart, J. G. 1999. "Castañeda: A Continental Philosophical Guise." In *The Phenomenologic of the I: Essays on Self-consciousness,* ed. Castañeda, H-N, 17–31. Bloomington: Indiana University Press.
Heidegger, M. 1996 [1927]. *Being and Time.* Albany: State University of New York Press.
Hobson, P. 1980. "The Question of Egocentrism." *Journal of Child Psychology and Psychiatry,* 21:325–31.
———. 1993. "Through Feeling and Sight to Self and Symbol." In *Ecological and Interpersonal Knowledge of Self,* ed. U. Neisser, 254–79. Cambridge: Cambridge University Press.
———. 2004. *The Cradle of Thought: Exploring the Origins of Thinking.* Oxford: Oxford University Press.
Holenstein, E. 1985. *Menschliches Selbstverständnis.* Frankfurt: Suhrkamp.
Hornsby, J. and R. Langton. 1998. "Free Speech and Illocution." *Legal Theory,* 4:21–37.
Hull, J. M. 2001. *On Sight and Insight.* Oxford: Oneworld Publications.
Humboldt, von, W. 1999 [1836]. *On Language: On the Diversity of Human Language Construction and Its Influence on the Mental Development of the Human Species.* Ed. M. Losonsky. Trans. P. Heath. Cambridge: Cambridge University Press.
———. 1907. Über den Dualis. *Gesammelte Schriften,* Band 6, 4–30. Berlin: Preussische Akademie der Wissenschaften.
———. 1907. "Über die Verwandtschaft der Ortsadverbien mit dem Pronomen in einigen Sprachen." *Gesammelte Schriften,* Band 6, 304–30. Berlin: Preussische Akademie der Wissenschaften.
Hume, D. 1967 [1739]. *Treatise of Human Nature.* Oxford: Clarendon Press.
Husserl, E. 1970 [1900]. *The Logical Investigations.* Trans. J. N. Findlay. London: Routledge and Kegan Paul.
———. 1997 [1907]. *Thing and Space: Lectures of 1907.* Trans. R. Rojcewicz. Dordrecht: Kluwer Academic.
———. 2002 [1912]. *Ideas Pertaining to a Pure Phenomenology and to a Phenomenological Philosophy: Second Book.* Trans. R. Rojcewicz and A. Schuwer. Dordrecht: Kluwer Academic.

———. 1982 [1913]. *Ideas Pertaining to a Pure Phenomenology and to a Phenomenological Philosophy: First Book.* Trans. F. Kersten. Dordrecht: Kluwer Academic.

———. 1970 [1938]. *The Crisis of European Sciences and Transcendental Phenomenology: An Introduction to Phenomenological Philosophy.* Trans. D. Carr. Evanston: Northwestern University Press.

———. 1988. *Cartesian Meditations: An Introduction to Phenomenology.* Dordrecht: Kluwer Academic.

———. 1991. *On the Phenomenology of the Consciousness of Internal Time.* Trans. J. B. Brough. Dordrecht: Kluwer Academic.

———. 2005. *Phantasy, Image Consciousness, Memory (1898–1925).* Collected works, vol. 11, 48. Dordrecht: Springer.

Imbens-Bailey, A. and A. Pan. 1998. "The Pragmatics of Self- and Other-reference in Young Children." *Social Development* 7 (2): 219–33.

Jaffe, J. and S. Feldstein. 1970. *The Rhythms of Dialogue.* New York: Academic Press.

———. and S.W. Anderson. 1979. "Communication Rhythms and the Evolution of Language." In *Of Speech and Time: Temporal Speech Patterns in Interpersonal Contexts,* ed. A. W. Siegman and S. Feldstein. Hillsdale, NJ: L. Erlbaum Associates.

———. et al. 2001. "Rhythms of Dialogue in Infancy: Coordinated Timing in Development." *Monographs of the Society for Research in Child Development,* 265, vol. 66, no. 2, i–149.

Jakobson, R. 1990. "Shifters and Verbal Categories." In *On Language,* ed. L. R. Waugh and M. Monville-Burston. Cambridge: Harvard University Press.

Jasnow, M. and S. Feldstein. 1986. "Adult-like Temporal Characteristics of Mother–Infant Vocal Interactions." *Child Development* 57:754–61.

Jay, M. 1993. *Downcast Eyes: The Denigration of Vision in Twentieth-century French Thought.* Berkeley: University of California Press.

Jespersen, O. 1922. *Language: Its Nature, Development, and Origin.* New York: H. Holt and Co.

———. 1924. *The Philosophy of Grammar.* London: George Allen and Unwin.

Kaye, K. and A. Wells. 1980. "Mothers' Jiggling and the Burst-pause Pattern in Neonatal Sucking." *Infant Behavior and Development* 3:29–46.

Lawlor, L. 2002. *Derrida and Husserl: The Basic Problem of Phenomenology.* Bloomington: Indiana University Press.

Legerstee, M., and H. Feider. 1986. "The Acquisition of Pronouns in French Speaking Children." *International Journal of Psychology* 21:629–39.

Levinas, E. 1969. *Totality and Infinity: An Essay on Exteriority.* Trans. Alphonso Lingis. Pittsburgh: Duquesne University Press.

———. 1984. "Martin Buber, Gabriel Marcel and Philosophy." *Martin Buber: A Centenary Volume.* Trans. Esther Kameron. Ed. Haim Gordon and Jochanan Block. New York: Ktav Publishing House for the Faculty of Humanities and Social Sciences, Ben-Gurion University of the Negev.

———. 1990. *Time and the Other.* Pittsburgh: Duquesne University Press.

———. 1990a. "Diachrony and Representation." In *Time and the Other.* Pittsburgh: Duquesne University Press.

———. 1991. "Martin Buber and the Theory of Knowledge." *The Philosophy of Martin Buber.* La Salle, IL: Open Court.

———. 1993. "Apropos of Buber: Some Notes." *Outside the Subject.* Stanford: Stanford University Press.

———. 1998. "Dialogue: Self-consciousness and Proximity of the Neighbor." In *Of God Who Comes to Mind.* Stanford: Stanford University Press.

———. 1999. *Alterity and Transcendence.* Trans. Michael B. Smith. New York: Columbia University Press.

Lewis, M. and D. Ramsay. 2004. "Development of Self-recognition, Personal Pronoun Use, and Pretend Play during the Second Year." *Child Development* 75 (6): 1821–31.

Loveland, K. 1984. "Learning about Points of View: Spatial Perspective and the Acquisition of 'I/you.'" *Journal of Child Language* 2:535–56.

———. 1993. "Autism, Affordances, and the Self." In *The Perceived Self: Ecological and Interpersonal Sources of Self Knowledge,* ed. U. Neisser, 237–53. Cambridge: Cambridge University Press.

Lyons, J. 1968. *Introduction to Theoretical Linguistics.* London: Cambridge University Press.

———. 1977. *Semantics: 1 vols. and 2.* Cambridge: Cambridge University Press.

Marbach, E. 2000. "The Place for an Ego in Current Research." In *Exploring the Self,* ed. D. Zahavi, 75–94. Amsterdam: John-Benjamins.

McNeill, D. 2005. *Gesture and Thought.* Chicago: University of Chicago Press.

Marcel, G. 1991. "I and Thou." *The Philosophy of Martin Buber.* Ed. Paul A. Schilpp and Maurice Friedman, 41–8. La Salle, IL: Open Court.

Martin, G. B. and R. D. Clark. 1982. "Distress Crying in Neonantes: Species and Peer Specificity." *Developmental Psychology* 18:3–9.

Mass, N. 1947. *The Little Grammar People.* Sydney: Angus and Robertson.

Meltzoff, A. N. and A. Gopnik. 1993. "The Role of Imitation in Understanding Persons and Developing and Theory of Mind." In *Understanding Other Minds: Perspectives from Autism.* Oxford: Oxford University Press.

———. and K. Moore. 1977. "Imitation of Facial and Manual Gestures by Human Neonates." *Science* 198:75–78.

———. 1989. "Imitation in Newborn Infants: Exploring the Range of Gestures Imitated and the Underlying Mechanisms." *Developmental Psychology* 25:954–62.

———. 1994. "Imitation, Memory and the Representation of Persons." *Infant Behavior and Development* 17:83–99.

Mensch, J. 1988. *Intersubjectivity and Transcendental Idealism.* Albany: State University of New York Press.

Merleau-Ponty, M. 1994 [1945]. *The Phenomenology of Perception.* London: Routledge.

———. 1964. "Philosopher and his Shadow." *Signs,* 159–81. Evanston: Northwestern University Press.

———. 1968. *The Visible and the Invisible.* Evanston: Northwestern University Press.

———. 1973. "Dialogue and Perception of the Other." *The Prose of the World,* 131–46. Evanston: Northwestern University Press.

———. 2000. "The Child's Relations with Others." *The Primacy of Perception*. Trans. W. Cobb, 96–155. Evanston: Northwestern University Press.

———. 2003. *Nature: Course Notes from the College de France*. Compiled with notes by Dominique Seglard. Trans. Robert Vallier. Evanston: Northwestern University Press.

Muhlhausler, P. and R. Harre. 1990. *Pronouns and People: The Linguistic Construction of Social and Personal Identity*. Oxford: Basil Blackwell.

Oshima-Takane, Y. 1988. "Children Learn from Speech Not Addressed to Them: The Case of Personal Pronouns." *Journal of Child Language* 15:94–108.

———. E. Goodz, and J. L. Derevensky. 1996. "Birth Order Effects on Early Language Development: Do Secondborn Children Learn from Overheard Speech?" *Child Development* 67:621–34.

Papousek, H., and M. Papousek. 1979. "Early Ontogeny of Human Social Interaction." In *Human Ethology: Claims and Limits of a New Discipline*, ed. M. von Cranach, K. Koppa, W. Lepenies, and P. Ploog, 456–78. Cambridge: Cambridge University Press.

Perez-Pereira, M. 1999. "Deixis, Personal Reference, and the Use of Pronouns by Blind Children." *Journal of Child Language* 26:655–80.

Piaget, J. 1959 [1923]. *The Language and Thought of the Child*. London: Routledge.

———. and B. Inhelder. 1956. *The Child's Conception of Space*. Trans. F. J. Langdon and J. L. Lunzer. London: Routledge and Kegan Paul.

Plato. *Symposium*. Ed. K. Dover. Cambridge: Cambridge University Press.

Ricard, M., P. Girouard, and T. Gouin Decarie. 1999. "Personal Pronouns and Perspective Taking in Toddlers." *Journal of Child Language* 26:681–97.

Rochat, P. 2001. "Dialogical Nature of Cognition." In *Rhythms of Dialogue in Infancy: Coordinated Timing in Development*, ed. J. Jaffe et al. Monographs of the Society for Research in Child Development 265, vol. 66, no. 2.

Rome, S. and B. 1964. *Philosophical Interrogations: Interrogations of Buber, Wild, Wahl, Blanshard, Weiss, Hartshorne, Tillich*. New York: Holt, Rinehart and Winston.

Rommetveit, R. 1978. "On Piagetian Cognitive Operations, Semantic Competence, and Message Structure in Adult–Child Communication." In *The Social Context of Language*, ed. I. Markova, 113–50. Chichester, NY: Wiley and Sons.

Rorty, R. 1980. *Philosophy and the Mirror of Nature*. Oxford: Blackwell.

Rosenstock-Huessy, E. 1988 [1924]. *Practical Knowledge of the Soul*. Norwich, VT: Argo Books.

———. 1970. *Speech and Reality*. Norwich, VT: Argo Books.

Rosenzweig, F. 1985 [1921]. *The Star of Redemption*. Notre Dame: Notre Dame Press.

———. 2000 [1925]. "The New Thinking." *Philosophical and Theological Writings*. Indianapolis: Hackett.

Ryle, G. 2000 [1949]. *The Concept of Mind*. London: Penguin Books.

Sartre, J. P. 1956 [1943]. *Being and Nothingness: An Essay on Phenomenological Ontology*. New York: Philosophical Library.

———. 1972. *The Transcendence of the Ego*. Trans. F. Williams and R. Kirkpatrick. New York: Octagon.

Schelling, W. J. 1990. *Vorlesungen über die Methode (Lehrart) des akademischen Studiums*. Hamburg: Meiner, Germany.

Schutz, A. 1957. "The Problem of Transcendental Intersubjectivity in Husserl."

Collected Papers 3. Ed. I. Schutz. *Phaenomenologica,* no. 22. The Hague: M. Nijhoff.

———. 1957. "Discussion—Comments by Eugen Fink on Alfred Schutz's Essay, 'Problem of Transcendental Intersubjectivity in Husserl.'" *Collected Papers 3.* Ed. I. Schutz. *Phaenomenologica,* no. 22. The Hague: M. Nijhoff.

———. 1967. The *Phenomenology of the Social World.* Evanston: Northwestern University Press.

Segal, J. 1993. "Speech and Language Development." In *First steps: A Handbook for Teaching Young Children Who Are Visually Impaired,* 70–82. Los Angeles: Blind Children's Center.

Simms, E. 1999. "The Countryside of Childhood: Reflections on a Hermeneutic-phenomenological Approach to Developmental Psychology." *The Humanistic Psychologist* 27 (3).

Soffer, G. 1999. "The Other as Alter Ego: A Genetic Approach." *Husserl Studies* 15:151–66.

Spelke, E. S. 1991. "Physical Knowledge in Infancy: Reflections on Piaget's Theory." In *The Epigenesis of Mind: Essays on Biology and Cognition,* ed. S. Carey and R. Gelman. Hillsdale, NJ: Erlbaum.

Spitz, R. 1963. "The Evolution of the Dialogue." In *Drives, Affects, and Behavior, Vol. 2,* ed. M. Schur. New York: International University Press.

Stahmer, H. 1968. *Speak that I May See Thee! The Religious Significance of Language.* New York: Macmillan.

Stawarska, B. 2002. "Memory and Subjectivity: Sartre in Dialogue with Husserl." *Sartre Studies International* 8 (2): 94–111.

———. 2004a. "Anonymity and Sociality: The Convergence of Psychological and Philosophical Currents in Merleau-Ponty's Ontological Theory of Intersubjectivity." *CHIASMI International,* 5:295–309.

———. 2004b. "The Body, the Mirror and the Other in Merleau-Ponty and Sartre." In *Ipseity and Alterity: Interdisciplinary Approaches to Intersubjectivity,* ed. S. Gallagher and S. Watson, 175–86. Rouen: Presses Universitaires de Rouen.

———. 2006. "Mutual Gaze and Social Cognition." *Phenomenology and the Cognitive Sciences* 5/1: 17–30.

———. 2007. "Persons, Pronouns, and Perspectives: Linguistic and Developmental Contributions to Dialogical Phenomenology." In *Folk Psychology Reassessed,* ed. M. Ratcliffe and J. Hutto, 79–99. Dordrecht: Springer.

Stern, D. 1974. "Mother and Infant at Play: The Dyadic Interaction Involving Facial, Vocal and Gaze Behaviors." In *The Effect of the Infant on its Caregiver,* ed. M. Lewis and L. Rosenblum, 105–21. New York: Wiley.

———, et al. 1977. "The Infant's Stimulus World During Social Interaction." In *Studies in Mother–Infant Interaction,* ed. H. R. Schaffer, 177–202. New York: Academic Press.

Strasser, S. 2004. "Buber and Levinas: Philosophical Reflections on an Opposition." Ed. Atterton, P., M. Calarco, M. Friedman. *Levinas and Buber: Dialogue and Difference.* Duquesne: Duquesne University Press.

Stetter, C. (1999). *Schrift und Sprache.* Frankfurt am Main: Suhrkamp.

Strawson, P. F. 1958. "Persons." *Minnesota Studies in the Philosophy of Science, Vol. 2,* ed. H. Feigl, M. Scriven, and G. Maxwell, 330–53. Minneapolis: University of Minnesota Press.

———. 1991. "Self, Mind, and Body." In *The Nature of the Mind*, ed. David M. Rosenthal, 58–62. Oxford: Oxford University Press.

Tanz, C. 1980. *Studies in the Acquisition of Deictic Terms*. Cambridge: Cambridge University Press.

Theunissen. 1986. *The Other: Studies in Social Ontology of Husserl, Heidegger, Sartre, and Buber*. Trans. C. Macann. Cambridge: MIT Press.

Tomasello, M. 2003. *Constructing a Language: A Usage-based Theory of Language Acquisition*. Cambridge: Harvard University Press.

Trevarthen, C. 1979. "Communication and Cooperation in Early Infancy: A Description of Primary Intersubjectivity." In *Before Speech: The Beginning of Human Communication*, ed. M. Bullowa, 321–48. Cambridge: Cambridge University Press.

———. 1993. "The Self Born in Intersubjectivity: The Psychology of an Infant Communicating." In *The Perceived Self: Ecological and Interpersonal Sources of Self Knowledge*, ed. U. Neisser, 121–73. Cambridge: Cambridge University Press.

Urwin, C. 1978. "The Development of Communication between Blind Infants and Their Parents." In *Action, Gesture, and Symbol: The Emergence of Language*, ed. A. Lock. London: Academic Press.

———. 1979. "Preverbal Communication and Early Language Development in Blind Children." Papers and Reports in Child Language Development 17:119–27.

Valery, P. 1948. *The Living Thought of Descartes*. London: Cassell.

Vandevelde, P. 1996. Vergenwärtigung et présence originale chez Husserl. *Recherches Husserliennes*, 6:91–116.

Vygotsky, L. 1978. *Mind in Society: The Development of Higher Psychological Processes*. Ed. M. Cole. Cambridge: Harvard University Press.

Wales, K. 1996. *Personal Pronouns in Present-day English*. Cambridge: Cambridge University Press.

Warren, D. F. 1994. *Blindness and Children: An Individual Differences Approach*. New York: Cambridge University Press.

Webster, A. and J. Roe. 1998. *Children with Visual Impairments: Social Interaction, Language and Learning*. London: Routledge.

Wertsch, J. 1991. *Voices of the Mind: A Sociocultural Approach to Mediated Action*. Cambridge: Harvard University Press.

Wimmer, H. and J. Perner. 1983. "Beliefs about Beliefs: Representation and Constraining Function of Wrong Beliefs in Young Children's Understanding of Deception." *Cognition* 13:103–28.

Wittgenstein, L. 1960. *The Blue and Brown Books*. New York: Harper.

Wolff, P. H. 1963. "Observations of the Early Development in Smiling." In *Determinants of Infant Behavior, Vol. 2*, ed. B. M. Foss, 113–38. New York: Wiley.

Zahavi, D. 1999. *Self-awareness and Alterity: A Phenomenological Investigation*. Evanston: Northwestern University Press.

———. 2001. *Husserl and Transcendental Intersubjectivity*. Trans. E. A. Behnke. Athens: Ohio University Press.

Zeltner, H. 1959. "Das Ich und die Anderen. Husserls Beitrag zur Grundlengung der Socialphilosophie." *Zeitschrift fuer philosophische Forschung* 13:288–315.

INDEX

Adelson, E., 115, 116
Adualism, 96–99
Alson, D., 109
Andersen, E., 116
Anderson, S. W., 113
Anscombe, G. E. M., 64–66, 82
Apel, K.-O., 33, 38
Austin, J. L., 140–41, 181–82, 191n11
Automatic Vocal Transition Analyser, the (AVTA), 107–9

Bakeman, R., 108
Baron-Cohen, S., 118
Bateson, M. C., 105
Beauvoir, S., 15
Beebe, B., 105, 109, 110, 113
Benveniste, E., 12, 17, 26, 63, 69, 75–78, 82, 87, 89, 102, 132, 138, 140
Bernet, R., xiv, 20, 21, 40, 48, 189n7, 190n12
Bhat, D. N. S., 62, 69, 70, 73, 76
Body, the
    Body schema, 99
    Living versus natural, 47
    Proprioception, 100, 133
    Twinlike form of: in Aristophanes' myth, 154; in prenatal life, 157–59
    Vulnerability, 187–88
Brown, J., 108
Buber, M., 39, 75, 77, 102, 141–44, 148, 149–53, 157–60, 175, 191n1, 192n5
    Butler, J., and, 187
    Ecological psychology, and, 157
    Levinas, E., relation to, 161
        Ethics: differing conceptions of, 167–68, 172–73, Talmudic-rabbinical inspiration, 168; Hasidic inspiration, 168
    I-you relation: formalism of, 172–73
    Reciprocity: as totalizing, 162–63; and informal address 163–64, 165; as a commercial relation (*Wechselwirkung*), 164; as a facing relation (*Gegenseitigkeit*), 164; physicalist construal of, 165–66; a non-physicalist notion of, 166; in teacher-student relations, 167; in parent-child relations, 167
    Relation: differing conceptions of, 171–72
    Temporality, as diachrony, 169–70
    Merleau-Ponty, M., 170–71
    Phenomenology, and, 135–36, 162
Budwig, N., 191n12
Butler, J., 186–88

Castañeda, H.-N., 36, 81–89, 132, 177, 189n2, 190n11
Cavarero, A., 186–87
Charney, R., 120–31, 191n12
Chiat, S., 121, 124, 128, 130, 191n12
Clark, E. V., 100, 124
Classical phenomenology, ix, 1, 5, 135
    Egology, pure, 20; epistemic quest, 4–5; Speechless thought, 136, 144–45; traditional theory of sociality, 4–5
    Cognition hypothesis, 93–94
Cohen, H., 135
Community, 14, 25, 34, 48, 72, 75, 81, 156, 187–88
Contagious crying, 100
Cromer, R. F., 93
Crown, C., 109, 110, 111

De Villiers, P. A., 120, 124
De Villiers, J. G., 120, 124
Depraz, N., 190n10
Derevensky, J. L., 122
Derrida, J., 7, 15, 17, 169, 189n3
    Expression and indication, 9–10; phonocentrism, 10–13, 16; phonophobia, 13; writing, 11
Descartes, R., 3–4, 25, 84, 85, 87, 93, 189n6
    Ego, the, 19–20, 25, 64–65, 132, 142
Dialogic dimension of meaning, ix, 16, 78, 152, 177–80

Dialogic tradition in philosophy, ix, xi, 13, 39, 81, 162, 163, 175
Dialogical phenomenology, ix, xi, 15–16, 135, 174, 176–78
  Ethics and politics, 186–88; factuality, 39; interdisciplinarity, 16–17, 53, 91–92, 130, 175–76; linguisticality, 39, 87; practice of, the, 180–81
  Transcendental phenomenology: relation to, 176; methodology, 177; transcendental/natural distinction, 179. *See also:* I-you connectedness, grammar, deep
Dunlea, A., 116

Ear, the, 139, 146
Ebner, F., 135, 139
Ego, the (or the I), transcendental, x, 18, 20, 82, 84, 190n7
  Epistemic bias in, x, 3, 5, 18–19, 35–38, 49, 63–64, 81, 82, 84–85, 89, 176; eye, the, 21; Husserl's arguments for: simple cogito, in, 20–22; I-you distinction, 21; ordinary language critique of, 22–23, 24–26, 27–32, 35–38, 81–88; personal pronoun acquisition, 87; primal ego, 49–50; re-presentation, and, 40–43; self-containment of consciousness, 21, 40–43; solitude of, 29; synthetic unity of apperception, 21–22; voice, the, 10–13, 15; *we*, exclusion of, 29, 48
Ego, the, empirical, 18, 27
Ego, the, transcendent, 18, 22, 65. *See also:* Pronouns, the "I," Pronouns, "I" and "you," Sartre, spatial deixis
Egocentric tradition, the, 4, 77, 135, 171, 174
Egocentrism
  Linguistics, 57–60
  Personal pronoun acquisition model: 120–31; empirical evidence for, 123–28; illogicality of, 128–29; language pragmatics, and, 129–31
  Phenomenology, 17–25, 28–50, 57–60, 93
  Philosophy of language, 82–88
  Psychology, 91, 93–99
Ethics. *See:* Buber, M., Levinas's relation to
Evans, Gareth, 190n10

Feider, H., 123
Feldstein, Stanley, 105–10
Fichte, J. G., 121
Fink, E., 23–24, 29, 49, 50
Fraiberg, S., 114–16, 117

Gallagher, S., 104
Gouin Decaries, T., 119
Girouard, P., 119
Gomez, J. C., 191n6
Goodz, N. S., 121, 122
Gopnik, A., 100
Gospel, St. John's, 191n3
Grammar, deep
  Addressability, 138–39, 144–45
  Categories, in: future tense, the, 143; imperative mode, the, and love, 143–44; present tense, the, and encounter, 144, 150–51; subjunctive mode, the, and hope, 143
  Dialogue, 179; dialogical and declarative discourse, 140–41; performativity, 142–43, 145; phenomenological perspective, 139; speaker/addressee roles, 72, 155–56; Speech-based, 137–38; social research, organon of, 137
  Superficial grammar, critique of: conjugation table, the, 137–38; pervasive indicative mode, the, 139–44
Gurwitsch, A.,
  Consciousness, the phenomenology of, 4–5; occasional expressions and intersubjectivity, 14; epistemic bias in phenomenology, 18; "I"-"you," 59

Habermas, J., 33, 38
Hart, J. G., 190n11
Hegel, G. W. F., 21, 146
Heidegger, M., 15
Hinds, J., 70
Hobson, P., 95, 118
Holenstein, E., 58–59, 63, 65
Hornsby, J., 181–84
Hull, J. M., 79
Humboldt, von, W., 14, 59, 60, 76, 150, 153 57, 159–60, 190n7
Hume, D., 40, 65, 179
Husserl, E., 4, 6–15, 17–23, 25, 28–30, 32–36, 38, 40–50, 56, 57, 58, 62, 74, 82, 84, 93, 169, 171, 174, 177, 189n5, 190n11
  Dialogue, 13; expression and indication 8–10, 13–14; Cartesian influence, 18–21; *Cartesian Meditations*, the, 19–20; *Ideas I*, the, 20–21; *Logical Investigations*, the, 6–16; soliloquy, 13, 15, 17

I-you connectedness, ix, 5–6, 16; 49, 53, 162, 174–75, 178

INDEX

A priori of relation, the, 158; air, the, 144, 157–58; alterity, 148–49; "between, the" 149–50, 163, 169, 171
Duality, xi, 76–77, 150, 153–60
  Dual number, the: in Humboldt, 153–55; in Plato, 155; one, the and the many, 154–55, 160, 175
  Twinhood, 154, 159, 175; in prenatal life, 157–60
  Reversibility, 171
Husserl, 7; ethics and politics, 186–88; greeting, 152; plurality, relational, 34, 73–75, 155; Present, lived, 150–51; speech, 60–61, 68–72, 75–78, 79–80, 138–39, 141, 146, 151–53, 155–56; storytelling, 186–87; temporality, 168–70; thinking, 15, 113, 147, 156, 178–79, 180–81; transcendental phenomenology, neglected in, 31–32, 35, 38, 79–80; vulnerability, 187–88; word-pair, 152. *See also:* I-you reversibility, grammar, deep
I-you reversibility, 31, 58–60, 77–78, 86, 89–90, 91, 122, 132
Imbens-Bailey, A., 129
Imitation, in infancy, 99–100
Index
  Existential relation, 62, 69; message (or speech-act), 62
Intersubjectivity, transcendental, 14, 32–34, 35–38, 46–48, 75
  A priori of subjectivity, an 33; aggregate of Is, x, 30–31, 35, 38; genetic account of, 45–46; Husserl's later thought, 49–50; multiple solipsism, 30–31; ownness, the sphere of, 46–47; pairing or coupling, 47; solipsism, 33, 48, 50; world constitution, 33, 48. *See also:* Mensch, J., Schutz, A., Soffer, G., Theunissen, M.
Intersubjectivity, linguistic pragmatic, 33, 38
Intuitionism
  in Castañeda, H.-N., 85–87
  in Husserl, E., 12, 20

Jaffe, J., 105, 106–10, 113, 191n9
Jaffe-Feldstein, the dialogic model of interaction
  Adult conversations, 105–8; conversational congruence, 108–11; dialogicity, 110; empathy, 108; infancy, 108–11; later development, consequences for, 110–11; partner and context discrimination in, 111, stranger, attunement to, 111; turn taking pattern, 109, 110; turn rule, the, 106–7
  Vocal states: parsing,106; coding, 107–8
Jakobson, R., 17, 26, 61, 128
Jasnow, M., 109, 110
Jaspers, K., 135
Jay, M., 21
Jespersen, O., 26, 61, 73, 74, 121
Joint attention, 101–2
  Mutual attention, 101
Jopling, D., 191n4

Kant, I., 4, 21–22, 83–84, 177
Kaufmann, W., 192n5
Kaye, K., 105
Kekelis, S., 116
Kern, I., 189n7

Langton, R., 181–84
Language
  Acquisition of, 93, 98, 114, 131; mystification by, 26–27; ordinary, x, 5, 22–23; 25–28, 34, 81, 84–86; transcendental predication, 23–25, *lingua naturalis,* 24; transcendentalese, x, 22–32, 28–32, 31–38, 64–66, 75, 78, 80–81, 82–86
Legerstee, M., 123
Levinas, E., 15, 148, 149, 152, 154, 161, 162–73, 187
Lewis, M., 116
Liberation phenomenology, 188
Lightbown, P. M., 121
Locke, J., 4,
Loewith, K., 153
Loveland, K., 118–20, 121
Lyons, L., 12, 17, 55, 56, 57–58, 60–61, 69, 70, 73, 104

Mann, B., 188, 190n6
Marbach, E., 21, 39–45, 189n7
Marcel, G., 135, 166
Martin, G. B.,100
Mass, N., 54, 68
Mays, K., 109
McNeill, D., 191n10
Meltzoff, A. N., 92, 100, 191n3, 191n4
Mensch, J., 29, 49–50
Merleau-Ponty, M., 15, 30–31, 89, 132, 169–71
Moore, K., 92, 191n3, 191n4
Murungi, J., 188

Ocularcentrism, 21, 79, 139
Onion, The, 92, 190n1
Oshima-Takane, Y., 122
Oxford English Dictionary, 190n1, 190n2

Pan, A., 129
Papousek, H., 105
Papousek, M., 105
Peirce, C. S., 61, 128
Performativity, 27, 38, 61, 63, 140–43
Perez-Pereira, M., 117
Perner, J., 191n5
Perspective
  Grammaticalization of, 130; imitation, in, 100; mentalistic construal of, 98; perceptual ability, 100; self-other, distinction, 99; spatial orientation, 118–20; speech, in, 59, 77. *See also:* spatial deixis, protoconversation
Piaget, J., 91, 92–99, 100. 101, 103, 120, 130, 132, 190n2
Plato, 147, 150, 153, 154, 155, 157–60, 179
Polycentrism, ix, x, 57–64, 82, 88, 93–95, 98, 103, 118–20, 129–33, 174
Pointing, 62, 90, 101–2
  and I-you relations, 102
Primary intersubjectivity, 103–4
Pronouns
  Definition and types, 54–55; function: anaphoric, 55; deictic, 55–56, 60–64; subjective and occasional expressions, 56; indexicals, 56. *See also:* pronouns, personal, spatial deixis
Pronouns, personal (or person deixis)
  Acquisition of, dominant model, 87–88, 90, 121, 122–31; speech-role-referring (ROLE) hypothesis, 123–26, 128–29; person-referring (PERSON) hypothesis, 124–26; person-in-speech-role-referring (PERSON-ROLE) hypothesis, 124–28
  Gender, 29, 69; Noun substitutes (or *pro-nomen*), traditionally defined as, 53–55, 67–68; number, 29, 73–75; Performative function of, 38, 61, 142–43, 145; Semantic poverty of, 62–63, 69–70; Shifter, the, 61–62, 66; Spatial deixis, connected with, 59–60, 174; spatial perspective, and, 118–20
  Traditional grammar of: conjugation table, 68–69, 137–39; symmetry between the three persons, illusion of, 69–70, 76

Vision, importance of, 117. *See also:* symbol, index, protoconversation, pronouns, the "I," pronouns, "I" and "you"
Pronouns, the "I"
  Ambiguity of, 85; context-dependence of, 12, 66, 104
  Concept, of: transcendental, individual, 17; linguistic, general, 17, 62
  Emphatic quality of, 142–43; future tense, and, 143; *I*-guises, 84; mentalistic subject, and, 23, 82–87, 121, 132–34; non-referring expression, 65–66; objective expression, contrasted with, 6–8, 23; quasiname, as, 65; Reduction to the "I" in Modernity, the, 3–4, 147; subjective and occasional expression, as, 6–8, 12, 23; soliloquy, in, 8, 11, 14–15; Subjective and objective use of, 27–28, 67–68; subjunctive mode, 143; writing, in, 11
  Grammar, the, in ordinary language, x, 22, 26, 27–28, 31, 34, 37–38, 66, 67, 85–86
  Grammar, the, in transcendentalese: x, 22–26, 28–32, 64–66, 82–86; a substantive form, 28–32; an indeclinable nominal, 29–32, 35–38; a nonnumerical singular, 29–31, 33–35; a nonobjectifiable subject, 31–32
  Indexicality (or internal reflexivity) of, 35–37, 82–83; addressability, tied to, 86–89, 133–34; guaranteed speaker reference, distinct from, 63, 65; immunity to error through misidentification, 37; objectified self-knowledge, contrasted with, 37–38, 82–85; self-awareness, 36–38, 82–84, 85–86, 121
  Performative function of, 61, 63, 68; socialized discursive role of, 35, 63–64
  Speech acts, used in the service of ,129, 131; Syncretic use of, 115, 127–28. *See also:* Ego, transcendental, Grammar, deep, Pronouns, "I" and "you"
Pronouns, "I" and "you"
  Acquisition of, protoconversational model: xi, 39, 89, 90, 93–94, 112–14, 132–34, 175, 180; and gestural communicative hypothesis, 113
  Addressed and non-addressed speech, exposure to, 122, 131; Autism, challenges with, 118, 124
  Blindness: as impediment to the acquisition of, 114–17, 131; reversal errors in,

115, 124; perspective taking, 116–17; protracted syncretism, 115–16; self-recognition, 116
Conversational competence, 90, 133; discourse-language distinction, 76
Grammar, the, in ordinary language: complementarity, 76–77; asymmetry, 77; reversibility, 77–78; third person, distinct from, 69–70, 73–75, 75–76, 79–80
Grammar, the, in transcendentalese, 78, 80–81
Horizontal relations in, 71
Indispensable to speech, 60–61, 70; interlocutory pronouns, or interlocutives, 76; microstructure of language, as, 112; participant involvement in discourse, and, 69, 72; person deixis, and, 56–57, 60–61, 155–56
Self-deprecating and honorific expressions: 70–72; vertical relations in, 70–72;
Spatial perspective, correlated with, 118–20. *See also:* I-you reversibility
Pronouns, the third person
Demonstratives, and, 70; dispensable, 69–70; nonparticipant, 69, 141; nonperson, as, 69, 78–80; proforms, or substitutive pronouns, 76
Pronouns, "we"
Community, and, 30, 34, 48, 72–75, 160
Grammar, the, in ordinary language: "I"-"you," contingent on, 34, 73–75, 160; inclusive and exclusive, 73–74; intradiscursive, relational plurality in, 73–74, 76; irreducible to an aggregate of individuals, 30, 34–35, 48
Grammar, the, in transcendentalese: extradiscursive, external plurality in, 75; tied to the traditional view of language, 75
Phenomenological reduction, and, 29, 48; *we*-consciousness, 34
Proper names, and pronouns, 29, 37, 60, 65, 142–43, 161–62
Protoconversation (or dialogic relations in infancy), x, 91, 103–5, 112, 114, 117, 132–33, 175
Conversational competence, and, 91, 103–4; "intuitive motherese," in, 110; Macrostructure of language, as, 112; mutual influence in, 99, 103, 104, 109, 140; protogrammar, and, 130–31; proto-speaker and proto-addressee roles in, 112
Turn-taking, in, 90, 94, 103, 105, 117, 132–33; role-switching, in, 90, 94, 103, 130, 132–33. *See also:* Jaffe-Feldstein, the dialogic model of, pronouns, "I" and "you"
Psychology, developmental, x, 81, 94, 120, 174, 175

Ramsay, D., 116
Reference
Denoting, 66–67; indexing, 66
Re-presentation (or presentation) 40–43
Empathy, in, 44–45; imagination, in, 41–42, 45; memory, in, 41, 45; picture-consciousness, and, 40–41, 43; third-person stance, in, 46
Ricard, M., 119
Rochat, P., 110, 112–13
Roe, J., 116
Rogoff, B., 91
Rome, S., 160, 161, 165, 166, 167, 172
Rome, B., 160, 161, 165, 166, 167, 172
Rommetveit, R., 92, 93
Rorty, R., 21
Rosenstock-Huessy, E., 135, 136–45, 146, 161–62, 191n3
Rosenzweig, F., 3, 135, 136, 137, 146–48, 169
Ryle, G., 56, 190n4

Sartre, J. P., 15, 41
Transcendental ego, critique of: 22, 43–44, 65; gaze, the, and objectification, 79–80, 190n9
Scheler, M., 47
Schelling, W. J., 156
Schopenhauer, A., 146
Schutz, A., 29, 30, 33, 46–50
Segal, J., 116
Showalter, C. J., 76
Soffer, G., 39, 45
Social ontology, 46
Phenomenology, and, 48; philosophy of dialogue, and, 49; speech-based method of, 136–37, 147
Sociolinguistics, x, 6, 27, 28, 80, 81, 174
Spatial deixis, 57–60, 174–75
Absolute *here*, and, 57; acquisition of, 90; "here"-"there" reversibility, 58; perspective, and, 58–59; transcendental

ego, and, 59; vision, dependence on, 117
Speech
  Ethical and political ramifications of, 63, 184–88; expression and indication, and, 9–10
  Free, 183–84; generative faculty, as, 156; gesture, and, 113–14; occasional expressions, and, 7; living, ix, 16, 49, 61, 78, 136–45
  Piaget's theory, in: egocentric, 96–99; socialized, 97–98
  Pornographic, 183; received view of, 67–68; sociality, and, 137, 155, 163; transcendent/transcendental distinction, and, 72; writing 11–13. *See also:* protoconversation, speech act theory
Speech act theory
  Feminist theory, applications in, 181–85
  Illocutionary disablement (or silencing), 183–85
Speech roles, 77
  Addressee, ix, x, 4–5, 23, 29, 31, 38, 56–57, 59–61, 63–64, 69, 70, 72–74, 78, 86, 89–90, 93, 97, 104, 106, 112, 121–27, 131, 140, 143–44, 155–56, 163, 175, 178, 185
  Speaker, x, 4, 7, 8, 12, 14, 17, 22, 23, 26, 31, 36, 38, 56–60, 61, 62, 63–64, 66, 67–69, 70–72, 73–75, 76–78, 83, 87, 89–91, 97, 104, 107, 109, 112, 120–22, 123–31, 132, 140–44, 146, 155–56, 163, 181–85
  Preserved in direct address with nominal terms, 70–72
  Translinguistic universality of, 60–61, 70
  Tied to individuals, 70–71
Spelke, E. S., 92

Spitz, R., 104–5
Stahmer, H., 146, 191n2, 191n3
Stawarska, B., 190n8, 190n9, 190n9, 191n7, 191n8, 192n1
Stern, D., 105, 109, 110, 113
Strasser, S., 167
Strawson, P. F., 25–26, 36, 84
Symbol
  and conventional rules, 61–62, and code, 62

Tanz, C., 112, 120, 124
Theory of mind, 100–103
  False belief tasks, 100
Theunissen, M., 35, 46, 48–49, 190n13, 190n13
Three Mountain task, 94–95
Tomasello, M., 101
Trevarthen, C., 103, 110

Urwin, C., 117

Valery, P., 142
Vandevelde, P., 45, 190n11
Vygotsky, L., 113, 189n4

Wales, K., 70
Warren, D. F., 116
Webster, A., 116
Wells, A., 105
Wertsch, J., 91
Wimmer, H., 191n5
Wittgenstein, L., 26–28, 67–68, 72
Wolff, P. H., 102

Zahavi, D., 32–39, 48
Zeltner, H., 35